Emerging Developments in Pre-Therapy

A Pre-Therapy Reader

Edited by

Garry Prouty

PCCS BOOKS
Ross-on-Wye

First published in 2008

PCCS BOOKS Ltd
2 Cropper Row
Alton Rd
Ross-on-Wye
Herefordshire
HR9 5LA
UK
Tel +44 (0)1989 763 900
www.pccs-books.co.uk

This collection: © Garry Prouty, 2008.

Parts I, II, and Chapters 6 and 9 © Garry Prouty; Chapter 1 © Marlis Pörtner;
Chapter 2 © Dion Van Werde; Chapter 3 © Penny Dodds; Chapter 4 © Aldo Dinacci;
Chapter 5 © Hans Peters; Chapter 7 © Margaret Warner & Judith Trytten;
Chapter 8 © Ton Coffeng.

All rights reserved.
No part of this publication may be reproduced, stored in a retrieval system, transmitted or utilized in any form by any means, electronic, mechanical, photocopying or recording or otherwise without permission in writing from the publishers.
The authors have asserted their rights to be identified as the authors of this work in accordance with the Copyright, Designs and Patents Act 1988.

**Emerging Developments in Pre-Therapy:
A Pre-Therapy Reader**

A CIP catalogue record for this book is available from the British Library

ISBN 978 1 906254 09 4

Cover design by Old Dog Graphics

Printed by Cpod, Trowbridge, UK

CONTENTS

PREFACE		i
PART I	A BRIEF HISTORY OF PRE-THERAPY	3
PART II	A REVIEW OF PRE-THERAPY	13
PART III	EMERGENT DEVELOPMENTS	23

PRACTICE

Chapter 1	Pre-Therapeutic Approaches for Working with People with 'Special Needs' *Marlis Pörtner, Switzerland*	25
Chapter 2	The Falling Man: Pre-Therapy applied to somatic hallucinating *Dion Van Werde, Belgium*	39
Chapter 3	Pre-Therapy and Dementia Care *Penny Dodds, UK*	49

THEORY

Chapter 4	ECPI: Objective Evaluation for the Pre-Therapy Interview *Aldo Dinacci, Italy*	75
Chapter 5	The Development of Intersubjectivity in Relation to Psychotherapy and Its Importance for Pre-Therapy *Hans Peters, the Netherlands*	87
Chapter 6	Pre-Therapy and the Pre-Expressive Self *Garry Prouty, USA*	105

PART IV	RELATED DEVELOPMENTS	115
Chapter 7	Metaphact Process: A new way of understanding schizophrenic thought disorder *Margaret Warner and Judith Trytten, USA*	118
Chapter 8	The Therapy of Dissociation: Its phases and problems *Ton Coffeng, the Netherlands*	147
Chapter 9	The Hallucination as the Unconscious Self *Garry Prouty, USA*	164
Index		181

PREFACE

Garry Prouty

Western humanistic psychology has traditionally focused on higher levels of human functioning such as self-actualization. In contrast, Pre-Therapy focuses on the lower levels of functioning such as regression and dissociation associated with having 'special needs,' learning disability, traumatization, dementia and psychotic withdrawal in people with diagnoses of schizophrenia. Pre-Therapy is a commitment to understand and treat these regressed levels of 'Being in the World' and represents a paradigm shift within Western humanistic psychology.

Pre-Therapy is also a cultural conserve. It maintains a consistent 'non-directive' position derived from mid-century Rogerian psychology. It also embraces 'a concrete phenomenology.' In Martin Buber's language, this is described as 'pointing at the concrete.' Pre-Therapy enables the therapist to contact the patient's regressed levels of communication through the concreteness of the contact reflections.

What is important about this text is not Pre-Therapy itself, which is fully available in other books and papers (see Prouty, Van Werde & Pörtner, 2002; Sanders, 2007), but the expansion beyond itself to a second generation of theorizing and applications.

For the reader not familiar with Pre-Therapy, Part I outlines a brief history of the approach, and Part II is a review of the theory itself. Part III contains independent developments in practice and theory—their commonality being rooted in Pre-Therapy. They are the emergent developments. Part IV contains related developments that are less explicitly connected to, but nevertheless influenced by, Pre-Therapy.

REFERENCES

Prouty, G, Van Werde, D & Pörtner, M (2002) *Pre-Therapy: Reaching contact-impaired clients*. Ross-on-Wye. PCCS Books.
Sanders, P (Ed) (2007) *The Contact Work Primer*. Ross-on-Wye: PCCS Books.

Preface

Part I

A Brief History of Pre-Therapy

A Brief History of Pre-Therapy

GARRY PROUTY

INTRODUCTION

Over the past 40 years (1966–2006), through books, articles, translations, seminars, lectures, and hospital visits, as well as research and training programs, Pre-Therapy has become known as a theory and practice of psychotherapy inspired by the suggestions of Carl Rogers (1957) and Fritz Perls (1969). Through this activity, Pre-Therapy has been introduced in Russia, China, Japan, Greece, Romania, Slovakia, Switzerland, the Czech Republic, Austria, Germany, Italy, Spain, France, the Netherlands, Belgium, England, Scotland, Denmark, and Portugal, as well as the United States, Canada, Australia and Korea.

There are two personal roots for this work. First, my brother 'Bobby' was dually diagnosed as schizophrenic and developmentally disabled. This enabled me to have an intuitive grasp of such problems. Second was the profound mentoring of Dr. Eugene Gendlin, of the University of Chicago, who encouraged and supported my earliest efforts at practice and theorizing. A short autobiography is available in Prouty, Van Werde and Pörtner (1998/2002).

THE BIRTH

Pre-Therapy was 'born' in Palos Park, Illinois in 1966 in a very small rehabilitation workshop attached to the Lt. Joseph Kennedy School for Exceptional Children—a residential school for developmentally disabled and mentally ill youngsters. Clients were also received from other community facilities. My role was chief psychologist. The 'birth' was not deliberate but was parented by three forces: (1) my family experience with this type of person; (2) my client-centered/experiential training; (3) the availability of these client types. The period (1966–1970) was the period of practical clarification for the method. My taking a new job as Professor of Mental Health at Prairie State Community College (1970) offered a gestation period lasting through several years of teaching. I finally published the first article on the Pre-Therapy method which was a simple advance in reflective technique for retarded and chronic schizophrenic populations (Prouty, 1976).

A NEW STAGE

The work gradually became known among local psychologists and psychiatrists who, in part, were initially skeptical. Their argument was that my success was the result of my own individual talent or gift with these clients—certainly a flattering criticism. However, in their view, certainly no new principles were involved! Of course, part of the refutation came with students who were also able to do the work (Sharon Pietrzak, Mary Ann Kubiak, and Melinda Cronwall). While driving to teach student practicums at the local state hospital, I could see smoke stacks. These reminded me of the Nazi concentration camps. The huge facility (with a capacity of 8,000 people) was filled with chronic psychotic persons, all medicated but without psychotherapy. Some patients were actually in chains at the time.

Dr. Efie Hinterkopf and Dr. Les Brunswick, of nearby Governors State University, attended the practicum seminars as guests, and we spent many satisfying afternoons discussing Pre-Therapy and highlighting the problems students brought. During these meetings Hinterkopf and Brunswick suggested a pilot study to explore Pre-Therapy.

It was at this time (1979) that I realized I was proposing new principles not articulated by Rogers or Gendlin. I was not exploring the core conditions or the experiencing process, but something different—reality, affect, and communication, later recognized as psychological contact (Hinterkopf, Prouty & Brunswick, 1979). The clients were chronic schizophrenics averaging 20 years of hospitalization. The criticism and expectation was that any patients receiving attention in a state hospital situation would show improvement. Consequently, the experimental group received six months of Pre-Therapy, and the control group received six months of recreational attention without therapy. The results in terms of gain scores showed a greater proportion of communications about reality and affect as compared with failure to communicate these.

This model was the first attempt toward what later became the empirical foundations of Pre-Therapy. This early work led to an appointment as a research associate at the Institute for Developmental Disabilities, University of Illinois (1980).

THE FATES

In 1980, after the election of Ronald Reagan as president, the social philosophy of the USA changed to a severe economic conservatism, and program cuts occurred everywhere. Because the Pre-Therapy program was the newest and in the earliest stages of development, the University of Illinois dropped it. My thought at the time was 'this is the end of Pre-Therapy.' At this point, the Fates stepped in.

For a number of years, I had received postcards from European universities and training centers requesting copies of my publications. At that time, I paid little attention to this, just thinking, 'this is odd' and 'oh well.' I then made the most important decision of my professional life when I wrote a very naïve letter to the Netherlands asking if they accepted Americans into their conferences, in the hope of receiving a program slot. To my great surprise, I received a letter saying they would develop a full five-day conference on my work alone.

So, in October 1985, my wife Jill and I landed in Amsterdam, the beginning of a twenty-year-plus European odyssey. On the trip over, I fantasized about returning to the continent of Husserl—an intellectual full circle in phenomenology. We made our way to De Klokkenberg Hospital, Breda, in the Netherlands, as the guests of Dr. Bart Santen. The way I remember the experience was that for three days my wife and I trudged to the meeting, I spoke for five to six hours a day, and no one said anything to us—just speaking amongst themselves in Dutch. My heart sank; I thought I had failed. My comment to Jill was 'well, we had a great trip and that was that.' On the third afternoon, however a Dutch psychiatrist said, in English, 'It's a breakthrough.'

It was from this meeting that many core Pre-Therapy people came: Dr. Wim Lucieer, psychiatrist; Dr. Hans Peters, special educator; Dr. Luc Roelens, psychiatrist; Dr. Ton Coffeng, psychiatrist—all of whom have contributed to Pre-Therapy over the years. We went home satisfied. A few months later, we received an invitation from De Klokkenberg for a second week of workshops focused on practice.

CARL ROGERS

In 1986, the Chicago Counseling and Psychotherapy Center, the original training and research center for Rogers at the University of Chicago, invited him for a symposium held at the University of Chicago Law School Auditorium (White & White, 2005). The symposium participants consisted of Carl Rogers, Eugene Gendlin, Nat Raskin, Natalie Rogers, and myself. The speaking sequence was Carl Rogers, Eugene Gendlin, and then myself. After a break, Natalie Rogers and Nat Raskin spoke. It was a memorable and intense experience to follow the two masters from whom I had learned everything. As I proceeded to outline Pre-Therapy, my wife Jill reported that Rogers immediately started taking notes. I finished, and Rogers commented: 'Garry's work is important' and I felt like a knight of the realm! During the break, I was standing with Jill and my daughter Gwen, when Rogers walked up to us. He said directly to me, 'You have killed the Buddha' and 'Don't let the bastards get you down,' and then he walked away. I took the words to heart, and many times since, during difficult experiences, I have turned to that personally meaningful encounter for inspiration. Rogers died several months later.

The later Eighties and early Nineties reflected a surge in Pre-Therapy publication by myself and others, thereby establishing the clinical value of the approach. Jill Prouty, realizing the growth of our activities, formed the Pre-Therapy International Network in Amsterdam (1995) for scholarly interchange. We have met annually for the last decade at St. Camillus Hospital in Ghent, Belgium where Dion Van Werde assumed the coordination of our meetings.

COLLEAGUES

TON COFFENG

Ton Coffeng, MD and psychiatrist, has been a longtime associate of the Pre-Therapy group. His contribution has been the application of Pre-Therapy to multiple personality clients and trauma victims (Coffeng, 2005). He theoretically identified 'contact' as 'pre-experiential,' thereby giving insight about 'contact' as a precursor to experiential process.

ALDO DINACCI

Dr. Aldo Dinacci is an Italian psychologist and mathematician who founded the Italian Institute for Pre-Therapy Research and Practice in Bologna. He also founded the International Pre-Therapy Review. His contributions include the development of the Objective Evaluation Criterion for the Pre-Therapy Interview—ECPI (2000). This is an instrument for measuring the communicative effects of Pre-Therapy. As well, Dr. Dinacci computerized the international bibliography for Pre-Therapy writings (www.pretherapy.com).

HANS PETERS

Hans Peters, a social pedagogue and psychologist from the Netherlands, has explored the research on imitation and intersubjectivity as innate potentials (Peters, 2005). The contact reflections of Pre-Therapy are in line with these basic human capacities that are available within a few hours of birth. Pre-Therapy develops or restores the intersubjective, making psychological contact possible. Such an approach seems to explain the therapeutic results of Pre-Therapy with developmentally disabled, contact-impaired clients who are psychotic and/or brain-damaged. In an earlier paper, Peters (1999) described Pre-Therapy as a primary therapy for the severely contact-impaired and as a secondary application with more 'in contact' clients.

MARLIS PÖRTNER

Marlis Pörtner is a Swiss psychologist who has played an important role in the development of Pre-Therapy. We first met at a Chicago workshop given by Eugene Gendlin. Our mutual interest was counseling clients with 'special needs'—in fact, severe learning disabilities—notably overlooked in the client-centered literature due to Rogers' views that client-centered therapy required 'normal' intelligence. We met a second time at a client-centered workshop in Brazil (1989). During the early and middle Nineties, we worked together in Germany where Marlis worked as translator, clinical colleague, and finally as an independent lecturer and author.

Marlis was responsible for spreading Pre-Therapy for those with special needs throughout the German-speaking world especially to institutions in Austria, Germany and Switzerland. She had considerable experience consulting with residential facilities and had clearly developed a way of teaching caregivers the attitudes and methods that enabled person-centered care. She combined this with Pre-Therapy, providing a helpful environment for people with special needs. This work resulted in *Trust and Understanding*, initially written in German (Pörtner, 1996) and later translated into English (Pörtner, 2000/2006), Dutch and Danish. Her next book, in German, *Brücken Bauen* (2003) was a further development of concepts for person-centered care as well as for client-centered psychotherapy with people with special needs—not seeing them as remodeled to the wishes of caregivers. It also highlighted facilitating changes of self-concept (Rogers) and developing and strengthening the contact functions (Prouty). Marlis's latest book, on geriatric care, *Being Old is Different* (2005/2008), expands the principles developed in *Trust and Understanding* to the aged. In addition was Marlis's contribution to Prouty, Van Werde and Pörtner (1998/2002), written from the USA, Belgium, and Switzerland and translated by her for a German publisher. In sum, Marlis Pörtner spread Pre-Therapy into the institutional services for people with learning special needs throughout the German-speaking world and contributed her own person-centered caregivers approach.

PETE SANDERS

Pete Sanders has played a profound role in the development of Pre-Therapy in three ways: the first is evidenced through PCCS Books' publication of Pre-Therapy literature. Second, and equally important, is his writing for and editing of, the *Pre-Therapy Primer* (PCCS Books, 2007). Finally are his efforts, through workshops and presentations, to introduce Pre-Therapy to the counseling and psychotherapy world in the UK.

ANN-LOUISE SILVER

Ann-Louise Silver, MD, psychoanalyst and psychiatrist, opened new doors for Pre-Therapy. We first met at a symposium on schizophrenia at the American Psychological Association in Washington, DC (2000). She is currently president of the American chapter of ISPS, the International Society for the Psychological Treatments of the Schizophrenias and other Psychoses (www.isps.org) (www.isps-us.org). Viewing Pre-Therapy and Pre-Symbolic Experiencing as psychoanalytically compatible, she invited me to give the Frieda Fromm-Reichmann Memorial Lecture at the Washington School of Psychiatry in 2002.

She followed this with suggestions to publish in the *Journal of the American Academy of Psychoanalysis and Dynamic Psychiatry* and to present at several psychoanalytic conferences. She sponsored my being invited to serve as a Scientific Associate of the American Academy of Psychoanalysis and Dynamic Psychiatry. For the first time in 40 years, a Rogerian was connected to American psychiatry. Her personal and professional support has been profound.

LISBETH SOMMERBECK

Lisbeth Sommerbeck, a Danish psychologist, wrote a very successful introductory text for the client-centered reader interested in psychotic or near-psychotic clients (Sommerbeck, 2003). The book is valuable in that it focuses on the institutional interface between psychiatry and client-centered therapy—an approach never done before. She also introduced the beginning client-centered student to Pre-Therapy, which she believes should be a part of every client-centered training, since most therapists encounter near-psychotic, or episodic people. Sommerbeck founded such a training program near Copenhagen, thus introducing Pre-Therapy into Denmark as part of the client-centered tradition.

DION VAN WERDE

Dion Van Werde is a Belgian psychologist who has played a very prominent role in the history of Pre-Therapy. He is responsible for the spreading of Pre-Therapy throughout Belgium, the Netherlands, and on into France and Germany and was a Fellow at the Chicago Counseling and Psychotherapy Center. He is a staff psychologist at St. Camillus Hospital in Ghent, Belgium, where he founded a milieu therapy ward for people with a diagnosis of acute schizophrenia, based on Pre-Therapy principles. This has become a model for other hospitals in Belgium and the Netherlands He is also co-author, along with Marlis Pörtner, of *Prae-Therapie* (1998/2002) a theoretical and clinically descriptive text. Since 1996, Dion has served as Coordinator of the Pre-Therapy International Network.

SUMMARY

There are three identifiable stages in the history of Pre-Therapy. The first period (the American Phase) consisted of the early work in the United States where the basic concepts and methods were worked out. This was from the period 1966–1985. The second phase from 1985–2005 can be called the European Phase, during which new practice forms were developed. It is fair to say we are entering a third phase of development, with geriatrics emerging as a focus of interest through the work of Penny Dodds, RN, Lecturer, Brighton University, England. She is currently conducting research on the teaching of nurses in Pre-Therapy with geriatric clients. Dave Deady, RN (Paisley University, Scotland) introduced Pre-Therapy directly into nurses' training. Marlis Pörtner and Dion Van Werde are starting seminars on geriatrics in continental Europe. The newer connections with psychoanalysis-psychiatry also can offer networking possibilities.

REFERENCES

Coffeng, T (2005) The therapy of dissociation: Its phases and problems. *Person-Centered and Experiential Psychotherapies*, 4 (2), 90–105.

Dinacci, A (2000) Objective Evaluation Criterion for the Pre-Therapy Interview. *International Pre-Therapy Review*, 1, 31–5.

Hinterkopf, E, Prouty, G & Brunswick, L (1979) A pilot study of Pre-Therapy applied to chronic schizophrenic patients. *Psychosocial Rehabilitation Journal*, 3, 11–19.

Perls, F (1969) The ego as a function of the organism. In *Ego, Hunger and Aggression* (p 139). New York: Random House.

Peters, H (1999) Pre-Therapy: An approach to mentally handicapped people. *Journal of Humanistic Psychology, 39* (4), 9–29.

Peters, H (2005) Pre-Therapy from a developmental perspective. *Journal of Humanistic Psychology, 45* (1), 62–81.

Pörtner, M (1996) *Ernstnehmen – Zutrauen – Verstehen*. Stuttgart: Klett-Cotta. [English edition, *Trust and Understanding: The person-centered approach to everyday care for people with special needs*. Ross-on-Wye: PCCS Books, 2000, 2nd edn 2007]

Pörtner, M (2003). *Brücken Bauen*. Stuttgart: Klett-Cotta.

Pörtner, M (2005) *Alt Sein ist Aanders*. Stuttgart: Klett-Cotta. [English edition, *Being Old is Different*, Ross-on-Wye: PCCS Books, 2008]

Prouty, G (1976) Pre-Therapy: A method of treating pre-expressive psychotic and retarded patients. *Psychotherapy: Theory, Research and Practice, 13*, 290–4.

Prouty, G, Van Werde, D & Pörtner, M (1998) *Prä-Therapie*. Stuttgart: Klett-Cotta. [English edition, *Pre-Therapy: Reaching contact-impaired clients*. Ross-on-Wye: PCCS Books, 2002, reprinted 2008]

Rogers, CR (1957) The necessary and sufficient conditions of therapeutic personality change. *Journal of Consulting Psychology, 21* (2), 95–103.

Sanders, P (Ed) (2007) *The Contact Work Primer: Introduction to Pre-Therapy*. Ross-on-Wye: PCCS Books.

Sommerbeck, L (2003) *The Client-Centered Therapist in Psychiatric Contexts: A therapists' guide to the psychiatric landscape and its inhabitants*. Ross-on-Wye: PCCS Books.

White, C & White, C (2005) Reminiscing and predicting: Beyond words, speech and commentary. *Journal of Humanistic Psychology, 45* (3), 384.

Part II

A Review of Pre-Therapy

A Review of Pre-Therapy

GARRY PROUTY

Pre-Therapy is embedded within the non-directive tradition of client-centered psychotherapy (Prouty, 2005). For full clinical, theoretical, and philosophical descriptions, see Prouty (1994, 2002) and Prouty, Van Werde and Pörtner (2002), and for a brief illustrative summary see Sanders (2007).

Rogers (1957) defined psychological contact as the first condition of a therapeutic relationship and as a precondition to treatment: hence the coinage 'Pre-Therapy.' Rogers, however, did not provide therapeutic technique or operational concepts for the measurement of this precondition. Pre-Therapy is the therapeutic use and scientific study of psychological contact. The theory is structured in three parts: (1) contact reflections; (2) contact functions; and (3) contact behaviors.

CONTACT REFLECTIONS

Contact reflections are the techniques of Pre-Therapy. Characterized by their very concrete and non-directive nature, they are a very literal following of the client's 'regressed' expressive process. The presence of an empathic contact with the client's 'regressed' world provides an access for developing relationship.

Here 'regression' does not have its traditional psychiatric meaning of a return to lower levels of functioning and meaning. We see 'regression' as the opposite: as the organism's attempt to achieve higher and fuller meaning—a movement from lower pre-expressive levels to congruent communication. We have based this conclusion on the observation of contact reflections. (A full theoretical description is available in Prouty, 1998, which appears as Chapter 6 in this volume.)

Another characteristic of contact reflections is their ultra-concrete nature or 'a pointing at the concrete' (Buber, 1964: 547). Client cognition and therapeutic responses are coordinated by the quality or property of concreteness. Numerous psychiatric scholars (Arieti, 1955; Friedman, 1961;

Goldstein, 1939; Goldstein & Scheerer, 1941; Gurwitsch, 1966; Mazumdar & Mazumdar, 1983) have documented the concrete nature of 'schizophrenic' cognition. This necessitates very concrete therapeutic responses, i.e. Pre-Therapy.

METHOD

There are five contact reflections: (1) situational; (2) facial; (3) word-for-word; (4) bodily; and (5) reiterative.

Situational Reflections (SR) are imbedded in living concrete situations, environments, or milieu and constitute our 'Being in the World'. As such, these reflections facilitate reality contact with the client. An example could be 'Johnny is sitting on the floor' or 'Mary is holding the ball.'

Facial Reflections (FR) The human face, described as the 'expressive organ,' contains not-yet-formed affect. These facial reflections facilitate affective experiencing for the client. Examples are 'You look sad' or 'You look angry.' A more concrete example is 'There are tears in your eyes.'

Word-for-Word Reflections (WWR) Many learning disabled, regressed, dissociated, thought-disordered and geriatric clients, and people with special needs present symptoms of incoherence. For example, people with a diagnosis of schizophrenia often present neologisms, word-salads, and echolalia. Pre-Therapists are trained to reflect the words they can understand 'word-for-word.' For example, '(unintelligible) ring (unintelligible) house (unintelligible) horse.' Even though the sentence cannot be understood logically, the therapists can reflect individual words they have understood: 'ring,' 'house,' 'horse.' What is therapeutic is the client's experience of being 'received' or 'affirmed' as a communicator. On occasion, sounds are reflected.

Body Reflections (BR) Many clients express bizarre body symptoms such as echopraxia or catatonia. Meddard Boss (1994: 102–4) presented the concept of 'bodying forth,' meaning that bodily symptomatology is a form of 'Being in the World' and as such expresses the person's existence. Body reflections are empathic responses to 'bodying forth' that result in a shift toward more verbal expression. Prouty and Kubiak (1988) demonstrated this in a therapeutic exploration of catatonia. There are two types of body reflections: (1) verbal, such as 'Your arm is in the air' or 'You are lying on the floor' and (2) postural reflections—sensitive 'mimicry'—with the therapist's own body.

Reiterative Reflections (RR) Not specific techniques, these embody the principle of 're-contact.' If any particular contact reflection produces a response, the therapist should repeat it. There are two types of reiterative reflections: short-term and long-term. Short-term responses usually follow client-reactions to a contact reflection. A client was continually touching her forehead. This was bodily reflected continuously. As the client said, 'Grandma,' this was reiterated until the client finally expressed congruent feeling about her real-life grandmother. Long-term reiterations can be applied when 'threads of meaning' keep reappearing from session to session.

SUPPLEMENTAL TECHNIQUE

Krietemeyer (Krietemeyer & Prouty, 2003) used additional creative techniques in developing psychological contact with a totally withdrawn and isolated girl who was learning disabled and showing psychotic symptoms. For example, she used silent mutual awareness as a contact. She also rolled a ball of yarn into the client's room which the client rolled back. This facilitated reality contact. Additional reality development occurred when the therapist used a drum and the client responded with finger tapping. This approach eventually led into a verbally communicative relationship.

CONTACT FUNCTIONS

The contact functions are an evolution from Fritz Perls' concept of 'contact as an ego function' (1969: 139) into 'contact as ego functions (with the emphasis on the 's').' Full philosophical and theoretical descriptions are available (Prouty, 1994, 2003). Contact as ego functions is defined as (1) reality contact, (2) affective contact, and (3) communicative contact.

Reality Contact (contact-with-the-world) is defined as the awareness of people, places, things, and events. Things are a part of our lived existence. We turn handles, we throw balls, we touch stones, etc. Things are a definite part of our reality sense.

Affective Contact (contact-with-the-self) is our response to the world and others, defined as the awareness of moods, feelings, and emotions. Mood is affect that is subtle, diffuse, and general. It often is background. I can go to a football game and have anxious and depressed moods having nothing to do with the current reality. Feelings are a more pronounced form of affect. They are clearer and have a specific locus. The intensity of feeling is stronger than mood, and it is not subtle. It is more foreground than background. I feel sad that my grandmother is deceased and no longer here to care for me. Emotions are more intense still, and more clearly linked to an event. My emotion is rage if you are attacking my child or wife.

Communicative Contact is the symbolization of reality (world) and affect (self). Communicative contact is more than the transmission of information. It is the meaningful expression of our perceived world and self to others. It conveys denotative and connotative meanings from our experiential universe. It enables psychological contact with the other. We live in language.

THE CONTACT FUNCTIONS IN THERAPY

This therapeutic vignette illustrates the restoration of psychological contact (Prouty, 1994). Dorothy, an older woman, was one of the more regressed women on X Ward. She was mumbling something, as she usually did. This time, I could hear certain words in her confusion. I reflected only the words I could clearly understand. After about ten minutes, I could hear a complete sentence.

> *Client: Come with me.*
>
> *Therapist: (WWR) Come with me. [The client led me to the corner of the dayroom. We stood there for what seemed a very long time. Since I couldn't communicate with her, I watched her body movements and closely reflected these.]*
>
> *Client: [Dorothy put her hand on the wall and said 'cold.']*
>
> *Therapist: (WWR-BR) [I put my hand on the wall and repeated 'cold.']*
>
> *[She had been holding my hand all along, but when I reflected her, she would tighten her grip. Dorothy began to mumble word fragments. I was careful to reflect only the words I could understand. What she was saying began to make sense.]*
>
> *Client: I don't know what this is anymore [touching the wall – REALITY CONTACT]. The walls and chairs don't mean anything anymore [Existential autism].*
>
> *Therapist: (WWR-BR) [Touching the wall] You don't know what this is anymore. The walls and chairs don't mean anything to you anymore.*
>
> *Client: [Dorothy began to cry – AFFECTIVE CONTACT. After a while, she began to talk again. This time, she spoke clearly – COMMUNICATIVE CONTACT]. I don't like it here. I am so tired—so tired.*
>
> *Therapist: (WWR) [As I gently touched her arm, it was I who tightened my grip on her hand. I reflected ...] 'You're tired, so tired.'*
>
> *Client: [Dorothy smiled and told me to sit in a chair directly in front of her and began to braid my hair.]*

CONTACT BEHAVIORS

Contact behaviors are the emergent behaviors resulting from Pre-Therapy contact reflections. They are the operationalized aspect of psychological contact. Reality contact is operationalized as the client's verbalization of people, places, things, and events. Affective contact is operationalized as the facial or bodily expression of affect. It is also operationalized verbally through the use of 'feeling words' such as 'sad' or 'happy' or 'scared.' Communicative contact is operationalized as social words or sentences.

EXPLORATORY STUDIES

An early exploratory pilot study, Hinterkopf, Prouty and Brunswick (1979), utilizing the Pre-Therapy method, found significant increases for gain scores in reality and communicative contact for patients with chronic schizophrenia, when compared with a control group receiving recreational therapy. The patients in the study had an average hospitalization of 20 years, thereby providing an exploration of the genuinely chronic part of the schizophrenic continuum lacking in prior client-centered research.

A single-case study (Prouty, 1990) measured the effects of the Pre-Therapy method on a dual-diagnosed schizophrenic/autistic and mental disability with a Stanford-Binet IQ of 17. Large increases of reality, affective, and communicative contact were measured by client frequency of contact per minute. A supportive clinical evaluation was provided by an independent psychologist who was unaware of the purpose of the study. He reported an improved ability to tolerate frustration and reduced aggressiveness. He also reported internalized self-control mechanisms as well as greater emotional and behavioral stability. This study provided the first client-centered exploration of the extreme lower end of the intellectual continuum.

Prouty (1994), in another single-case study, measured the inter-rater agreement of psychological contact scaling. The client, a young woman hospitalized with schizophrenia/mental disability, received Pre-Therapy. There were two sets of observations: one set for a single day and one for a three-month period. The single-day observations consisted of 24 pairs of rater scorings drawn from the beginning, end, and middle of the sessions: (1–20, 40–60, 80–100 percentiles). A correlation coefficient of 0.9847 was obtained with a p value of .0001. The pairwise t-test produced a value of 2.3738 with a p value of 0.0526. These results indicated no difference at the .01 or .05 level of significance. The three-month set of observations consisted of nine pairs of mean scores from independent raters that obtained a correlation coefficient of 0.0966 with a p value of .0001, presenting strong evidence against the null hypothesis. The pairwise t-test resulted in a value of 0.0964 with a p value of 0.3528. These results indicated no difference between the raters, suggesting that the observations were based on actual behavioural changes in the client.

Another small-scale study by DeVre, (1992), with her colleagues Van Werde and Deleu, further confirmed positive correlation coefficients and developed evidence for the reliability of the Pre-Therapy scale. There were three clients. The first two were clients with chronic schizophrenia, and the third had mental retardation. The first measure of agreement between raters was k = .39. After much difficulty, translation improvements from English to Flemish were made. The same raters, with a second client, obtained k = 0.76. Again, the same raters with a third client obtained k = .87. The reliability was obtained by independent psychiatric nurses trained in the Pre-Therapy scale. Their first attempt produced a low measure k = .39. With improved English to Flemish translation, the nurses produced a k of .87 with a .0005 level of significance. Again, the tentative conclusion is that this agreement between raters is based on actual changes in the client.

Dinacci (1997) produced a video study of clients receiving Pre-Therapy. The study consisted of one therapist, as well as two experimental and two control patients originally diagnosed with 'mental disability/schizophrenia' and hospitalized for 30 years. The study produced strong clinical and quantitative evidence for marked communicative increases in the near-mute clients, using the Evaluation Criterion for the Pre-Therapy Interview (ECPI) scale (see chapter 4, this volume), which measures verbal coherence and severe levels of disorganization. Reporting a beta-coefficient of .77, Dinacci found a corresponding confidence level of 97.5% that the differences will fall between 16.195 and 28.257 communicative units. Controlling for first-session differences, Pre-Therapy patients averaged 22.226 units higher communicative scores than the control group with the significance was at p .02. This statistical evaluation revealed that the changes in client communication scores fell within the range predicted by a much larger sample and were not the result of extraneous variables.

For a full and complete review of Pre-Therapy studies see Dekeyser, Prouty and Elliot (2008).

REFERENCES

Arieti, S (1955) *An Interpretation of Schizophrenia*. New York: Robert Brunner.
Boss, M (1994) *Existential Foundations of Medicine and Psychology*. London: Jason Aronson.
Buber, M (1964) A phenomenological analysis of existence versus pointing at the concrete. In M Friedman (Ed) *The Worlds of Existentialism*. New York: Random House.
DeVre, R (1992) Prouty's Pre-Therapy. Master's thesis. Department of Psychology, University of Ghent, Belgium.
Dekeyser, M, Prouty, G & Elliot R (2008) Review of Research Insturments and Findings. Person-Centered & Experiential Psychotherapies, 7 (1), 37–55.
Dinacci, A (1997) Ricera sperimentale sul trattamento psicologico de pazenti schizopfrenici con la Pre-Terapia. *Psicologia della Persona*, 2 (4), 3–8.

Friedman, G (1961) Conceptual thinking in schizophrenic children. *Genetic Psychology Monographs, 63*, 149–96.

Goldstein, K (1939) The significance of special tests for the diagnosis and prognosis of schizophrenia. *American Journal of Psychiatry, 96*, 575–88.

Goldstein K & Scheerer, M (1941) Abstract and concrete behavior: An experimental study with special tests. *Psychological Monographs, 53* (2), 51.

Gurwitsch, A (1966) Gelb-Goldstein's concept of 'concrete' and 'categorical' attitude and the phenomenology of ideation. In *Studies in Phenomenology and Psychology* (pp 359–89). Evanston, IL: Northwestern University Press.

Hinterkopf, E, Prouty, G & Brunswick, L (1979) A pilot study of Pre-Therapy applied to chronic schizophrenic patients. *Psychosocial Rehabilitation Journal, 3* (13), 11–19.

Krietemeyer, B & Prouty, G (2003) The art of psychological contact: The psychotherapy of a mentally retarded psychotic girl. *Person-Centered and Experiential Psychotherapies, 2* (3), 151–61.

Mazumdar, D & Mazumdar, T (1983) Abstract and concrete behavior of organic, schizophrenic and normal subjects on the Goldstein-Scheerer Cube Test. *Indian Journal of Clinical Psychology, 10* (1), 5–10.

Perls, F (1969) The ego as a function of the organism. In *Ego, Hunger and Aggression.* New York: Random House.

Prouty, G (1990) Pre-Therapy: A theoretical evolution in person-centered experiential psychotherapy of schizophrenia and retardation. In G Lietaer, J Rombauts, & R Van Balen (Eds*) Client-Centered and Experiential Psychotherapy in the Nineties* (pp 645–58). Leuven: Leuven University Press.

Prouty, G (1994) *Theoretical Evolutions in Person-Centered/Experiential Therapy: Applications to schizophrenic and retarded psychoses.* Westport, CT: Praeger (Greenwood Press).

Prouty, G (1998) Pre-Therapy and the pre-expressive self. *Person-Centred Practice, 6* (2), 80–8.

Prouty, G (2000) Pre-Therapy and the pre-expressive self. In T Merry (Ed) *Person-Centred Practice: The BAPCA reader* (pp 68–76). Ross-on-Wye: PCCS Books.

Prouty, G (2002) Pre-Therapy as a theoretical system. In G Wyatt & P Sanders (Eds) *Contact and Perception, Vol 4 of Rogers' Therapeutic Conditions: Evolution, theory and practice* (pp 54–62). Ross-on-Wye: PCCS Books.

Prouty, G (2003) Pre-Therapy: A newer development in the psychotherapy of schizophrenia. *Journal of American Academy of Psychoanalysis and Dynamic Psychiatry, 31* (1), 59–73.

Prouty, G (2005) Forms of non-directive psychotherapy: The non-directive tradition. In B Levitt (Ed) *Embracing Non-directivity: Reassessing theory and practice in the 21st century* (pp 28–39). Ross-on-Wye: PCCS Books.

Prouty, G & Kubiak, M (1988) The development of communicative contact with a catatonic schizophrenic. *Journal of Communication Therapy, 4* (1), 13–20.

Prouty, G, Van Werde, D & Pörtner, M (2002) *Pre-Therapy: Reaching contact impaired clients.* Ross-on-Wye: PCCS Books.

Rogers, CR (1957) The necessary and sufficient conditions of therapeutic personality change. *Journal of Consulting Psychology, 21* (2), 95–103.

Sanders, P (Ed) (2007) *The Contact Work Primer: Introduction to Pre-Therapy.* Ross-on-Wye: PCCS Books.

Part III

Emergent Developments

Editor's Commentary on Marlis Pörtner

The clinical value of Marlis Pörtner is that she expands the scope of contact reflections from individual therapy to institutional helping roles. She then combines these two functions into a wider concept—the Pre-Therapy approach. Another valuable contribution is that she often bases contact on highly practical client situations, such as putting on shoes or coats, opening windows, closing doors, etc. This is a more 'humanizing' response than a behaviorally directed program or a psychiatric/symptomatic approach. Yet another valuable contribution is her emphasis on developing client-autonomy—sorely needed for this often infantilized population.

CHAPTER 1

Pre-Therapeutic Approaches for Working with People with 'Special Needs'

MARLIS PÖRTNER

INTRODUCTION

The term 'special needs' embraces a wide variety of people who are impaired in many different ways: learning disabilities, psychological disorders, genetic deficiencies, congenital or developmental brain defects, physical disabilities combined with not having been offered adequate opportunities for education, etc. Being able to do justice to the variety of these very different personalities and better understand them requires an individual approach. Therefore the person-centred approach including Prouty's pre-therapeutic concepts is particularly suitable for this field. This chapter will describe how, in my experience, Pre-Therapy proves to be helpful in psychotherapy as well as in everyday care for people who, in some way or other, suffer from a mental disability. It will also describe some experiences of other psychotherapists and caregivers.

DISCOVERING PRE-THERAPY

The first time I met Garry Prouty was at a Gendlin workshop in Chicago, where he presented his work with chronic psychiatric patients and 'mentally retarded' persons—as they were then called. It was for me a revelation as well as an encouragement. Two aspects particularly impressed me. One was how true Prouty's approach remained to client-centred principles while at the same time opening new ways to reach people who, so far, had been hardly accessible for psychotherapy. The other was his conviction—illustrated by amazing case examples—that delusions and hallucinations symbolise concrete experiences.

Becoming acquainted with Garry Prouty and his work reinforced my own experience that the client-centred approach is particularly suitable for this field. I no longer felt isolated in working with these clients. More than 25 years ago, when I started as a psychotherapist, psychotherapy was barely available for people with special needs. None of my colleagues had any experience with these clients. We all had learned that Rogers considered an average level of intelligence indispensable for a therapeutic process and we had our doubts about whether client-centred—or any psychotherapy—would work at all for people with special needs. I had to break new ground supported by my equally inexperienced colleagues in our supervision group and find my own way to cope with the specific demands of this field. The therapies with my first two disabled clients showed that the client-centred approach did work for them (Pörtner, 1990).

The case vignettes Prouty presented at the Chicago workshop were outstanding examples of empathically understanding even clients with extremely bizarre or incoherent ways of behaviour and expression. Prouty did not content himself with a vague general way of 'being empathic', but developed concrete methodical means to facilitate contact with severely impaired persons. By not restricting contact to the interpersonal aspect, but defining it on three different levels as contact with reality, contact with oneself, and contact with others, he built a bridge which made it possible to reach even severely disabled persons with whom apparently there was no way to communicate. The different forms of Prouty's contact reflections correspond to the different contact levels and facilitate contact on all three of them. Beyond the verbal reflections we know from client-centred psychotherapy, they embrace non-verbal ways of communication, thus opening new possibilities of relating to another person's inner world—as strange and unintelligible as it might appear.

My clients were not as severely disabled as those Prouty describes, but for me too, Pre-Therapy offered a valuable and natural completion of the person-centred approach. I experienced it to be useful in two areas of working with people with special needs: psychotherapy and everyday care.

PSYCHOTHERAPY

During the course of the 1980s, it began to be recognised that psychological disorders are frequent among people with mental disabilities, even more so than among the average population (Gaedt, 1987; Lotz & Koch, 1994). The German author Barbara Senckel identifies the reasons: 'in addition to limitations due to disabilities', in traumatic experience like 'fundamental lack of acceptance and esteem; repeated experience of being abandoned and of separation; disparagement, neglect, isolation; heteronomy, pressure to conform, control; lack of self-determination (even where it would be possible) and no prospects in life' (Senckel, 1998: 37, translated from German by this author [MP]). Looking at the histories of persons with mental disabilities we time and again find such experiences.

There is obviously a need to make psychotherapy available to people with special needs. Unfortunately, still only very few practitioners are interested in this field and willing to face its specific demands. However, since the late 1980s, the issue, at least in conferences and the literature, has been increasingly discussed. Psychotherapists of different schools have proposed their ideas (Lotz, Koch & Stahl, 1994; Lotz, Stahl & Irblich, 1996) and it is interesting to discover that most of the specific requirements they postulate correspond exactly to client-centred principles. It is not surprising that empathic understanding is even more essential with clients who, on a cognitive level, seem barely accessible. It might be the only way to get in touch with their strange and sometimes bizarre world.

As it is often hard to distinguish whether a specific behaviour is due to mental disability or a symptom of a psychological disease, traditional diagnostic categories only partly apply. Though people with special needs do suffer from the same psychological disorders as anyone else—such as depression, bipolar disorder, anxiety, compulsiveness, psychotic episodes, posttraumatic syndrome, etc.—with many symptoms 'it is not clear if they allow the same conclusions with a mentally disabled person as with one who is not disabled' (Senckel, 1998: 21, translated from German by MP). In this context it is a clear advantage of the person-centred approach that it does not focus on diagnostics, but on trying to understand the client's subjective world. This is particularly important with disabled persons who 'have only a limited range of behaviours and reactions to express all kinds of states of mind' (Senckel, 1998: 21, translated from German by MP). Prouty's concept of 'pre-expressive' (Prouty, 1994, 1998; Prouty, Van Werde & Pörtner, 1998/2002) allows a deeper understanding of people whose ways of behaving or expressing themselves at first seem incoherent and incomprehensible.

I talk about 'pre-therapeutic approaches' rather than 'Pre-Therapy' because, in my experience with mentally disabled people, pure Pre-Therapy is hardly ever exclusively used. Not that there are no potential clients, but within the existing structures, the chances of very severely disabled and/or non-verbal persons getting psychotherapy are extremely rare. It is not sufficiently recognised as yet that these people too need their individual ways of experiencing and feeling to be understood and responded to. However, slowly, here and there, it is beginning to be recognised—sometimes as a consequence of positive experiences with supportive communication.

An outstanding example is what the German psychologist Barbara Krietemeyer achieved with Laura, a severely disabled, extremely aggressive and auto-aggressive woman. By patiently over a long period just staying near her, yet at some distance, and later by very sensitively reflecting her subtle non-verbal signals, she facilitated a remarkable change process with Laura that no one would have thought her capable of. It is interesting that Krietemeyer, trained in client-centred psychotherapy, intuitively used contact reflections, though at that time she did not know about Pre-Therapy (Krietemeyer, 2000; Krietemeyer & Prouty, 2003; Pörtner, 2000: 103–13).

Also with not so severely disabled clients, who are capable of verbal expression, there are often moments or sequences in psychotherapy when contact reflections are the only adequate response. According to the person's current contact level, these quite naturally intertwine with 'regular' client-centred responses and allow the therapist to more accurately follow a person who is constantly switching levels, which frequently happens with people with special needs.

> EXAMPLE
> Catherine used to fantasise about accidents, ambulances, doctors and hospitals. Sometimes she told me that she had to go the hospital today to help the doctors, or that she had been there yesterday and something had been done to her. It took me a while to realise that, hidden behind these fantasies, there was the real memory of a traumatic experience: her sterilisation. Scattered through many therapy sessions, in tiny fragments, the memory emerged. Each time Catherine then abruptly changed the subject and did not come back to it for some time. Obviously, only in this way and at this tempo was she able to cautiously approach the painful memory.

This corresponds exactly with what Dion Van Werde describes as 'grey-zone functioning' (Prouty, Van Werde & Pörtner, 2002: 81–90): a blurred area between the pre-expressive and expressive level where it is often not clear if what the client expresses is real or delusional. In order that it may become clearer, the therapist has to carefully follow the client on his or her way through this blurred area. Though Van Werde's concept refers to psychotic patients, it is also extremely helpful for understanding clients with mental disabilities. Catherine's 'fantasies' belonged to this grey zone in that they were fragments of a real memory and at the same time delusional in how they were mingled with Catherine's actual life as if they were happening at the moment. Working with Catherine provided me with concrete evidence of Prouty's assumption that delusions are symbolisations of concrete experiences.

Prouty's definition of contact functions is crucial for working with people with special needs, as these functions are frequently impaired or not sufficiently developed. Therefore, restoring, developing and strengthening contact functions—be it on all three or on one of the three levels—is a major issue in psychotherapy (Pörtner, 2003/2007). Often it is the client's contact with him- or herself—emotionally as well as physically—that is the most impaired.

> EXAMPLE
> At the beginning Alex was unable to tell me anything about himself and reacted completely bewildered when I referred to what he felt or experienced. 'I don't know,' was the only answer he was capable of, deeply withdrawn in his chair. To verbally reflect his posture was to risk making him feel mocked. But by reflecting it with my body, I got more in touch with how he must feel. So over the following sessions I patiently continued to refer to it now and then, and after some time his answers changed to: 'Do you think so?' or 'Should I?' I then replied that I did not know, but would like to help him find out. With time, he began to answer with 'yes' or 'no', or 'just a little' to reflections like 'you look somehow sad' or 'you seem quite happy today'. More and more he got in contact with his feelings and slowly learned to find his own words to express them.

It seems to be extremely important for clients to feel that the therapist is also with them, on this confusing and sometimes even threatening pre-expressive level.

> EXAMPLE
> Nora initially did not speak at all, although she was quite able to express herself verbally. For some weeks we communicated only with gestures and facial expressions. Slowly, an emotional contact developed between us and, after some time, she began to talk about issues such as what had happened during the week, why she was angry or happy or sad, etc. With time she went through amazing changes that considerably improved the quality of her life and her relations with the other inmates of the community. However, till the very end of the therapy, she switched back, from time to time, to our earlier non-verbal style of communication—often in a quite playful, mischievous way. Probably she needed to make sure that I was still there, on the pre-expressive level as well.

Dion Van Werde told me that he is observing the same phenomenum with psychotic patients. Apparently clients need the security of knowing that the therapist will 'be there' when for some reason they have to shift to a pre-expressive level.

Some years ago Michael Kief, a psychologist working in a big organisation for disabled people in Germany, participated in several workshops with Garry Prouty. Since then he has often used contact reflections and finds them very helpful, particularly with people suffering from post-traumatic stress disorder, which is frequent among people with special needs. He gives two examples.

EXAMPLES

1. Michaela suffers from post-traumatic stress disorder as a consequence of continuous physical maltreatment during the first four years of her life. It shows in provocative-aggressive behaviour linked with anxiety fits, in pronounced emotional instability and in stereotypical verbal expression. It was not possible to verbally work through the traumatic experience with her, as she refused to get into that issue. So the therapy soon turned to body-oriented methods (massage). In addition, the therapist tried to introduce elements of 'somatic experience' according to Peter Levine (Levine, 1998), yet her willingness to co-operate was limited. In order to bring the escaping Michaela back to the actual situation and anchor her there, he successfully worked with contact reflections. They made her quiet down, interrupted the verbal stereotypes and, now and then, initiated authentic comments on the actual situation. A particularly important issue was, with the help of body reflections, to get her more in contact with her body that, due to the early maltreatment, she felt completely alienated from.

2. Peter, after a severe car accident and having remained in an 'awake coma' (Apallic Syndrome) for about four months, has recovered quite well in his orientation. But, due to the frontal brain damage, he has lost the capability of controlling his impulses. Peter behaves extremely aggressively, scratching, biting, beating and screaming furiously. He sometimes seems terribly frightened, as if he is living through the accident again; sometimes he is hallucinating about non-existing threats. As he refused to cooperate, the therapist's attempts to get into conversation with him failed. However, with contact reflections the therapist was able to initiate some kind of contact. Peter then calmed down and became more aware of himself. He seemed, within this context, to be able to accept the therapist's presence, whereas otherwise he openly rejected him.

How helpful and necessary it is to work on a person-centred basis with disabled clients and to integrate contact reflections I experienced once more when, to my surprise, I was asked for supervision by a behaviour therapist.

EXAMPLE
Paul works with mentally disabled clients in a clinical setting, which also offers residential facilities. He felt at his wit's end with these clients and at the same time under pressure from carers and doctors who expected that, as a behaviour therapist, he would within a short time correct or eliminate the unwanted behaviours of the people they referred to him. It was interesting for me to learn that this idea is much more a projection of others rather than the psychotherapist's concept of behaviour therapy. Yet, Paul did not feel in a sufficiently strong position to withstand the pressure and convincingly support his view.

Based on his own case material, I introduced him to client-centred principles and to Prouty's contact paradigm. Learning to respond to a client's experiencing and feelings rather than just discussing facts opened Paul to a totally new dimension, allowing him more differentiated and useful ways of interaction with his clients. Furthermore he discovered that situational reflections were particularly helpful with people who feel embarrassed with the therapeutic situation and don't know what to say or do. This is often so with disabled clients who, as a rule, do not choose to see a therapist, but are sent by their carers. Without being intrusive, situational reflections help them to feel more comfortable and slowly clear a way for contact. Paul finds this way of working much more satisfactory. He now feels more confident in what he is doing, as well as more relaxed and patient when progress in a therapy is slow or sometimes hardly visible.

Of course, a few suggestions within the context of supervision cannot sufficiently provide a comprehensive knowledge of how to work in a person-centred way, but even so this behaviour therapist found it extremely helpful. Once more it proves the substantial contribution client-centred psychotherapy integrating Pre-Therapy has to offer in this specific field. The more it is to be regretted that this chance for the person-centred approach to spread its sphere of activity is far from being realised, as long as there are not more psychotherapists motivated to work with people with special needs.

EVERYDAY CARE

Pre-therapeutic approaches are useful not only in psychotherapy but also in everyday care, where there are even more opportunities to foster contact functions. Dion Van Werde proves it with the 'Contact Ward' he founded at the Psychiatric Clinic Sint-Camillus in Ghent, Belgium, which has been working successfully now for nearly 20 years. Everybody working on this ward has learned when and how to use contact reflections in order to foster and anchor the patients' contact functions. In addition, several aspects of the ward—activities, therapies, interior decoration etc.—were reconsidered with regard to their impact on contact functions and modified if necessary. Van Werde's concepts are exemplary, for working with his patients and also for working with people with special needs.

For people with special needs, everyday care is at least as important, or even more so, than psychotherapy. Good effects of psychotherapy will not last if they are not supported in daily life. If there is too big a discrepancy between what disabled people develop in the therapy sessions and what is required and tolerated by their surroundings, they will get confused and perhaps feel even worse than before. Problems, instead of being diminished, are likely to be aggravated.

On the other hand, a sensible way of care could make unnecessary many a psychotherapy. Therefore, it is desirable that caregivers too work in a person-centred way. Not that they should do therapy, this is not their task, but their daily work has to be based on person-centred principles. What this means concretely is described in *Trust and Understanding* (Pörtner 1996/2008 and 2000/2007). Based upon long experience in consulting and supervising staff, I developed a specific concept for person-centred everyday care. It is being adopted by more and more organisations in Austria, Germany and Switzerland. They experience that working this way does not only improve the quality of life of people with special needs, but is much more satisfying for the caregivers as well. In these countries the concept is also part of several educational programmes for social workers, caregivers, etc. And in Scotland, a very successful training programme for social workers, organised by Altrum (a federation of charities) in partnership with Queen Margaret University, is based on the concepts of *Trust and Understanding*.

Within a person-centred concept of everyday care, pre-therapeutic approaches apply in two different ways:

THE CONTACT PARADIGM AS POINT OF REFERENCE
An essential aspect of care is providing life conditions and activities that foster contact functions instead of damaging them even more. Unfortunately the latter happens frequently, though involuntarily, be it with regard to occupational, educational and physical programs, housework duties or leisure activities.

EXAMPLE
In an exhibition of Gauguin's paintings—one of these 'in vogue' exhibitions everybody is going to, crowded to a point that makes it difficult to see the paintings at all—I catch sight of a group of people with special needs, looking quite distraught, with their extremely nervous carers trying to keep them together and quiet. In vain: one of the women is screaming in a very loud voice: 'When do we go home?' and is vigorously hushed by the carers. It would have been better if they had listened to her, as she was absolutely right. Feeling that in these unfamiliar surroundings—a strange building, the crowd, pictures of exotic people and landscapes—she began to lose her reality contact. Her question clearly expressed the need to get back on firm ground.

Caregivers have a tendency to arrange greatly overcharged programs for people in their care. I often am startled by the ambitious schedules of my disabled clients—schedules that would stress even me. Not wilfully do carers act this way, but motivated by the wish to do a good job. They forget though, that demanding too much of a person with special needs is likely to aggravate existing or even cause new behaviour disorders. 'Less is more' is a motto worth being paid heed to when working in this field.

CONTACT REFLECTIONS
By using contact reflections, carers, in different ways, will be better equipped for some essential demands of everyday care, such as:

RECOGNISING, UNDERSTANDING AND RESPONDING TO A PERSON'S EXPERIENCING
This is an essential task of person-centred care. Contact reflections make it possible to work with people who are non-verbal or express themselves in rudimentary or bizarre ways. Caregivers report that by using contact reflections they are more often in contact with their clients and understand better how they feel and what they need.

FOSTERING CONTACT
Contact cannot be established once and for all, but will come and go. Therefore, contact functions need to be consistently fostered in order to inhibit their decrease or decline. Daily life offers numerous opportunities to stimulate and reinforce a person's contact with her experiencing and with the reality around her.

For example, on a walk, the caregiver might say: 'You take big steps', 'You hold my hand firmly' (body reflections), 'We are walking along the river', 'It is raining' (situational reflection). Or at the shower: 'You are shivering' (body reflection), 'The water is too cold' (situational reflection), 'The water feels nice and warm', (combined body/situational reflection). Or 'You are smiling', 'You look sad' (facial reflections). Or, responding to a person's oral expression: 'Paff paff', 'Mama', 'Brrrr!' (word-for-word reflections).

ADEQUATELY RESPONDING TO GREY-ZONE FUNCTIONING

To fully accept a person implies also accepting her occasional functioning in the grey zone. In everyday care—other than in psychotherapy—to follow somebody in this blurred area does not mean working on or trying to decipher delusional material, but helping the person to restore reality contact, while at the same time recognising her subjective world. For example, by reflecting: 'Catherine is telling me what she sees at the hospital. We all are sitting in the kitchen now, having breakfast.'

OVERCOMING CRITICAL SITUATIONS, REDUCING TENSION AND AVOIDING ESCALATION

For example, with a person who is hurting herself, the carer might stop her by using body reflections—be it verbally or by doing the same to himself (of course, without really hurting himself) and perhaps saying 'ow!' It helps a person become aware of what she is doing to herself and realise that it hurts. Situational reflections can help to loosen tension and break a vicious circle, especially in situations which recur again and again. For example: 'We are turning in circles', 'You say yes, I say no', 'You are shouting at me', 'We are both upset', 'We are speaking very loudly'.

Carers report that at the beginning they felt self-conscious about using contact reflections, especially body reflections, but once they get used to it, they find it extremely helpful. They observe that bizarre behaviours often diminish when being reflected. It is a reassuring experience, which makes them feel more relaxed and more competent.

EXAMPLE

George is a caregiver in a German organisation for people with special needs where work is consistently based on the concepts of *Trust and Understanding*. He tells me that using pre-therapeutic elements helped him to make contact with Franz, a severely handicapped man who most of the time lies on the floor, withdrawn into himself. The staff could not bear just letting him lie there and, despite his resistance, tried again and again to keep him away from the floor and sitting in a wheelchair. Franz did not like it at all and, whenever he had a chance, crawled back to the floor. George then, from time to time, tried to also lie down on the floor, at a little distance from

Franz, and just wait. Slowly he felt a very subtle contact developing. Franz still lies on the floor most of the time, is still very withdrawn, but he now looks around sometimes and seems to be aware of what is going on around him. His body appears less tense. The staff too are more relaxed since they gave up forcing Franz to sit on a chair. They sometimes sit or lie on the floor for a while, seeking eye contact with Franz. They discovered that accepting Franz where he is, and meeting him there, is less stressful for Franz and for themselves and therefore much more satisfying.

Seen from the outside, such changes might not seem significant. But for a severely impaired person like Franz, these subtle details make a substantial difference in terms of life quality and well-being.

CONCLUSION

Embedded in a person-centred way of working, pre-therapeutic approaches are helpful and necessary in psychotherapy as well as in everyday care for people with special needs. Person-centred principles allow an individual approach to the very different personalities who are in some way or other mentally and/or intellectually impaired, thus helping to understand them better. Pre-therapeutic concepts are indispensable with these clients, particularly with the severely disabled, as they open possibilities to communicate with people who apparently are not able to express themselves or do so by incomprehensible and bizarre behaviours.

It would be worthwhile for person-centred organisations to engage themselves more in this sphere of activity. Working with people with special needs and integrating pre-therapeutic approaches should be an issue in the curricula of regular client-centred training programmes. This way more psychotherapists would be motivated to work with such clients. For those who are interested and decide to do so, additional seminars should be offered where they can train and refine their practice and deal in depth with its specific conditions and requirements. Specific training programmes for person-centred everyday care should be created for professionals working in this field.

The person-centred-approach is in a position to substantially contribute to the quality of life and well-being of people with special needs—a chance that hopefully will increasingly be perceived and realised by its adherents.

REFERENCES

Gaedt, Ch (Ed) (1987) *Psychotherapie bei geistig Behinderten. 2. Neuerkeröder Forum.* Neuerkeröder Anstalten: Eigenverlag.

Krietemeyer, B (2000) Wege aus der inneren Isolation. *Kerbe, 2* (2), 21–2.

Krietemeyer, B & Prouty, G (2003) The art of psychological contact: The psychotherapy of a retarded psychotic client. *Person-Centered and Experiential Psychotherapies, 2* (3), 151–61).

Levine, PA (1998) *Trauma-Heilung. Das Erwachen des Tigers.* Essen: Synthesis Verlag.

Lotz, W & Koch, U (1994) Zum Vorkommen psychischer Störungen bei Personen mit geistiger Behinderung. In W Lotz, U Koch, & B Stahl (Eds) *Psychotherapeutische Behandlung geistig behinderter Menschen: Bedarf, Rahmenbedingungen, Konzepte* (pp 13–39). Bern: Hans Huber.

Lotz, W, Koch, U, & Stahl, B (Eds) (1994) *Psychotherapeutische Behandlung geistig behinderter Menschen: Bedarf, Rahmenbedingungen, Konzepte.* Bern: Hans Huber.

Lotz, W, Stahl, B & Irblich, D (Eds) (1996) *Wege zur seelischen Gesundheit für Menschen mit geistiger Behinderung: Psychotherapie und Persönlichkeitsentwicklung.* Bern: Hans Huber.

Pörtner, M (1990) Client-centered therapy with mentally retarded persons: Catherine and Ruth. In G Lietaer, J Rombauts & R Van Balen (Eds) *Client-Centered and Experiential Psychotherapy in the Nineties* (pp 659–69). Leuven: Leuven University Press.

Pörtner, M (1996) *Ernstnehmen, Zutrauen, Verstehen: Personzentrierte Haltung im Umgang mit geistig behinderten und pflegebedürftigen Menschen* (2008, 6th revised and extended edition). Stuttgart: Klett-Cotta. [English edition (2000), see below]

Pörtner, M (2000) *Trust and Understanding: The person-centered approach to everyday care for people with special needs.* (2007) 2nd revised and extended edition. Ross-on-Wye: PCCS Books.

Pörtner, M (2002) Psychotherapy for people with special needs: A challenge for client-centered psychotherapists. In JC Watson, RN Goldman, & MS Warner (Eds) *Client-Centered and Experiential Psychotherapy in the 21st Century: Advances in theory, research and practice* (pp 380–6). Ross-on-Wye: PCCS Books.

Pörtner, M (2003) *Brücken bauen. Menschen mit geistiger Behinderung verstehen und begleiten.* (2007) 2nd revised and extended edition. Stuttgart: Klett-Cotta.

Prouty, G (1994) *Theoretical Evolutions in Person-Centered/Experiential Therapy: Applications to schizophrenic and retarded psychoses.* Westport, CT: Praeger.

Prouty, G (1998) Pre-Therapy and the pre-expressive self. *Person Centred Practice, 6* (2), 80–8.

Prouty, G, Van Werde, D, & Pörtner, M (1998) *Prä-Therapie.* Stuttgart: Klett-Cotta. [English edition (2002) *Pre-Therapy. Reaching contact-impaired clients.* Ross-on-Wye: PCCS Books]

Senckel, B (1998) *Du bist ein weiter Baum: Entwicklungschancen für geistig behinderte Menschen durch Beziehung.* München: Beck.

Editor's Commentary on Dion Van Werde

The work of Dion Van Werde is important because of his pioneering development of a Pre-Therapy milieu treatment for schizophrenic clients. As with Pörtner, Van Werde differentiates between individual psychotherapy and institutional helping roles. He sees institutional helping roles as providing 'contact work'. The goal of contact work is the strengthening and support of the client's contact functions—not a full psychotherapeutic process. This specific paper is unique in several ways. First, it shows the combination of individual therapy with contact work. Second, it results in a psychological treatment of a highly psychotic patient with unusual symptoms. Third, it resulted in considerable improvement for the client. The last two results are rare in today's chemical Zeitgeist.

CHAPTER 2

The Falling Man:
Pre-Therapy applied to somatic hallucinating

DION VAN WERDE

> 4. Because wisdom will not enter into a soul that deviseth evil, Nor dwell in a body that is held in pledge by sin.
> 5. For a holy spirit of discipline will flee deceit, And will start away from thoughts that are without understanding, And will be put to confusion when unrighteousness hath come in.
> 6. For wisdom is a spirit that loveth man, And she will not hold a blasphemer guiltless for his lips; Because God beareth witness of his reins, And is a true overseer of his heart, And a hearer of his tongue.
> *Book of Wisdom* (Ch. 1: 4–6)

This article describes a piece of therapy undertaken in a multidisciplinary residential psychiatric setting. It involved working with a man named 'Henry' with the utmost incongruence between himself and the experiencing of his body. During treatment, and especially with the help of individual sessions based on Pre-Therapy, the client literally achieved a 'new balance' with the result that he no longer insisted on vehemently and physically correcting his hallucinatory body problems. He mastered the problematic relationship with his body sufficiently to leave the hospital and move to vocational training and a paid job.

The article assumes a certain familiarity with Pre-Therapy as described by Prouty (1976, 1990, 1994 and on pages 13–22, this volume); Van Werde (1994a, 1994b, 1998); Prouty, Van Werde and Pörtner (2002); Sanders (2007); and Van Werde and Prouty (2007). Readers should understand specifically the use of contact reflections—forms of reflection pointed towards concrete client behaviour by which the therapist makes contact with the client, and which are designed to establish or enhance the client's contact functions. Contact reflections take five forms (originally identified by Prouty, 1976): situational, facial, body, word-for-word and reiterative.

Van Werde, D (2002) The falling man: Pre-Therapy applied to somatic hallucinating. *Person-Centred Practice, 10* (2), 101–07. By kind permission of The British Association for the Person-Centred Approach.

THE CLIENT

The client, Henry, a man of average intelligence and in his early twenties, was an inpatient at our psychiatric hospital for approximately one year. Six years earlier, following a *fugue* (a sudden flight from home) and his subsequent return, Henry's parents had taken him to a psychiatrist. He was always bad tempered, and he and his parents quarrelled endlessly. At the time of the initial referral, he had just come back from a Scouts' camp, exhausted from a series of late nights with an average of only two hours of sleep: 'It was hot there and I wanted to feel myself awake so badly', was his comment. He was then referred to a psychiatric hospital. He went home after seven weeks with a prescription for a maintenance dose of neuroleptic drugs (Melleril® 100 mg a day). The fights at home stopped and the family was relatively satisfied. Henry's parents decided to take him out of school and have him started as an assistant in a friend's grocery store. Gradually Henry became interested in the Bible—he clearly prayed more than before. Working and studying lost importance for him. He felt himself getting more holy: 'I looked radiant. I often stood in front of the mirror and found myself beautiful.' At the same time, he had compulsive thoughts to injure other people: to 'hit them in the face'. The patient had to discipline himself not to give in to these thoughts: 'They were all thoughts that made me unhappy and gave me a headache. I was always busy with them.'

This situation worsened and a year later the client was convinced that he had to exorcise the Devil to let God enter:

> There are good things in myself, but they can't come out. My heart is like a stone, my body needs to be refreshed. The Holy Spirit lives in my abdomen, I need to let God come in from above, to have him make contact with the Spirit and expel the Devil out of my body. I let everything come to my heart. I must proclaim my guilt and sweat water and blood, 100% intense.

From that time on, the client started to literally practise what he said. He developed a way of falling and screaming that was designed to put an end to his sinful life. The way he experienced his body was very bizarre. He had the idea that his organs had changed places. Thus, he believed that his shoulders had narrowed and that the part between his shoulders had descended in the direction of his belly and pubic region. The falling was meant to shock his body in such a way that his organs returned to where they belong. He would jump in the air and throw himself on his knees to the floor, accompanied by a gruesome noise, especially since he felt that while falling he must confess all his sins. Once he had been admitted to our ward (aged 21), we could hear the repetitive falling, together with a hardly understandable recitation of sins. This falling and screaming put the whole ward under tremendous strain.

THE THEORY

We would describe the problem as one of somatic hallucinating involving a delusional interpretation of a bizarre bodily perception. When somebody is suffering psychosis—in this case a psychosis concerning the body—contact is lost and psychosomatic balance is disturbed. Functioning, both psychological and physical, is out of personal control and is in conflict with collective expectations, rules, norms and so on. On top of this the person is afraid of holding still and looking at his experiences that 'pop up' and tend to take over, since they are so powerful and overwhelming. This leads to alienation, stress and isolation.

The conceptualisation of treatment, especially from the perspective of Pre-Therapy, is to accompany the person in their search for contact. The application of Pre-Therapy to a ward milieu is extensively described in Prouty, Van Werde and Pörtner (2002) and more briefly in Van Werde (2007). In the treatment in the context of the psychiatric ward, the person is individually helped to restore his balance, to break the psychotic isolation, and to build up healthy functioning. Since we work in an institution and we are in charge of 24 patients, we have to confront the client continuously with the demands on him or her caused by living with others, and not functioning in a vacuum. There are the realities of the fellow patients, the house rules, the timetables, and so on. A part of our task, even our mission, is to find a way to bridge the patient's individual needs and the structural limitations of an institution and a regime. As to individual needs, we make sure that we stay attuned to the emotional world of the people we work with in order to facilitate psychotherapeutic process if at all possible; at the same time we have no difficulty in actively integrating reality elements in our work. However, we are aware that in the last instance it is the client who decides what should be done and, taking everything into account, what is best for him or her.

We try to stay with whatever presents itself, even when, for ourselves, the things that occur are new and, at first sight, incomprehensible. Staff need regular support to be able to live this phenomenological attitude continuously, to tolerate all the bizarre behaviours, and to continue to trust experiential processes (Deleu & Van Werde, 1998). Experiencing this attitude enables the patient to build up their strength from within and eventually start the psychotherapeutic process (hence 'Pre-Therapy'). All this since he is reconnecting with parts of his functioning that had become alien even to him.

What follows is a brief description of the therapy of Henry (the 'falling man') over approximately one year of inpatient treatment.

THE THERAPY

Most of the time and in almost every social situation, 'the falling man' could act normally, albeit on a superficial level. He even overachieved in being courteous and helpful. However, especially when alone, he could lose himself easily and plunge into his own swamps of bizarre pre-expressive functioning. Hidden by his family, almost nobody knew of his psychiatric admission; it was a well-kept secret. This situation fortified his psychological isolation.

Once he arrived on our ward, the problem of ensuring ward structure and keeping up house rules very soon conflicted with moments of this client's pre-expressive functioning. His dangerous behaviour necessitated intervention in his process. If we continued to let him do his 'exercises' (as he called it), we would burden the other patients with incomprehensible noises of repetitive falling and fast spoken words. This was one consideration in limiting his behaviour; another came from our responsibilities and concern for his physical safety. Several times he did real damage to himself by falling on the floor. At one point, fluid on his knees needed draining off. Another referral to general hospital occurred when he lost fluid from his nose (possibly of cerebral origin). Other limits that were set and measures that were taken during his stay included forbidding him to sit in other patients' rooms and sing and pray aloud during the night. As much as nursing staff and myself were able to, we tried to stay with his process and, in doing so, to help him to re-contact his own proactive forces. We did this not only by listening to his words and paying attention to his behaviour, but also always consciously trying to capture the facial signs of concurrent affective life and offer it back to him, often by means of facial reflections (FRs). Thus, when he came out of his room after the nurses had reminded him that it was time for coffee (situational reflections [SRs]), they reflected (FR) 'You smile' or 'You look puzzled' (FR) or even 'You look anxious' (FR). Sometimes they went to the toilet or the bathroom to reflect that they heard him on the corridor or in the bathroom (SR). This was done both empathically to be with his falling and screaming in places that he thought private, and also situationally to offer him realities about the noise, sound volume, etc. of his behaviour. They reflected his sitting in front of the television (SR) that was turned off and looking like he was daydreaming (FR). They reflected him saying that he had pain in his coccyx (word-for-word reflections [WWR]) but also his smiling (FR) at the same time. Sometimes these reflections brought him into contact with the reality of his body and even with his life which, until that moment, had been transposed into pre-expressive bizarre behaviour (for instance, pain and smiling). Little by little he contacted his doubts, his shame, his need for reassurance, his being afraid of the future and so on. Treatment did not become standardised but stayed tailor-made—but nevertheless within certain boundaries. Parallel to his self-abuse (falling, exaggerated jogging, binge-eating, staying awake at night to pray, hurting his toes by repetitive exercises to stretch his pelvis), nursing staff talked to him about how to take care of his body e.g. sitting in the sun to dry out pimples, using a different shampoo to deal with dandruff and so on. In this sense, working on contact in general and working on contact with his body in particular was not reduced to focusing only on the bizarre and the damage done. It stayed as open as possible, thus including positive aspects of attention and care for oneself. Other actions undertaken by the nurses included having him draw up his activities for one week and discuss with him the lack of spare moments. They told him about pain as a valuable signal given by the body. They informed him about the dangers of damaging his knees and head. They repeatedly explained to him why he was given medication to sleep and why sleeping is important.

Gradually through his treatment an opening up towards other people, reality in general and his body, together with a unfreezing of his affective life became visible. Over the year cracks appeared in the façade of being perfect and without problems. More and more people became aware of his bizarre praxis of falling and confessing: first the nurses, then the psychotherapist—Henry started demonstrating his 'exercises' in his office—and even his fellow patients. When we gave him this reality-information, it really shook him up, since this undermined his routine of exercising and disturbed his frozen social balances. Nursing staff also became stricter as to what was allowed and what was not. All this intensified his psychological process. He began to talk about being abused as a child and felt like a lamb that had to be slaughtered. He believed he was bad and sinful and punished by God. Treatment skill was demonstrated in following the tempo of his process without compromising the ward's structure too much, nor being scared away by his actions. We were able to maintain him on our ward and had him participate in the programme without cutting across his psychological process. Concrete therapeutic steps were made.

The key episode in his treatment arose when the individual psychotherapist no longer tolerated Henry's falling 'exercises' in his office—which at that time was located on the ward itself. Since Henry had opened up and started consciously sharing this previously hidden aspect of his life, the therapist had not wanted to stop this process. So, after thorough deliberation, the psychotherapist suggested that they work together in a soundproofed room above the hospital gym. They would not be disturbed there, nor would they disturb anybody else. The offer to change location was responsive to the reality of life on the ward (in terms of the volume of noise and general disturbance) and it acknowledged the necessary limitations of the institution.

The first session above the gym involved a lot of talking and resembled the sessions in the office. Near the end of that particular session, the client himself proposed practising his falling. They agreed that a gym mat would be used to prevent severe physical damage. The next ten minutes were very intense. Henry would stand staring, his legs open wide, stretching his upper body, then proceed to confessing his sins whilst falling flat down on the mat, his hands pushing his pelvis up. The therapist used Pre-Therapy reflections intensively to stay with that process. These aimed to help Henry fully to contact his experiencing and what he was doing with and to his body, thereby shifting his level up from pre-expressive to expressive functioning: 'You are standing upright' (body reflections [BRs]), 'Your face looks pale' (FR), 'You stare' (FR), 'You fall down' (BR), 'I hear you fall down on the mat' (SR), 'You look very concentrated' (FR), 'I hear you call out your sins aloud' (SR), 'You fell again' (BR, reiterative reflection [RR]), 'Your knuckles are white' (BR), 'You put at lot of pressure on your pelvis' (BR), 'You look at me' (SR), 'We're above the gym' (SR), 'You said you wanted to exercise' (RR), 'It looks like you're in pain' (FR). To the latter Henry replied 'Of course I am in pain! Do you think that it doesn't hurt?' By saying this, he started contacting his feelings. His tempo slowed down. Then he wanted to stop the session and after the therapist had reiterated what had happened, they agreed to meet again some days later.

For the second session in the same location above the gym, Henry came a few minutes late. He started talking. After a while, he said that falling was not necessary anymore. The therapist was genuinely very surprised and asked the reason for his new position. Henry said that he had just visited the hospital priest; he had confessed all his sins and had been forgiven! This made it redundant to continue his falling in order to exclaim all his sins and change his body. Everything was OK now!

After this, we saw that Henry needed to fall less. He had made a therapeutic shift. A new balance was achieved and this evolution was consolidated. The client moved to a rehabilitation ward and was able to take up employment training. Some months later, he started a job and five years later, he was still working. No crisis intervention or admission has been necessary since. He lived with his parents again without too many difficulties. His GP regularly prescribed a minimal dose of neuroleptic drugs to support his balance. When contacted for follow-up and for asking permission to publish his case, he told his former psychiatrist that he still occasionally 'exercised', but far less intensely and far less frequently. It had never hindered him in his work. Follow-up after ten years showed that, after five years, he had given up independent employment as the pressure had been too great. Together with moving into a sheltered living accommodation, relatively satisfying conditions were set and are still held, to consolidate the balance achieved with such hard work: his stress was reduced by stopping the regular job and changing to working on a farm for some days a week on a voluntary basis.

CONCLUSION

As a person-centred team we experienced the importance and therapeutic relevance of welcoming and staying with any material that presents itself or that is jointly chosen to be looked at. The client's experiencing as well as the institutional demands are the continuous touchstones of everything that is undertaken. We learned that the restoration and strengthening of contact are the basic processes and outcomes of our work.

How do we conceptualise the psychotherapeutic process that took place—and what happened to the somatic hallucination? On admission, we saw that Henry's psychological space almost coincided with his experience, as if his organs had changed place and needed to be put in their right place again. Connected to this, but on a different level, was his self-awareness of being evil and punished. Falling and confessing his sins would forgive his sins and, also literally, put everything in place again. Social functioning had been impossible; his isolation was almost complete. On the ward, this person, including his problematic experiencing and behaving, was welcomed. Staff also acted normally towards clearly psychotic functioning. By not being absorbed in his 'bodily problem', as he himself obviously was, staff could gradually anchor the man back to reality (see Van Werde, 1998), and bring him into communication.

The hypothesis of Pre-Therapy—that contact and symptomatic functioning are inversely connected—appears plausible and proved. The more Henry engaged in the therapeutic process, the less he needed to block every feeling, every other human being, and every bit of 'shared reality' out of his life. Somatic hallucinating no longer dominated his total functioning. It shrank and dissolved little by little in healthy functioning. Generally, he started feeling and acting again with respect for his body, to sense its limits and possibilities.

In the end, the psychotic core was addressed. We saw Henry eagerly starting his exercising. Then, after having really contacted what he was doing, he refrained from plunging into that explosive and dark area of hidden meanings and engraved history. He decided to stop and, in a manner of speaking, accepted the shifted balance. Problematic functioning became less dominating in his life, although not completely resolved. Overall, he felt strong enough to take control of his own life again.

REFERENCES

Deleu, C & Van Werde D (1998) The relevance of a phenomenological attitude when working with psychotic people. In B Thorne & E Lambers (Eds) *Person-Centred Therapy: A European perspective* (pp 206–15). London: Sage.

Prouty, G (1976) Pre-Therapy: A method of treating pre-expressive psychotic and retarded patients. *Psychotherapy: Theory, Research and Practice, 13* (3), 290–5.

Prouty, G (1990) A theoretical evolution in the person-centered/experiential psychotherapy of schizophrenia and retardation. In G Lietaer, J Rombauts & R Van Balen (Eds) *Client-Centered and Experiential Psychotherapy in the Nineties* (pp 645–85). Leuven: Leuven University Press.

Prouty, G (1994) *Theoretical Evolutions in Person-Centered/Experiential Therapy: Applications to schizophrenic and retarded psychoses.* New York: Praeger.

Prouty, G, Van Werde, D & Pörtner, M (2002) *Pre-Therapy: Reaching contact-impaired clients.* Ross-on-Wye: PCCS Books.

Sanders, P (Ed) (2007) *The Contact Work Primer: Introduction to Pre-Therapy.* Ross-on-Wye: PCCS Books.

Van Werde, D (1994a) An introduction to client-centred Pre-Therapy. In D Mearns (Ed) *Developing Person-Centred Counselling* (pp 121–5). London: Sage.

Van Werde, D (1994b) Dealing with the possibility of psychotic content in a seemingly congruent communication. In D Mearns (Ed) *Developing Person-Centred Counselling* (pp 126–8). London: Sage.

Van Werde, D (1998) Anchorage as a core concept in working with psychotic people. In B Thorne & E Lambers (Eds) *Person-Centred Therapy: A European perspective* (pp 195–205). London: Sage.

Van Werde, D (2007) Contact work in a residential psychiatric setting. In P Sanders (Ed) *The Contact Work Primer* (pp 60–71). Ross-on-Wye: PCCS Books.

Van Werde, D & Prouty, G (2007) Pre-Therapy: Empathic contact with individuals at pre-expressive levels of functioning. In M Cooper, P Schmid, M O'Hara & G Wyatt (Eds) *The Handbook of Person-Centred Therapy* (pp 237–50). Basingstoke: Palgrave.

Editor's Commentary on Penny Dodds

The significance of Dodd's writings is her level of expertise in the area of dementia, and through this, she has been able to make an important clarification in the Anglo-American meaning of 'person-centered' approaches to dementia. In UK social care settings, the term refers to a broad philosophical approach valuing the uniqueness and sense of self of persons with dementia, special needs or other personal care and living support needs. In addition, in this setting, there is a moral emphasis on engaging the humaneness of demented persons. In UK and American counseling and psychotherapy settings, the term 'person-centered' refers to the specific psychotherapy of Carl Rogers and its subsequent evolutions. This distinction allows her to carefully differentiate Pre-Therapy from other contemporary treatment models.

Another valuable contribution by Dodds is her qualitative exploration of the learning process when teaching Pre-Therapy contact reflections. Dodds described the first learning stage as *surprise*, wherein the student is literally surprised at the client response to contact reflections. The student is surprised at the level of engagement that is brought forth. In this early phase the student comes to see that their usual patterns of communication with the client were not authentic engagement but based on their needs to ascribe meaning to the client.

The next stage can be described as *confusion and experimentation*. As the student is surprised and realizes that their communication was not authentic engagement but their own ascription of meaning, they come to experimenting with the newly acquired contact reflections. Given various episodes of contact, *staff reactions* become important.

Some students experience joy and profound depth in the real communication that occurs. Other students are frightened and overwhelmed when intense emotions are expressed by the client. Others exhibit a pattern of hesitancy when they discover that their work can evoke sorrow, or when the contact reflections produce no client response. Finally when the contact reflections become integrated, they appear to be done 'with a light touch.'

CHAPTER 3

Pre-Therapy and Dementia Care

PENNY DODDS

PERSON-CENTRED CARE AND PERSON-FOCUSED CARE IN DEMENTIA

The application of Pre-Therapy to dementia care remains relatively unexplored. Van Werde and Morton first considered the potential use of Pre-Therapy in this field, and its relation to existing approaches, in a critique of person-centred approaches in dementia care (Morton, 1997). In dementia care in the UK, the term 'person-centred' has, rather confusingly, been adopted as a broad generic term. It has come to mean seeing the person, rather than a task or an object. Its broad philosophical base values the subjective experiences of the person with dementia and stresses the importance of their relationships with others (McCormack, 2004). Being person-centred in this sense involves: valuing the uniqueness of individuals; focusing on how a person with dementia might retain their sense of self in the face of a diminishing ability to express themselves to others; and emphasising the crucial role that relationships can play in helping a person retain a sense of self-identity (Kontos, 2005). Drawing on social constructionist perspectives, a person with dementia is seen as having a preserved self, an external self and a relational self (Sabat & Harre, 1992; Aquilina & Hughes, 2006). Interactions with others help validate the external self. Attention to the relational self encourages staff working with people with dementia to provide opportunities and ways of communicating that can support a person with neurological changes in experiencing and expressing their own unique personhood (Kitwood, 1997). On a wider level, contemporary thought in dementia care in the UK is also exploring a moral model of care, in an expansion of the psychosocial model that has challenged the medical perspective over a number of years (Hughes, Louw & Sabat, 2006). Thus, much of the current dementia literature rests on the moral imperative to engage with the humanness of people with dementia, in order to counteract neurological changes that may get in the way of a person's ability to express their own sense of personhood.

At the level of practice, we have seen the emergence of a range of therapeutic approaches. For people in the earlier stages of dementia, cognitive behavioural approaches are widely advocated to enhance coping with relatively mild cognitive impairment, and memory enhancement or memory 'training' techniques are often employed (Zarit et al, 2004; Saczynski & Rebok, 2004; NICE-SCIE, 2006). When cognitive impairment has become more pronounced, person-centred approaches focus on providing opportunities to use existing memories to relive positive emotional states through reminiscence (Woods, Spector, Jones et al, 2005). Reminiscence hopes to help people with dementia to retain a sense of their own identity, of past roles and experiences. A biographical approach might be used to help strengthen their social selves by using storytelling and encouraging narratives from people with dementia. Validation therapy is also largely concerned with past experiences (Feil, 1993). Feil argues that in dementia, people return to the past to deal with unresolved conflicts, and has developed an approach that acknowledges the emotions that underlie words or actions that present as apparently confused or disoriented behaviour. The worker's role here is to engage in the emotional world of the person, accepting reality as it is experienced by the person with dementia. Tom Kitwood put forward the concept of 'Positive Person Work' (Cheston & Bender, 1999; Kitwood, 1997), in which attention is on the relationship between the person with dementia and the worker, with the aim of providing people with dementia greater opportunities for positive social and emotional experiences that may counteract some of the detrimental effects of the typical care environments and social interactions that surround people with dementia. As a result, the personhood of the individual with dementia is strengthened as workers focus on providing a variety of opportunities for positive constructive social interactions. There has also been a growth in activities-based approaches that aim to offer stimulation and enhance well-being (Pool, 2001; Abraham, 2005). In the later stages of dementia more creative media are often used, with a focus on providing and initiating positive experiences for the person with dementia. These might include using sensory experience, touch, movement and music, and the use of transitional objects such as dolls (Götell, Brown & Ekman, 2003; Aveyard, Sykes & Doherty, 2002; Sung & Chang, 2005; Nystrom & Lauritzen, 2005; Baker, Holloway & Holtkamp, 2003; Sherratt et al, 2004; Graham, 2004; Verity, 2006).

Thus in dementia care in the UK, the umbrella term 'person-centred care' tends to be used in two ways. One the one hand it is extolled as a desirable goal in social policy terms, in order to promote individually focused care as opposed to institutional care. On the other, it refers to an assortment of approaches, which, whilst they may have quite varied theoretical origins, share a desire to improve the social, psychological and environmental conditions that influence the quality of life for those living through a progressive cognitive impairment. Although person-centred dementia care values subjectivity and offers empathic and compassionate presence, in accordance with its general humanistic origins, there are, as Morton (2000) observed, differences between the meanings that it ascribes to the term 'person-centred' and those understood by the Rogerian person-centred psychotherapy tradition. In exploring this difference in terminology Morton clarified some of the differences between person-centred dementia care and Pre-Therapy, which is grounded in the Rogerian tradition (Morton, 2000). He concluded that Pre-Therapy used with people with dementia was person-centred, whereas the other approaches, whilst clearly influenced by the person-centred tradition, are not truly person-centred in purely definitional terms, rather they are 'person-focused' (Morton, 1999). Whilst this might seem like splitting hairs, it has drawn attention to some important differences between the two worlds of Rogerian psychotherapy and dementia care. In addition, Van Werde and Morton (1999) provided the opportunity to explore the potential for using Pre-Therapy with people with dementia which, to date, stands as the only substantial UK publication on the potential for Pre-Therapy to offer 'emotional palliative care' to people with dementia.

This scarcity of publications in the field of dementia does not, however, mean that the Pre-Therapy community is oblivious to the use of Pre-Therapy with people with dementia. Some cross-fertilization has already occurred in Europe, with psychiatrists, psychologists and psychotherapists from the Pre-Therapy Network taking Pre-Therapy into their own clinical areas, including mental health services for older people—for example, Paul Dierick in his role as psychiatrist, Stijn Leijssen using Pre-Therapy via the medium of music therapy with people with dementia, and Marlis Pörtner. Van Werde and Morton's contribution was particularly important in two ways. Firstly, it clearly outlined the key concepts of Pre-Therapy: contact functions, contact reflections and the differences in levels of expressiveness. This made it accessible to people working in dementia care by including it in an overview of therapeutic approaches in dementia care. Secondly, they provided an extensive episode of dialogue that shows how contact reflections are used with someone whose speech appears confused and disoriented. This is particularly significant because it demonstrates the immediate relevance to dementia care.

Working with people with dementia frequently requires us to enter into conversations with people who are using language in an unusual way; their talking is different: sentences are hard to understand, patterns of speech become disjointed, their talk can appear obscure as traditional rules of syntax and cohesion are affected (Bayles, 2003; Shakespeare, 1998). The speech patterns of people with dementia often appear more poetic or metaphorical and consequently staff are sometimes left floundering about how to respond

(Killick, 2002, 2005; Knocker, 2002). By providing an example of an actual dialogue, the concreteness of the contact reflections is clearly visible in a conversation and this is instantly recognisable to staff working in dementia. It is this concreteness of the contact reflections that provides the dementia literature with something that has often been absent or lacking—some detail about what to say. Much of the dementia literature can be criticised on the grounds that for all its emphasis on principles of particular approaches, workers are still often left with a difficulty in knowing what they should *actually* say. The clarity, and apparent simplicity, of the contact reflections make deciding what you should say much more obvious—you reflect.

PRE-THERAPY AND OTHER APPROACHES IN DEMENTIA CARE

Thus Pre-Therapy has the potential to add to the mosaic of positive approaches in dementia care. Indeed it shares some similarities with some existing work. John Killick (Killick & Allan, 2001) has described some inspirational work in communicating with people with dementia, building on literature which draws attention to the art of listening to their words in order to appreciate the experiential world of people with dementia (Goldsmith, 1996). Again we can see similarities with Prouty's theoretical origins, with both Killick and Goldsmith paying great attention to the importance of the subjective experience, asking us to listen and engage with people with dementia on an experiential and phenomenological level.

Killick directly refers to *making contact,* and the following description of his work illustrates a startling similarity with a Pre-Therapy approach. It appears that Killick's understanding of what it is to make contact is uncannily similar to Prouty's. Focusing on non-verbal communication, Killick describes contact work with the emphasis on the worker following and not directing an intervention. This contact-making approach is advocated when more traditional overtures in conversation result in no response from the person with dementia. Killick and Allan (2001) describe his practice accordingly:

> When developing relationships with certain people who do not speak, John has found in general the most effective way of establishing and developing contact is to confine himself to using only those channels of communication the person with dementia uses. The practice that we have called mirroring has developed in a natural way in the course of John's work, as a response to individual people and situations, and has become part of his overall approach. Others have developed similar approaches in related fields, such as work with people with learning

> difficulties (Nind & Hewett, 1994). It can include words, but is most powerful and moving when it occurs in a purely nonverbal manner. Put simply, it involves being engaged in a one-to-one interaction, focusing closely on the person's movements, and reflecting back what they do, and in the style they are doing it, essentially following the leads that they give. If they rock their body, and stroke the arm of the chair you would do so also. As well as doing what the other person is doing, mirroring demands that you do it in a similar way so that attention must be given to the speed at which the person moves, the degree of muscle tension or relaxation involved, and the way one movement or gesture merges into another. It requires a great deal of concentration and attention, and being highly sensitised to the whole range of nonverbal channels. (Killick & Allan, 2001: 54)

This illustrates how Killick establishes contact by using mirroring and non-verbal reflections of the person's body movements. In Prouty's terms this is one of the contact reflections—a bodily reflection. It is slightly ironic that Killick and Allan state that they have termed this practice mirroring, as if it is something new, when the practice of reflecting has been part of the Pre-Therapy literature since the 1970s (Prouty, 1976). But this similarity perhaps simply reflects the meeting of two different worlds.

There are also similarities between Pre-Therapy and other approaches in dementia care. Validation therapy (Feil, 1993), guides workers to *tune in,* whilst Tom Kitwood's *positive person work* requires staff to notice and attend to the person (Kitwood, 1997). Both state the need for an empathic presence on the part of the worker. Focusing on promoting emotional security for the person with dementia, Cheston and Bender (1999) draw attention to the importance of empathic listening and bearing witness to the uncertainty and fear that the dementia process may provoke.

Although Pre-Therapy has some similarities to existing practice in dementia care, it is important to also recognise the differences. Chief amongst these is the purity of Pre-Therapy (using non-directive contact reflections), which contrasts to common use of additional, more directive, strategies in dementia care. Feil recommends directive strategies (for example—questioning, initiating) on the part of the care worker. Kitwood describes principles of *positive person work*, yet their application frequently involves workers initiating interactions or activities rather than focusing on a non-directive approach, led by the experiential world of the person with dementia. Killick, whilst less directive, still includes prompting and questioning as part of the listening process. Person-centred approaches in dementia care thus encourage staff to utilise a combination of approaches to communication

Fig. 1. Components of approaches in dementia care compared to Prouty's Pre-Therapy

Listening (Killick)	Positive person work (Kitwood)	Validation therapy (Feil)	Pre-Therapy (Prouty)
Resisting talking	Recognition	Stimulate energy	Contact reflections:
Using silence	Negotiation	Mirroring	Situational
Eye contact	Collaboration	Music and movement	Facial
Facial expressions	Play	Exploring rhymes and	Bodily
Voice tone and pitch	Timalation*	unusual word combinations	Word-for-word
Touch	Celebration	Speaking their language to build trust	Reiteration
Pacing	Relaxation		
Going with the flow	Validation	Repeat their last words	
Prompting: suggesting ending to sentences that are unfinished	Facilitation	Linking – getting in tune with their emotions	
	Holding	Be empathic	
		Validate feelings	
Mirroring		Closeness and touch	
		Use life review themes	
		Use questions (non-aggressive, tying together past and present, tap free expression)	
		Re-phrasing their words	
		Use polarity	
		Imaging the opposite	
		Linking behaviour with unmet need	
		Use of ambiguity	
		Use of non-threatening factual words	
		Centring	

* Timalation: Kitwood's word meaning sensuous or sensual e.g. massage or aromatherapy. The aim is to provide reassurance, closeness and pleasure.

that is rooted in the subjective world of the person, whilst also drawing on other verbal and non-verbal strategies. See Figure 1.

All four approaches attend to the relationship between with the person with dementia, but Prouty differs from the three authors from dementia care in his emphasis on the concreteness of the reflections and in his breaking down of how a relationship is formed. For Prouty, the focus is gaining contact and the embodiment of experience through the facial, the bodily, the situation and through words. For the authors in dementia, the process of gaining contact is less explicit, but it is still the therapeutic goal, and the range of approaches that facilitate psychological well-being hope to achieve it. In other words, Prouty takes us back to the basics of establishing contact—the therapeutic approach *is* contact—whereas for Kitwood and Feil contact arises *through* their therapeutic approaches. Killick seems to be the nearest approach to Prouty, but his emphasis is on the overall importance of communication rather than on exactly how this can be achieved.

We can thus see how Pre-Therapy offers a potential to expand our understanding of how we can make relationships with people with dementia, and how the concreteness of the contact reflections give it an instant appeal. These considerations led towards two developments: (1) trying out the contact reflections with people with dementia, and (2) a research study exploring the introduction of Pre-Therapy to staff—primarily unregistered nursing assistants—working with people with dementia.

TRYING OUT CONTACT REFLECTIONS WITH PEOPLE WITH DEMENTIA

Early work using contact reflections with people with dementia seemed to confirm their potential and led to two case studies that illustrated their use with individuals with moderate to severe degrees of cognitive impairment (Dodds, Morton & Prouty, 2004). To illustrate the application of contact reflections with dementia, an extract of an interaction is presented here. The man with dementia spends a large part of his day walking around the ward, frequently behaving aggressively to staff and other residents. His ability to communicate verbally was extremely impaired resulting in his remaining generally silent. Much of his day is spent in isolation from others and the majority of his contact with staff is focused on practical tasks such as washing, dressing and eating. At the time of this interaction he was walking in the corridor, his eyes did not appear to be focused on anything in particular and he was walking slowly without any discernable purpose. At the beginning of the interaction he was approached slowly and, using the same pace and rhythm of his walking, the nurse began to walk alongside him. The nurse stays slightly ahead so that he can see that there is another person with him, as he often seems unaware of the presence of others around him. He was walking next to the wall and the nurse was in the middle of the corridor. This extract contains the dialogue and events that occurred in addition to notes on the use of the contact reflections. It shows how contact between Mr X and the nurse was slowly built.

> Nurse: (SR) *We're walking.*
> *[This is a situational reflection, however the nurse also reflects the movements bodily, emphasising the gestures of walking.]*
>
> Mr X: *[Mr X continues walking, making no eye contact, no change in behaviour.]*
>
> Nurse: (SR) *The rail is there.*
> *[The nurse reaches across and touches the rail. Whilst this may seem intrusive, there is a need to provide greater visual and non-verbal cues for people with dementia as the capacity to comprehend language may be severely impaired.]*
>
> Mr X: *[Mr X continues walking, making no eye contact, no change in behaviour.]*
>
> Nurse: (SR, BR, SR) *We're walking, your hands by your side, the rail.*
> *[Again the situational reflections of walking and the rail are enhanced by the nurse physically gesturing walking and touching the rail. The bodily reflection of his hands being by his side is also enhanced non-verbally by the nurse mirroring this movement.]*
>
> Mr X: *[The resident continues walking, making no eye contact, no change in behaviour.]*
>
> Nurse: (SR) *The wall is here.*
> *[The nurse touches the wall. The situational reflections of the rail and the wall involve the nurse reaching over and in front of the resident to touch them. This interrupts the field of vision of the resident. Again this could be seen as disrupting the world of the person, however, it still stands as an invitation for the person with dementia by drawing attention to the environment. In this way the worker is also placing her own body in the environment of the person with dementia and this itself may result in the person with dementia noticing the worker.]*
>
> Mr X: *[Mr X looks at the nurse's hand.]*
>
> Nurse: (SR) *Is here, you look at my hand on the wall.*
> *[Here we see that Mr X has started to notice the nurse's hand on the wall.]*
>
> Mr X: *[Mr X continues walking.]*
>
> Nurse: (SR, FR) *We're walking, your face is down.*
> *[The nurse continues to mirror the body posture and movements of Mr X. The nurse also non-verbally reflects his facial expression. This involves the nurse walking ahead and*

slightly turned towards Mr X, so that her face is within his field of vision.]

Mr X: *[Mr X touches the wall.]*

Nurse: (SR) *We're touching the wall, we're looking.*
[Repeats the movement of touching the wall.]

Mr X: *[Continues to touch the wall.]*

Nurse: (SR) *A picture here.*
[The nurse touches the edge of the picture frame, running her hand up and down the frame.]

Mr X: *[Mr X touches the frame.]*

Nurse: (BR) *Your hand on the frame.*

Mr X: *[Looks at the picture and looks at the nurse. Here we see the building of contact as he is more in contact with the environment (the wall, picture) and with the nurse (by looking at her face).]*

Nurse: (FR, SR) *You look at me and the picture.*
[The nurse strengthens the contact.]

Mr X: *[Mr X then touched the image on the picture, he then looks at the nurse and goes GRRRRR (a growl) and smiles. The image on the picture is a tiger.]*

RESEARCH ISSUES

Anecdotal accounts such as this, however, are not sufficient to meet the current demands within the UK healthcare system to demonstrate that our practice is 'evidence-based'. Such demands require that care and treatment be based on a robust body of evidence that supports their use. However, evidence-based practice is biased towards a techno-scientific positivist paradigm—in which the randomised double-blind control trial is seen as the gold standard of evidence. This bias is reflected in policy and guidelines that direct practice. Approaches that are more amenable to scientific study are more likely to be able to prove favourable outcomes and therefore more likely to 'prove' effectiveness. Consequently 'scientific' research is more likely to determine what is seen as good practice. The implications of this are that quantitative positivist research paradigms are difficult to apply to psychotherapy, where variables are difficult to exclude and it is more difficult to measure interventions and outcomes. As a result, alternative research paradigms—such as qualitative methodologies and methods—are commonly placed lower in the hierarchy of evidence (Roth & Fonagy, 2005). Pre-Therapy has begun to engage with the scientific perspective, using quantitative methodologies. The establishment of construct validity of the contact functions and the development of scales to measure contact have advanced work in this area, but at present this research does not include people with dementia as research subjects (Dinacci, 2000 (Chapter 4 this volume); Prouty & Dinacci, 2002; Prouty & Dekeyser, 2006). As a result we are currently at a point where there is no substantial research supporting the use of contact reflections in dementia care, despite a growing body of evidence in relation to other client groups such as people with schizophrenia. I do not mean to imply that Pre-Therapy should not be used, rather that we need to exercise caution in simply taking something from one area of practice (psychosis) and apply it to another (dementia), in spite of the immediate face validity of the usefulness of Pre-Therapy for dementia care.

In order for Pre-Therapy to gain greater recognition in dementia care we need further research. However, gaining recognition through research, which is inherently biased towards a scientific paradigm, poses a problem. Ethical and methodological barriers hamper research with people with dementia, despite a growing commitment to including people with dementia in research activity (Wilkinson, 2002). The study of interactions and social phenomena in dementia does not lend itself to scientific methods (Bond & Corner, 2001), and the dementing process renders people with severe dementia unable to give informed consent to participate in research and unable to comment on their experience of any research activity.

However, these barriers are not insurmountable and research governance requires clear protocols and ethical frameworks where people with dementia are included in research activity (Department of Health, 2001a, 2001b; Vass et al, 2003). If Pre-Therapy in dementia is to gain greater acceptance we need research that will be recognised by those in positions of power who sanction what is seen as effective practice, and this research needs to work with the challenges that are posed by researching people with dementia as well as use a range of established methodologies, both quantitative and qualitative.

CAN PRE-THERAPY BE LEARNT BY STAFF WORKING WITH PEOPLE WITH DEMENTIA?

Before we can get to the point of building a body of 'evidence', we need to address a fundamental question—*can* nursing staff learn to use Pre-Therapy contact reflections with people with dementia? In order to establish if something is useful, we need to know if people can use it. This is particularly important if a therapeutic approach that has developed within the world of psychotherapy, by psychotherapists, is to be imported into nursing practice. It is from this starting point that an exploratory research study was carried out, addressing this very question—the learning and using of contact reflections in dementia care.

The Pre-Therapy literature already provides ideas about introducing Pre-Therapy to nursing staff. Pörtner (2002) has given us accounts of how nurses' attitudes and perceptions can change as a result of staff embracing Pre-Therapy.

> Before Prouty, I called the patients' behaviours bizarre, disturbed or problematic, without thinking about the reasons of this behaviour or about methods how to deal with them. After Prouty, I tried to change my attitude. (Pörtner, 2002: 141)

However, the process of introducing Pre-Therapy to nursing staff has not always been smooth. Resistance has been experienced and projects are vulnerable to withering, resulting in the potential for change not being realised. Pörtner describes the introduction to nurses by Luc Roelens:

> Originally the programme was intended primarily for the nurses. The founders felt that the nurses had the most opportunity to apply and integrate Pre-Therapy into their daily work. Luc Roelens had not anticipated the solid resistance from the staff that came to oppose his idea. In most wards, there were two or three people interested in Pre-Therapy and willing to try it. But they felt quite isolated because the majority of the nurses could not see any good in this approach and resisted it. Sitting with a patient and trying to make contact, in the eyes of many nurses, was not 'real work' and not anything serious. Instead they felt if was their duty to 'do something'. On the wards where this attitude predominated, it was deadening for those who actually were motivated to try Pre-Therapy. (Prouty, Van Werde & Pörtner, 2002: 124)

In order to understand the complexities of introducing Pre-Therapy to dementia care environments, we need to firstly acknowledge that the vast majority of the day-to-day care is delivered by nursing or social care staff. In the UK, psychology and psychotherapy services for people with dementia are limited. If Pre-Therapy is to have any impact, therefore, we need to look more closely at how Pre-Therapy is learnt and used by the staff who deliver the majority of care. In the main, such staff are 'unqualified' in that they have no formal professional training in nursing. As well as holding in mind the composition of the workforce, we also need to consider the processes at work in introducing something new, and pay heed to the kind of difficulties that Pörtner refers to above. There is much more involved here than teaching something and expecting change. We have to work with the real context in which we are hoping that people will learn, and try out, something new.

THE RESEARCH PROJECT

The research project started with the specific question—'what happens when staff learn and use Pre-Therapy contact reflections?' The study used Action Research methodology and captured the experiences of staff as well as observations of how staff use the contact reflections (Dodds, 2008). The methodology was important. Action Research focuses introducing a change, researching the process of change, is context specific, collaborative and participatory (McNiff & Whitehead, 2006). In order to meet the challenge of providing research that is robust, and thus enhance its prospects of gaining acceptance by the research community, the study used qualitative methods and comparative analysis within the recognised methodology of Action Research (Miles & Huberman, 1994; Waterman, Tillen, Dickson & de Konig, 2001).

Preliminary findings from the study provide us with information in two areas: (1) how staff learn and use contact reflections; and (2) ideas about the influence of the context and nursing role which helps or hinders staff adopting contact reflections in their practice. These lead to tentative ideas about the application of Pre-Therapy to dementia care.

LEARNING AND USING PRE-THERAPY BY UNQUALIFIED NURSING STAFF

Early findings from the research show that the processes of learning and using contact reflections are far more complex than they first appears. On paper, the reflections seem straightforward. Indeed, staff would commonly react initially by saying that they seem familiar; they make sense and staff feel, to some extent, that they use them already. Once staff start using contact reflections, however, it becomes clear that the apparent simplicity is deceptive. In the early stages of learning and using contact reflections, staff appear to follow a pattern, namely: surprise, confusion, experimentation, reaction, hesitancy, integration. Perhaps not surprisingly, this resembles some theoretical ideas about how people acquire skills in any form of practice (Benner, 1984, 2004).

SURPRISE

Surprise arises from staff finding that there is a qualitative difference in doing the contact reflections—they *feel* different to do. Staff are then faced with reconsidering how they usually communicate with people with dementia, throwing into sharp relief that much of their interactions with people with dementia are based on offering commands, questions and statements rather that reflecting the concrete embodied experience of the person with dementia. Amongst some of the staff research subjects we have developed a 'shorthand' for how Pre-Therapy contact reflections differ from other ways of communicating. Staff begin to recognise that their usual patterns of communication may be *ventriloquism* (putting words into the mouth of another), or *hijacking* (where the worker initiates and takes the lead overriding the world of the person with dementia with the worker's world). Another surprise for staff is that they realise how their normal patterns of communication are based on their own world, rather than the world of the person with dementia. This is particularly evident where staff have to perform tasks or physical-oriented care. The experience is illustrated by quotes from the staff who participated in the research.

> ... yes for me it's entering that world, to me that's what it is ... it's showing them that they are not alone, it's being there with them and that does make sense, but I'm not much of an actor and this mimicking and doing the same things as they are doing takes a bit of practice for me actually, it's difficult to just start doing that and not task-orientated, give you a drink, if you're crying we'll give you something to eat, sort of nurses responses, we've got to watch that. (ANN/VHS2/29.12.04)

CONFUSION THEN EXPERIMENTING

After surprise, staff experience confusion and some discomfort in going through a process of unknowing and unlearning (Grech, 2004). The confusion is often generated by uncertainty about when to use a contact reflection and when to use another response. In terms of learning about Pre-Therapy, this indicates how staff are getting to grips with understanding the conceptual difference between an expressive state and a pre-expressive state. In relation to working with people with dementia, this seems further complicated by the emotional states of people with dementia which may be frequently highly expressive, albeit expressed in a way that appears disjointed or disoriented.

A period of experimenting happens with staff, as they begin to gauge who might benefit from contact reflections and when contact reflections are or are not appropriate. There have been insights from staff that the contact reflections might seem to be more appropriate with people who are quiet and withdrawn. This also has offered staff the opportunity to try and interact with people who frequently get overlooked in busy environments, where the norm is that the most vocal people tend to monopolise staff time and attention. Experimenting also means risking getting reactions that were not expected or reactions that lead staff to doubt the use of the contact reflections.

> ... and I got a ... well, ... not negative results, as you don't know what to expect, well he was a bit irritable with what I was doing when I was doing ... my mirror ... and I was doing whatever, and mirroring what he was doing and repeating what he was doing so he end up getting very irritated and then he just left me and I tried to follow him and that was it, and there's another lady who can't speak proper, I tried to do that as well, so that's the two, she also got very irritated in a sense that she clapped me [gestures being slapped]. (APP/VHS7/15.2.05)

REACTIONS IN STAFF

Some of the reactions to contact reflections by people with dementia have themselves led to powerful reactions in the staff. These have not always been comfortable for staff, and have led to further surprise that the contact reflections had brought about such a sudden expression of emotional contact from the person with dementia.

> The eye contact was with he and I ... virtually the whole time and he was holding my hands and shaking them and saying yes as if he was remembering something ... initially we thought perhaps he was laughing and when you looked at him there was no way was he laughing, I mean he had tears ... it was total raw emotion and not pleasant to see ... I wanted to cry, as I've never seen him like that. (AYL/VHS1/29.11.04)

Staff have also had experiences of receiving no response, and the constraints of the ward environment denying them opportunities for sustained periods of time in which to use contact reflections. Yet, where contact is established, the rapidity of the emotional connection has been a recurrent theme of the research. Staff have described a sudden change in the relationship using phrases like 'it was I was inside them ... I feel we really were looking at each other you know *really* looking ...'

The experiences described by staff can be considered in relation to Hans Peters' ideas around subjectivity, intersubjectivity and two-way intersubjective attunement (Peters, 2003, 2005 and Chapter 5, this volume). Peters expanded the concept of contact in Pre-Therapy, exploring the development of attunement, drawing on Stern's ideas of mirroring, reflection and affective/empathic attunement in child development (Peters, 2003, 2005 and Chapter 5 this volume). For Stern, imitation was not simply mechanical, but involved a degree of empathic attunement and intersubjectivity (Stern, 1985). Peters clarifies this, offering an explanation of subjectivity, by developing the idea of intersubjectivity.

- *Subjectivity:* how an individual sees, thinks and feels about the world.
- *One-way intersubjectivity:* the capacity of taking on the subjectivity of others, which requires empathic attunement to the other person. Within one-way intersubjective attunement the carer picks up the feelings from the child, and imitates or mirrors these. The child then understands that the carer response is related to the child's own original emotions and experience.
- *Two-way intersubjective attunement:* two people are reciprocally aware of each other's awareness of each other.

(Adapted from Peters, 2005)

In relation to Pre-Therapy, Peters views the Pre-Therapeutic relationship as one-way—the therapist uses contact reflections using intersubjectivity. The purpose is to move to mutual contact and a relationship based on two-way intersubjectivity. Traditional therapy requires two-way intersubjectivity. The aim of Prouty's Pre-Therapy is to restore the very basic contact functions and establish a relationship that can allow therapy to proceed. Peters (2005) proposes a secondary application. Where some contact is possible, but limited, he suggests that contact reflections can enhance or reflect the client's momentary level of functioning. The use of the contact reflections becomes a tool through which the therapist enhances *moments* of two-way intersubjectivity. What staff appear to describe are sudden moments where the relationship switches from one-way intersubjectivity to two-way intersubjective attunement which results in a powerful felt sense within the worker. For some staff this was shocking and upsetting, for others it felt like a privilege to be meeting the person within.

HESITANCY THEN INTEGRATION

Not surprisingly, the variety of responses to contact reflections from people with dementia results in a degree of hesitancy in staff. The hesitancy seems mainly to come from either fear of provoking sorrow or because they see no apparent reaction from the person with dementia. Those staff who begin to integrate the contact reflections into their own personal repertoire of communication skills find that the 'light touch' use of contact work helps them work more effectively with people. This becomes particularly relevant where staff are performing personal, often intimate care, which is an unavoidable reality of caring for a person with severe dementia. Some have found that by using contact reflections whilst encouraging a person to dress, wash or drink results in making these tasks easier. However, it may be that either this is the result of the contact reflections or of the enhanced sensitivity that may have arisen as a result of learning about the contact reflections and avoiding overly directive ways of interacting.

IMPLICATIONS OF SUDDEN EMOTIONAL CONTACT

Whilst the implications of the experiences of staff need to be more fully considered, there are two things that stand out in relation to staff learning and using contact reflections. The first concerns the implications for workers gaining sudden emotional contact in which the person with dementia is expressing intense and powerful emotions that are difficult for the member of staff to hold, or to contain. Given that the majority of staff are unqualified, they may not have the emotional capacity, or have received training in managing such emotional connection (Morse, Botorff, Anderson et al, 1992; Smith, 1992). This raises a difficult questions—should staff be exposing themselves to such unpredictable deep emotional contact without sufficient skills or experience? This difficulty is compounded by the matter of fact way in which some models of care quite happily state that an empathic presence underpins the relationships with people with dementia. If the consequences of being empathic, however, are that staff feel that they are 'opening a can of worms … which you can't put the lid back on it … with no magic wand to make it better …' (ANN/AYL/VHS1/29.11.04), then we might need to question the rhetoric and the reality of being empathic in dementia care. Dementia literature consistently calls for improvements in communication and being empathic is central to this. However, it is difficult to realise this where staff may not have the professional training or skills to contain the emotions of others, especially where staff have limited opportunities for support and supervision.

The hesitancy that some staff have shown in relating to people with dementia in a way that opens up a deeper and more emotional relationship may also be linked to how staff see their role in caring for people with dementia. Where staff view their nursing role as offering comfort and relieving distress, it goes against the grain to be using contact reflections which facilitate a person with dementia expressing emotions of distress and discomfort. Anxieties are raised as staff fear they will be unable to provide comfort, which is seen as part of the nursing role, and that witnessing distress may provoke additional feelings of powerlessness and hopelessness within themselves. So there is a potential conflict arising from using contact reflections which facilitate a two-way intersubjective attunement between a person with dementia and nursing staff.

REFLECTING *AND* DOING

A second issue arises in the integration of contact work into the existing duties of staff. Contact reflections, whilst concrete, need to be grounded in a person-centred ethos which may be contradictory or compete with the task-oriented work that staff need to carry out (Graneheim et al, 2005; Hansebo & Kihlgren, 2002). We should not underestimate the positive effects on job satisfaction and staff morale that delivering value-based compassionate care can offer, however it may be important to acknowledge the potential tension arising from trying to do both simultaneously (Berg, Hallberg & Norberg, 1998; Kendrick & Robinson, 2002). The experiences described by staff demonstrate that using contact reflections feels different for them, and this may reflect the complex decisions that staff have to make on a micro level about what to say. When a person with dementia is walking around, staff are presented with a range of possibilities—the person may be lost and looking for something practical such as the toilet, they may be lost in their own world and looking for someone who they knew from the past, or they may be responding to their environment and trying to get out. In such situations staff have to make a decision about what direction their interaction will take. For example, they may meet the need that the person with dementia cannot meet themselves by directing them to the toilet. Alternatively they may use their existing knowledge of the person and strike up a discussion about a deceased relative, or offer comfort and security in an attempt to make the person feel safe in an environment that may seem strange and frightening. Once contact reflections are added to the staff's repertoire, they have an additional choice—to stop, reflect and notice the person prior to any other form of directive or 'helping' intervention. Where staff feel that their role is to help and intervene, rather than leave the person with dementia to flounder, the contact reflections counter the urge to help and 'do something'. Consequently using contact reflections can feel to staff as if they are not doing something. This runs counter to a role concept which equates 'doing' with caring.

CONTEXTUAL FACTORS

Up to this point I have described the individual experiences of staff learning and using contact reflections. To broaden the investigation it is necessary to consider the context in which staff are attempting to use them (Innes, 2002;

Innes, MacPherson & McCabe, 2006). The research sites used in the study are unremarkable; all three are residential settings for the long-term care of people with dementia. Staffing ratios are approximately one member of staff to four or five people with dementia. As a rule, four staff will be on duty at any time; they work shifts and the composition of shifts varies on daily basis. An understanding of this context and its effects is integral to any examination of an attempt to introduce new therapeutic approaches amongst such nurses and care staff. The working patterns of professional disciplines such as occupational therapists, psychologists and psychotherapists differ from ward-based nurses. Such non-nursing disciplines can come and go from a ward; their working day might involve being in a number of different places, in the company of different individuals or groups. For the duration of a shift, nurses are perhaps as captive as the residents they care for. The concept of *relational autonomy* helps us understand how these differences between nurses and other professionals impact on the use of contact reflections in practice, in addition to accounting for some of the resistance that Pörtner described above. Non-nursing professionals have the space to exert individual autonomy over their practice. Nurses who work in unstable groups can be seen to be affected by the concept of *relational autonomy* (MacDonald, 2002; Sherwin, 1998; Donchin, 1995) where 'the complex webs of personal and institutional relationships that make possible, or sometimes hinder the making of real choices' (MacDonald, 2002: 195). This perspective shows how staff are not driven solely by individual autonomy over their own actions. Rather they are affected by other staff around them. On a very concrete level, this means that staff have to be aware of their own actions in relation to the actions of others. Throughout the day, the staff have to work as a single entity, ensuring that phones are answered, the safety of the overall environment is maintained by adequate levels of supervision and making sure that all staff know where each other are. This frequently impinges upon staff's ability to take time away from the whole care environment to work on a one-to-one basis with a single resident. Indeed, to do so may expose the staff member to being seen as a bad team player. The use of the contact reflections, therefore, has to fit into the existing working patterns of staff and the care they provide. Other than episodes of personal care, which are carried out in residents' bedrooms and bathrooms, much of the interactions that staff have with people with dementia are done in public areas, such as corridors, lounges and dining rooms. This means that staff are faced with trying out something new in the presence of colleagues, relatives, other residents and visitors to the wards. Thus the context itself may inhibit staff from trying something new. This has certainly been evident in the research where staff describe being embarrassed to use the contact reflections in front of other people for fear of looking silly.

> I just found it a lot easier to sit on my own with Mr X than in a room where there are members of staff walking by, that self-consciousness of appearing foolish or, no I think that's my stuff, my lack of confidence, my fear of being judged, so I think that's not about what I'm doing, that's about my stuff, does that make sense? It's not about my lack of belief about what I'm doing, it's just that what if I look stupid, what if the patient hits me in front of everybody ... (CAT/VHS12/22.3.05)

Staff have also reported discomfort with using the contact reflections in public spaces for fear they may appear disrespectful in the eyes of an onlooker, particularly when they are reflecting words or sounds which are incomprehensible to the member of staff. 'I just feel like I'm copying them and taking the mick I suppose, I don't feel quite comfortable doing that one' (ALI/VHS/16.5.05).

This concern was also expressed by a relative who, after receiving information about the research and the contact reflections, raised the question of dignity. Her concern was that the word-for-word reflections may appear to be parodying her mother. 'God knows she has little enough dignity as it is' (KP/RD/1.3.05). This may lead to further ideas of how the contact reflections challenge usual ideas about the rules of conversations. So adopting contact reflections requires an understanding that the delivery of the contact reflections needs to be subtle and done from a position of respect before people can accept that the process of reflecting is not mocking.

The introduction of Pre-Therapy to dementia care settings requires an awareness of the psychological group process such as conformity and affiliation to dominant group behaviours, which might work to prevent people learning, using and sustaining any change in their practice. In addition to the influence that working in groups, working in public, intergroup process and relational autonomy can have on new developments, attempts to introduce new practice may also come up against organisational and structural forces that can inhibit change. This point has already been raised by Mueller-Hergl (2003), who emphasises the need for managerial and organisational support for change in practice of staff. For workers to adopt new practice, a pivotal role can be played by staff in senior positions within units who have a willingness to role-model new approaches, which can sanction experimentation with new ways of working. Again, organisational constraints can militate against this, as senior nurses on units are increasingly distracted away from direct patient care and practice development by the requirement to spend time on the administrative tasks of running residential and inpatient units.

These individual, relational and organisation barriers to introducing Pre-Therapy might seem somewhat daunting, reflecting as they do the real world and lived experience of staff who work in these contexts. Such barriers do not, however, detract from the growing awareness that the contact reflections offer a medium for staff to develop their relationship-building skills with people with dementia. Staff repeatedly report using contact reflections that have led to unexpected levels of contact and understanding between themselves and individuals with dementia who have not responded to other approaches.

> I sat on the bed with him and just used the contact reflections and just finding out so much about him being in the merchant navy, how he got burnt, just sitting with him for a quarter of an hour and learning all about his experiences how he got pensioned off and where the burns were, just using those word-for-word reflections, again it's just wonderful really to have that time with him. (CAT/VHS12/22.3.05)

PRE-THERAPY AND DEMENTIA

To date, the research project has highlighted some areas where the practice of using contact reflections with people with dementia differs from using contact work with people with psychosis or other functional (as opposed to organic) mental health problems.

In relation to physical space and proximity, whereas in psychosis a worker may be very tentative about entering into the personal space of the client, in dementia care we frequently work in much closer physical contact. This is reflected in other dementia care approaches, such as Validation Therapy, in which physical closeness is encouraged. Close physical contact is an intrinsic aspect of dementia care as staff wash, dress, and toilet individuals and assist them with walking. We sit close to people and the nurse offers a physical presence to the person with dementia. This often involves staff using touch with tenderness and gentleness, fostering feelings of closeness with residents. It can also make contact reflections problematic for staff in the early stages, as the contact reflections seem distant in comparison to the close physical relationship that may be the norm. For example, to state that 'John is walking' rather than 'you (or we) are walking' may feel at variance with the intimate relationship between John and the staff who have washed and dressed him earlier in the day.

PRE-EXPRESSIVE OR DISORIENTED?

Another difference may stem from the nature of the dementing process. Contact reflections target people in pre-expressive states, yet people with dementia are frequently highly expressive and 'relational seeking', although the damage to language and cognitive impairment lead to this being conveyed in a way that can be difficult for staff to understand, or may appear to be pre-expressive. Where contact reflections have been used with people whose communication is distorted, perhaps as a way of trying to reflect back, allowing them time and space to try and express themselves more clearly, the effect has been very rapid emotional connections and engagement that staff may find difficult, especially if they are unable to meet the request of the person—for example to go home, to find their mother, to find a child that died.

AGNOSIA, DYSPHASIA AND CONCRETENESS

The concreteness of the contact reflections can also add complications. A concrete reflection might involve stating that 'the table is in front of you' (situational reflection). We know, however, that visuo-spatial impairments can lead the person with dementia to see something quite different from a table; in their mind's eye the table may be another object. Or, it may be that progressive linguistic disabilities have stripped the word 'table' of its meaning, or removed the person's capacity to convey the correct word. As a result, there seems to be a need to combine the concrete and the abstract by greater use of vague pronouns—for example *it* is in front of you, *it* is there, you are *here*, rather than you are in the sitting room, where the sitting room may have no meaning to the person with dementia.

In addition to conveying the concrete through the abstract, there is need for greater emphasis on the use of non-verbal reflections. In dementia care we are aware of the importance of non-verbal communication to enhance meaning between people, and we are also aware that the ability of people with dementia to read and interact non-verbally is often retained when their capacity for verbal communication is severely affected. Indeed, the need to strengthen contact reflections in dementia work by enhanced non-verbal reflection echoes the emphasis on the use of non-verbal media that already exists in the dementia literature.

So with facial reflections, it may be that the worker uses a non-verbal reflection of the person's facial expression, mirroring back to them the emotion. This may be more effective than using a verbal reflection such as 'your face is sad', as this relies on the cognitive capacity to understand words which may be compromised by the dementing process. There is also an argument in favour of greater use of sounds instead of words, so that a worker reflecting a person who is sighing would make the sounds and reflect the gesture of sighing with their own body language, rather than stating verbally: 'you are sighing'.

CONCLUSIONS

People using contact reflections were certainly surprised by the way that they facilitated people with dementia to express themselves and to relate to workers in ways beyond the seemingly possible. Anecdotally some staff have reported experiences which they felt were almost uncanny when they gained meaningful contact and attunement with people with dementia who were felt to be 'out of reach'. Even when these moments of clarity and lucidity were fleeting, the experience has been a powerful one for staff. Without being dismissive of the usefulness of Pre-Therapy, one outcome of staff learning to has been to temper other patterns of interacting which do not allow a patient the necessary space or time to formulate and relate to another—their own sense of themselves, their place in the world and how they are feeling. There is no doubt that by reflecting rather than intervening, staff are giving people with dementia a greater opportunity to be heard. This reinforces the somewhat discomforting thought that the non-demented population that cares for the person with dementia is sometimes making their lives more difficult, rather than easier (Kitwood, 1997).

There are questions that remain unanswered at present, for example, how does one makes decisions about when to use contact reflections, as there are times when it is appropriate for workers to provide positive directive approaches to people with dementia in order to enhance the quality of their lives. But the gentleness that flows from attempting to establish contact prior to performing care tasks or other approaches to a person with dementia is surely preferable to doing something in the absence of any relational contact. The concreteness of the contact reflections provides staff with an opportunity to see in practice how to begin to operationalise a person-centred approach, which requires noticing, reflecting and sensitivity to the experiential world of the person with dementia. Despite the difficulties of the context in which staff are required to use the contact reflections, it seems they can contribute to the current understanding of positive person-focused approaches in dementia care.

REFERENCES

Abraham, R (2005) *When Words Have Lost Their Meaning: Alzheimer's patients communicate through art.* Westport, CT: Praeger.

Aquilina, C & Hughes, JC (2006) The return of the living dead: Agency lost and found? In CJ Hughes, SJ Louw & SR Sabat (Eds) *Dementia: Mind, meaning and the person* (pp 143–61). Oxford: Oxford University Press.

Aveyard, B, Sykes, M & Doherty, D (2002) Therapeutic touch in dementia care. *Nursing Older People, 14* (6), 20–1.

Baker, R, Holloway, J & Holtkamp, C (2003) Effects of multi-sensory stimulation for people with dementia. *Journal of Advanced Nursing, 43* (5), 465–77.

Bayles, KA (2003) Effects of working memory deficits on the communicative functioning of Alzheimer's dementia patients. *Journal of Communication Disorders, 36* (3), 209–19.

Benner, P (1984) *From Novice to Expert: Excellence and power in clinical nursing practice.* London: Addison-Wesley.

Benner, P (2004) Using the Dreyfus model of skill acquisition to describe and interpret skill acquisition and clinical judgement in nursing practice and education. *Bulletin of Science, Technology & Society, 24* (3), 188–99.

Berg, A, Hallberg, IR & Norberg, A (1998) Nurses' reflections about dementia care, the patients, the care and themselves in their daily caregiving. *International Journal of Nursing Studies, 35,* 271–82.

Bond, J & Corner, L (2001) Researching dementia: Are there unique methodological challenges for health service research? *Aging and Society, 21,* 95–116.

Cheston, R & Bender, M (1999) *Understanding Dementia: The man with the worried eyes.* London: Jessica Kingsley.

Department of Health (2001a) *Seeking Consent: Working with older people.* London: Department of Health.

Department of Health (2001b) *Research Governance Framework for Health and Social Care.* London: Department of Health.

Dinacci, A (2000) EPIC: Objective evaluation criterion for the Pre-Therapy interview. *Pre-Therapy International Review, 1,* 31–40.

Dodds, P (2008) Pre-Therapy and Dementia: An action research project. Unpublished PhD thesis, University of Brighton.

Dodds, P, Morton, I & Prouty, G (2004) Pre-Therapy and dementia. *Journal of Dementia Care, 12* (2), 25–7.

Donchin, A (1995) Reworking autonomy: Towards a feminist perspective. *Cambridge Quarterly of Health Care Ethics, 4,* 44–55.

Feil, N (1993) *The Validation Breakthrough: Simple techniques for communicating with people with 'Alzheimer's-type' dementia.* London/Baltimore, MD: Health Professions Press.

Goldsmith, M (1996) *Hearing the Voice of People with Dementia.* London: Jessica Kingsley.

Götell, E, Brown, S & Ekman, SL (2002) Caregiver singing and background music in dementia care. *Western Journal of Nursing Research, 24* (2), 195–216.

Graham, J (2004) Communicating with the uncommunicative: Music therapy with pre-verbal adults. *British Journal of Learning Disabilities, 32,* 24–9.

Graneheim, UH et al (2005) Balancing between contradictions: The meaning of interaction with people suffering from dementia and 'behavioural disturbances'. *The International Journal of Aging and Human Development, 60* (2), 145–57.

Grech, E (2004) Hegel's dialectic and reflective practice: A short essay. *The International Journal of Psychosocial Rehabilitation, 8,* 69–72.

Hansebo, G & Kihlgren, M (2002) Carers' interactions with patients suffering from severe dementia: A difficult balance to facilitate mutual togetherness. *Journal of Clinical Nursing, 11* (2), 225–36.

Hughes, JC, Louw, SJ & Sabat, SR (2006) *Dementia: Mind, meaning and the person.* Oxford: Oxford University Press.

Innes, A (2002) The social and political context of formal dementia care provision. *Aging and Society,* 22, 483–99.

Innes, A, MacPherson, S & McCabe, L (2006) *Promoting Person-Centred Care at the Front Line.* York: Joseph Rowntree Foundation. (Also available at www.jrf.org.uk.)

Kendrick, KD & Robinson, S (2002) 'Tender Loving Care' as a relational ethic in nursing practice. *Nursing Ethics,* 9 (3), 291–300.

Killick, J (2002) Creativity and dementia: 'Holding a rainbow in our hands'. Text of Presentation. Accessed 30th September 2003 at www.dementia.com.au/papers_2002/John_Killick_Creativity_and_Dementia.

Killick, J (2005) Making sense of dementia through metaphor. *Journal of Dementia Care,* 13 (1), 22–3.

Killick, J & Allan, K (2001) *Communication and the Care of People with Dementia.* Buckingham: Open University Press.

Kitwood, T (1997) *Dementia Reconsidered: The person comes first.* Buckingham: Open University Press.

Knocker, S (2002) Play and metaphor in dementia care and drama therapy. *Journal of Dementia Care,* 10 (2), 33–7.

Kontos, PC (2005) Embodied selfhood in Alzheimer's Disease. *Dementia,* 4 (4), 553–70.

MacDonald, C (2002) Nurse autonomy as relational. *Nursing Ethics,* 9 (2), 194–201.

McCormack, B (2004) Person-centredness in gerontological nursing: An overview of the literature. *International Journal of Older People Nursing,* 13, 31–8.

McNiff, J & Whitehead, J (2006) *All You Need to Know about Action Research.* London: Sage Pulications.

Miles, MB & Huberman, AM (1994) *Qualitative Data Analysis: An expanded sourcebook* (2nd edn). London: Sage Publications.

Morse, JM, Botorff, J, Anderson, G, O'Brien, B & Solberg, S (1992) Beyond empathy: Expanding expressions of caring. *Journal of Advanced Nursing,* 17, 809–921.

Morton, IR (1997) Beyond validation. In IJ Norman & SJ Redfern (Eds) *Mental Health Care for Elderly People* (pp 371–91). London: Churchill Livingstone.

Morton, IR (1999) *Person-Centred Approaches to Dementia Care.* Bicester: Winslow Press.

Morton, IR (2000) Just what is person-centred dementia care? *Journal of Dementia Care,* 8 (3), 28–9.

Mueller-Hergl C (2003) Focus on the change agent. *Journal of Dementia Care,* 11 (6), 8–10.

NICE-SCIE (2006) *Dementia: Supporting people with dementia and their carers.* Draft guidelines for consultation. London: National Institute for Health and Clinical Excellence and the Social Care Institute for Excellence.

Nystrom, K & Lauritzen, S (2005) Expressive bodies: Demented persons' communication in a dance therapy context. *Health,* 9 (3), 297–317.

Peters, H (2003) Imitatie, intersubjectiviteit and pretherapeutische reflecties: Een samenhang in verschillen. *Tijdschrift Clientgerichte Psychotherapie,* 41, 168–81. English translation, Affective attunement, imitation and pre-therapeutic reflections: A coherence in disparities, obtained October 2003.

Peters, H (2005) Pre-Therapy from a developmental perspective. *Journal of Humanistic Psychology,* 45 (1), 62–81.

Pool, J (2001) Making contact: An activity-based model of care. *Journal of Dementia Care,* 9 (4), 24–6.

Pörtner, M (2002) Part 3: Pre-Therapy in Europe. In G Prouty, D Van Werde & M

Pörtner *Pre-Therapy: Reaching contact-impaired clients* (pp 123–67). Ross-on-Wye: PCCS Books.

Prouty, G (1976) Pre-Therapy: A method of treating pre-expressive psychotic and retarded patients. *Psychotherapy: Theory, Research and Practice, 13* (3), 290–5.

Prouty, G & Dekeyser, M (2006) Pre-Therapy: Early pilot studies. Unpublished manuscript.

Prouty, G & Dinacci, A (2002) Pre-Therapy: Early pilot studies. Chicago Counseling and Psychotherapy Center, and the Italian Society for Pre-Therapy Research and Practice: Bologna. Unpublished.

Prouty, G, Van Werde, D & Pörtner, M (2002) *Pre-Therapy: Reaching contact-impaired clients.* Ross-on-Wye: PCCS Books.

Roth, A & Fonagy, P (2005) *What Works for Whom? A critical review of psychotherapy research* (2nd edn). London: Guilford Press.

Sabat, SR & Harre, R (1992) The construction and deconstruction of self in Alzheimer's Disease. *Ageing and Society, 12,* 443–61.

Saczynski, JS & Rebok, GW (2004) Strategies for memory improvement in older adults. *Topics in Advanced Practice Nursing, 4* (1). Accessed 27th August 2006 at www.medscape.com/viewarticle/465740.

Shakespeare, P (1998) *Aspects of Confused Speech.* London: Lawrence Erlbaum Associates.

Sherratt, K et al (2004) Music interventions for people with dementia: A review of the literature. *Aging and Mental Health, 8* (1), 3–12.

Sherwin, S (1998) A relational approach to autonomy in health care. In S Sherwin (Ed) *The Politics of Women's Health: Exploring agency and autonomy* (pp 19–47). Philadelphia, PA: Temple University Press.

Smith, P (1992) *The Emotional Labour of Nursing.* London: Macmillan.

Stern, DN (1985) *The Interpersonal World of the Infant.* New York: Basic Books.

Sung, H & Chang, A (2005) Use of preferred music to decrease agitated behaviours in older people with dementia: A review of the literature. *Journal of Clinical Nursing, 14* (9), 1133–40.

Van Werde, D & Morton, IR (1999) The relevance of Prouty's Pre-Therapy to dementia care. In IR Morton (Ed) *Person-Centred Approaches to Dementia Care* (pp 139–66). Bicester: Winslow Press.

Vass, AA et al (2003) Research into communication patterns and consequences for effective care of people with Alzheimer's and their carers. *Dementia, 2* (1), 21–48.

Verity, J (2006) Dolls in dementia care: Bridging the divide. *Journal of Dementia Care, 14* (1), 25–6.

Waterman, H, Tillen, D Dickson, R & de Konig, K (2001) Action research: systematic review and guidance for assessment. *Health Technology Assessment, 5* (23), iii–157.

Wilkinson, H (2002) *The Perspective of People with Dementia: Research methods and motivations.* London: Jessica Kingsley.

Woods, B, Spector, A, Jones, C, Orrell, M & Davies, S (2005) Reminiscence therapy for dementia. *The Cochrane Library (4).* Chichester: Wiley.

Zarit, SH et al (2004) Memory Club: A group intervention for people with early-stage dementia and their care partners. *Gerontologist, 44* (2), 262–9.

ACKNOWLEDGMENT

I would like to thank Ian Morton for his valuable contributions to this chapter.

Editor's Commentary on Aldo Dinacci

The measurement of Pre-Therapy was originally calculated along three dimensions: reality, affect and communication. However, Aldo Dinacci constructed an instrument called the Evaluation Criterion for the Pre-Therapy Interview (ECPI), which measured *only* the communicative dimension. It did so with important differences to the original theoretical formulation. The original calculation of social communication was simply to count the number of words or sentences expressed by the client. The ECPI, on the other hand, measures language (dis)organization. The concept of 'Communicative Sign' is any change in client verbal or non-verbal behavior which immediately follows a stimulus offered by the therapist. Application of the ECPI results in six measures of language organization:

1. The ratio of communicative signs and therapist stimuli is the *Reaction Index*: a measure of general client reactivity.
2. *The Expressive Modality Index* is a measure of the relevance of client responses and a measure of the extent to which the responses are verbal.
3. *The Verbal Expressiveness Index* is a measure of verbal coordination.
4. *The Coherence Index* is the percentage of time the client performed coordinated verbal expressions.
5. *The Physical Expressiveness Index* measures the relative frequency of all communicative signs that involve touch.
6. The mean of all previous indices is the *General Interview Index*. As yet, there is no data on reliability.

The value of this measuring system is that it shows more than simple increases in communication. It illustrates the language organization itself both in pathology and therapeutic change which is certainly helpful to the clinician.

CHAPTER 4

ECPI:
Objective Evaluation Criterion for the Pre-Therapy Interview

ALDO DINACCI

There are various questionnaires and tests available which were designed to evaluate psychiatric clients with regard to aspects such as the seriousness of the phenomenon, residual potentiality, course of the illness, and others, such as the ABI (Adaptive Behaviour Inventory by Brown & Leigh, 1986), the PIRS (Psychological Impairment Rating Schedule) defined in the studies on interactive behaviour by Trower, Bryant and Argyle (1978) and Eckman and Oster (1979), and the DAS II (Disability Assessment Schedule) by Jablensky, Schwarz & Tomov (1980).

The latter two tests have been used in the pilot study by the World Health Organisation, begun in 1986 with the objective of perfecting a set of tools for evaluating functional disabilities and disabilities in psychologically disturbed individuals. These same tests have been used for follow-up on the same subjects in more recent studies (De Jong, Giel & Stoof, 1986). The ABI has been used for screening patients in the psychiatric institution where the Pre-Therapy interviews to which this work refers took place.

However, when working with people who are in Pre-Therapy (Dinacci, 1990), it is often not possible to have a satisfactory guarantee of the effectiveness of any given evaluation method, because of the condition of these clients. On the other hand, the very nature of Pre-Therapy calls for the use of these tools with those very subjects who, because of the seriousness of their disorder, seem to be beyond the reach of any type of therapy and, therefore, of any system of measurement. For an example of applying this scale see Prouty, 2002: 596.

However, there are certain tasks (establishing if and when to start a client in Pre-Therapy, evaluating the effect of different techniques of contact, and others) which call for a test that meets two basic requirements: it must be applicable to all cases, regardless of the condition of the client, and it must be as objective as possible.

Dinacci, A (2000) ECPI Objective Evaluation Criterion for the Pre-Therapy Interview. *International Pre-Therapy Review*, 1, 31–7. By kind permission of the editors.

I use the term 'objective' here to indicate that the test must give the same results, or at least that there must be only minimal variations in the results, regardless of who does the evaluation. In creating this test, we must start from Prouty's definition of 'contact' (with self, with others, and with the world) and from his 'reflections,' from 'touch contact' and positive reinforcement.

It is important to define exactly what I mean by the term 'communicative sign' used in this paper. This term indicates 'any variation in the client's state of stillness and/or motion that is correlated, immediately and chronologically only, with the therapist.' Using this definition, a 'communicative sign' (referred to as 'CS' from here on) may be assumed to be the minimum unit in the process of re-establishing contact, as defined by Prouty (1994) and Perls (1969). In keeping with this definition, it is evident that a CS may be verbal or non-verbal. It is just as evident that the therapist's behaviour—and especially the stimuli s/he offers to the client—is also evaluated in CSs. By this definition, a CS is clearly recognisable, and therefore counting the number of CSs is not a problem.

Time is the other variable to be considered. This is done both in terms of how long the communication (defined as a succession of CSs) lasts, and according to the numerical relationship CS/T.

Set up this way, the Objective Evaluation Criterion for the Pre-Therapy Interview (ECPI) depends entirely upon the phenomenology of the client while taking into consideration only two variables and the relationship between them. These two variables are easy to measure accurately. Practically speaking, the ECPI breaks up communication into elementary units that are easily recognizable (CSs) and evaluates these units. The communication picture is then put back together, using a method for calculating the client's ECPI scores.

The stimuli the therapist offers during the session must be considered 'stimuli', and therefore the 'response' ('Contact Reflections,' Prouty, 1994) must be evaluated in terms of CSs.

THE EVALUATION TECHNIQUE

In order to obtain a significant ECPI score, an interview must last not less than ten minutes. However, slightly shorter interviews may be evaluated for preliminary purposes only. For more accurate evaluations, it is advisable to hold interviews of approximately 20–25 minutes length. In any case, the length of the interview must be decided after taking into consideration how the session is proceeding in general and taking care, when possible, not to end the session if the client's behaviour seems to advise against it.

Note the following:

- A 30-minute interview cannot be evaluated as two 15-minute interviews.
- Evaluations of first interviews lasting less than 20 minutes have proved inaccurate.
- Evaluations of 10-minute interviews are admissible only with the purpose of evaluating variations in behaviour during the course of prolonged Pre-Therapy.

The ECPI can be used essentially for the following two types of evaluations, accompanied by corrective co-efficient: (1) Quantitative evaluations; and (2) Qualitative evaluations. The quantitative evaluation uses two types of scores: (A) Stimulus-reaction (numerical score); and (B) Stimulus-reaction (modal score). It is essentially a test of the patient's coordination, divided into (C) verbal expressiveness coordination, (D) verbal/non-verbal expressiveness coordination, and (E) physical coordination.

QUANTITATIVE EVALUATION

A. NUMERICAL SCORE

The numerical score is obtained by counting the number of stimuli offered by the therapist and the number of responses (CSs) given by the client. Using our definition of the CS, there is no difference between verbal and non-verbal responses for the purposes of this evaluation. Whether or not the response seems more or less related to the stimulus is not important either.

When all points (see below) have been assigned, the percentage of responses given by the client is written onto a chart in column A. The score in column A is called the *Reaction Index*, abbreviated as 'RI.'

B. MODAL SCORE

1. No reaction	0 points
2. Non-verbal reaction apparently not related to the stimulus	2 points
3. Verbal reaction apparently not related to the stimulus	1 point
4. Verbal and non-verbal mixed reaction apparently not related to the stimulus	3 points
5. Non-verbal reaction related to the stimulus	4 points
6. Verbal or mixed reaction related to the stimulus	5 points

The sum of the points assigned to the client represents the rough score (R). To obtain the standard score to record on the chart, divide the rough score (R) by the number of stimuli offered (S) multiplied by five. The formula is as follows:

Standard score = Rough Score / Number of stimuli × 5

The standard score is then recorded in column B, called the *Expressive Modality Index* (EMI).

C. VERBAL EXPRESSIVENESS COORDINATION

The term 'Verbal expressiveness coordination' refers to the client's ability to speak coordinately.

1. Uncoordinated and apparently meaningless sentences	0 points
2. Meaningful, but uncoordinated sentences	1 point
3. For each sentence generically linked to the preceding sentence	3 points
4. For each sentence clearly consistent with the preceding sentence	5 points
5. In case of silence interrupted by action on the part of the therapist:	
• If there is an apparently related response	5 points
• If followed by a complete, unrelated sentence	3 points
• If followed by a complete, meaningless sentence	1 point
• No response	0 points

The rough score (R) is obtained by adding together all the points assigned to the client. The standard score (S) in column C is obtained with the following formula:

- Standard score C = Rough Score / No. of interactions × 5

- Standard score C is recorded, naturally, in column C. Score C is called the *Verbal Expressiveness Index* (VEI).

D. COORDINATION OF VERBAL AND NON-VERBAL EXPRESSIONS

Standard score D, written in column D, is easily obtained by taking the percentage of time (T), including separate intervals, during which coordination has been noted, and by comparing this to the total time of the interview. Score D is called the *Coherence Index* (CI).

E. BODY CONTACT
1. For each reaction to body contact created by the therapist   1 point
2. For each contact initiated by the client   1 point

To obtain the standard score, divide the sum of rough scores (R) by the number of interactions noted, using this formula:

Standard scores = Rough Score / No. of interactions

The score in column 'E' is called the *Physical Expressiveness Index* (PEI). There may be differences in theory between therapists, some of whom may not include physical contact with the patient as part of their way of conducting an interview. In these cases, the ECPI can be used, nonetheless, simply by omitting the assignment of points in column 'E.' In order not to alter the procedure for obtaining the final score, use the simple mathematical correction explained in paragraph 3.2.

CORRECTIONS

The ECPI uses three types of corrections:

1. score correction
2. control correction
3. mathematical correction

1. Score correction:
1.1. If the client tends to speak continuously and uninterruptedly in an unrestrainable manner, write 0 in column C.

1.2. If the repetition or unrestrained speech stops, with or without the intervention of the therapist, and then begins again, diminish the score in column C as follows:

  A. if the interval lasts less than one minute ($I < 1'$), write 0.70 in the 'correction' box.

  B. if the interval lasts more than one minute ($I > 1'$), write 0.80 in the 'correction' box.

1.3. If the client gesticulates continually without speaking, even stopping for short intervals,

  A. if continual and unrestrained, write 0 in column D.

  B. if tends to be continual but susceptible to modification related to stimulus by the therapist, write 0.80 in the corresponding 'correction' box.

2. Control correction:

2.1. If the client repeats the same sentence or the same group of sentences, record the score for response evaluation only once.

2.2. Follow the same procedure for non-verbal communicative signs.

3. Mathematical correction:

3.1. If points have also been recorded in column E, multiply the total score by 0.20.

3.2. If no points have been recorded in column E, multiply the total score of the preceding columns (A–D) by 0.25. This is the case when the therapist does not use the physical contact, and the client does not seek this type of contact, either.

The mathematical correction gives a final score which we will call the *General Interview Index* or GII. The GII score always falls between zero and one hundred, and it facilitates an immediate interpretation and comparison.

THE CLIENT'S CHART

The client's chart includes four forms (see pp. 82–5). The first serves to briefly record basic information regarding the client. The second serves to record rough scores for each interview and to calculate percentages and relative corrections. The third is made for easier calculation. The fourth allows grouping data from each interview so as to have a detailed overview of the interview along with the respective indexes (RI, EMI, VEI, CI and PEI). It includes the following:

- date of sessions
- time of sessions
- separate scores
- sum total
- mathematical correction
- General Interview Index

SINGLE INDICES

Both the ECPI score sheet (p. 83) and standard score sheet (p. 85) can be adapted and drawn very simply, both for the GII and for the separate single indices (RI, EMI, VEI, CI and PEI), depending upon the requirements of the study in question.

REFERENCES

Brown, L & Leigh, JE (1986) *Adaptive Behavioral Inventory*. Austin TX: PRO-ED. [Italian translation, 1987, Trento: Inst. Erickson]

De Jong, A, Giel, R & Stoof, C (1986) Relationship between symptomology and social disability, *Social Psychiatry, 21*, 200–5.

Dinacci, A (1990) *Pre-Terapia: Una nuova opportunità per il trattamento psicoterapeutico nella schizofrenia*. Tesi di Specializzazione, Università di Siena.

Eckman, P & Oster, H (1979) Facial expression of emotion. *Annual Review of Psychology, 30*, 527–54.

Jablensky, A, Schwarz, R, & Tomov, J (1980) WHO collaborative study on impairments and disabilities associated with schizophrenic disorders: A preliminary communication—Objectives and methods. In E Stromgren, JA Dupont & JA Nielsen (Eds) Epidemiological research as the basis for the organization of extramural psychiatry. *Acta Psychiat Scand, Supplement 285* (62).

Perls, F (1969) *La terapia della Gestalt parola per parola*. Roma: Astrolabio.

Prouty, G (1994) *Theoretical Evolutions in Person-Centered/Experiential Therapy: Applications to schizophrenic and retarded psychoses* (pp 31–47). Westport, CT: Praeger.

Prouty, G (2002) Humanistic psychotherapy for people with schizophrenia. In DJ Cain & J Seeman (Eds) *Humanistic Psychotherapies: Handbook of research and practice* (pp 579–601). Washington, DC: American Psychological Association.

Trower, P, Bryant, B & Argyle, M (1978) *Social Skills and Mental Health*. London: Methuen.

WHO (1980) *International Classification of Impairments, Disabilities, and Handicaps*. Geneva: WHO.

CLIENT CHART

Client _____

Chart No. _____

General Information _____

_____

Last name _____ First name _____

Date of birth _____ City _____

Physician/hospital _____

Diagnosis _____

_____

Length of hospitalization _____

Medicine used _____

Psychotherapeutic treatment undergone _____

_____

Family history _____

_____

_____

Current Public Health Service assistance _____

_____

Does the client live with his/her family?	[yes]	[no]
Is the client hospitalized?	[yes]	[no]
Is the client in day hospital?	[yes]	[no]

Began Pre-Therapy on _____

Therapist _____

ECPI SCORE SHEET

Date of Session _____ Sheet No. _____

No.	Interaction	A	B	C	D	E

Total this sheet

ECPI CALCULATION SHEET

Date of Session _____

Score A	Rough Points	No. of Interactions	×	100			=	Score A
Score B	Rough Points	No. of Interactions × 5	×	100			=	Score B
Score C	Rough Points	No. of Interactions × 5	×	100	×	Corr.	=	Score C
Score D	Time Recorded	Length of session	×	100	×	Corr.	=	Score D
Score E	Rough Points	No. of Interactions	×	100			=	Score E

NB The scores in the last column must be carried over to the Standard Score

ECPI STANDARD SCORE SHEET

Client _____ Therapist _____

Date of Session	Time Begun/Ended	A	B	C	D	E	Total	Math Corr	GII
No. of Sessions		RI	EMI	VEI	CI	PEI			
Total									

Editor's Commentary on Hans Peters

Hans Peters wrote on the relationship between intersubjective psychoanalysis, mirror neurons and Pre-Therapy. Intersubjective psychoanalysis refers to the study of the psychological field between patient and therapist. Introspection and empathy are its central methods. This approach sharply rejects knowledge based on objective methods. Exploring infant development literature, Peters concluded there was sufficient proof that intersubjectivity is an innate capacity and is available during the first hours of life. He also concludes that the emotional aspects of intersubjectivity are far more important than the cognitive. Also, that the infant can differentiate between its behavior and that of parents thereby distinguishing self from other.

Mirror neurons are suggested as the neurophysiological basis of intersubjectivity. Gallese (2002) describes how motor neurons respond. If monkey A observes monkey B picking up an object, almost immediately the associated neurons in monkey A become activated. This happens only if goal-oriented nature of the action is perceived. The same phenomenon is observed in humans. In a more elaborate form it is called the Shared Manifold Hypothesis. This means that when we enter a relationship with others we share a multiplicity of states. It is because of this shared manifold that empathy functions.

Pre-Therapy in these contexts can be understood in the following way:

> Pre-Therapy is a form of attunement on very young levels of development
> Pre-Therapy is a form of intersubjective contact
> Pre-Therapy is an intersubjective relationship
> Mirror neurons are the empathic basis for Pre-Therapy

REFERENCE

Gallese, V (2000) Action, goals, and their role in intersubjectivity: From mirror neurons to the 'shared manifold' hypothesis. Retrieved 23 October 2004, from www.mpipf-muenchen.mpg.de/MPIPF/MECA/docs/gallese.doc

CHAPTER 5

The Development of Intersubjectivity in Relation to Psychotherapy and its Importance for Pre-Therapy

HANS PETERS

THE CONCEPT OF INTERSUBJECTIVITY

SOME INTRODUCTORY REMARKS WITH REGARD TO THE HISTORY OF INTERSUBJECTIVITY

Intersubjectivity is a term which has been well known for years in psychoanalysis, though it has been used in multiple ways. This is partly due to the way in which research concerning intersubjectivity took place. The starting point of Atwood and Stolorow (1984) and Stolorow, Brandchaft and Atwood (1987) was the thesis that psychoanalysis '… seeks to illuminate phenomena that emerge within a specific psychological field constituted by the intersection of two subjectivities — that of the patient and the analyst … (Stolorow, Brandchaft & Atwood, 1987: 41). Psychoanalysis is considered here as a science of the intersubjective '… focused on the interplay between the differently organized subjective worlds of the observer and the observed. The observed stance is always one within, rather than outside, the intersubjective field' (Atwood & Stolorow, 1984: 41). Introspection and empathy were the central methods of observing others in which the observer was also the observed. Stolorow sharply rejected knowledge which had been gathered in other ways, for instance by the objective knowledge possessed by the analyst of the patient's life, of human development and human psychological functioning. Knowledge grounded in experimentally validated, objectively obtained research on the brain is also rejected: '… anything that is not in principle accessible to empathy and introspection does not properly fall within the bound of psychoanalytic inquiry' (Stolorow, Brandchaft & Atwood, 1987: 5). They thought it was impossible for the psychoanalyst to have objective knowledge concerning the life of the patient or concerning human development and human psychological functioning.

Peters, H (2006) The development of intersubjectivity in relation to psychotherapy and its importance for Pre-Therapy. *Person-Centered and Experiential Psychotherapies*, 5 (3), 192–207. By kind permission of The World Association for Person-Centered and Experiential Psychotherapy and Counseling.

Stern made a large contribution to the research on imitation in connection with the early development of intersubjectivity. In his research the notions of attunement (tuning in a broad sense) and affective attunement (a selective form of attunement) played a central role. As I have stated elsewhere, in Stern's view 'Parents ... do not just imitate the behaviors of the child; there must be an empathic attunement ... so that parents will react in a congruent way to the behaviors of the child' (Peters, 2005: 69). Reacting in a congruent way means that it is not a matter of strict imitation, as Vliegen and Cluckers (2001) stated, but that imitation in the sense of intersubjective communication means that the primary caregiver has to pick up the feeling from the child's behavior, has to imitate child's behavior, and that the child must be able to understand the response of the parents as something that has to do with the child's original, emotional experience and message. What strikes me is that the relation between mother and child is mainly described as being essentially from the mother to the child, which gives the impression of a one-way communication. The paragraph 'Intersubjective Relatedness' in Stern's book, *The Interpersonal World of the Infant* (1985/2000) described almost exclusively the way the mother reacted to the baby's behavior, but not the baby's reaction to the mother. In the later work of the Boston Change Process Study Group,[1] especially the study by Tronick (1998), the reciprocity of the relationship received a much stronger and more realistic emphasis. The study group acknowledged that empathy plays an important role within the domain of psychoanalysis, but Tronick also applied more objective research as, for instance, is seen in his work with regard to emotional connectedness and intersubjectivity and the damaging effect on the mental health of the child if there is a failure to achieve this connectedness. In his view the emotional state of the child is implicitly regulated in a dyadic way.

Gergely and Watson (1996), originally working from a psychoanalytic frame of reference but strongly influenced by *learning theory*, presented a theory of parental affect-mirroring and its role in the development of emotional self-awareness and control in infancy. 'It is proposed that infants first become sensitised to their categorical emotion-states through a natural social biofeedback process provided by the parent's "marked" reflections of the baby's emotion displays during affect-regulative interactions' (p. 1181). In other words, babies were able to store different kinds of emotions when parents gave feedback on certain emotional utterances.

Bråten (1998) and Trevarthen (1998, 2002a, 2002b) showed that babies from birth onwards are able to make goal-oriented contact. 'Minutes after a natural birth ... an awake newborn is immediately capable of coordinated

---

1. A research group founded in 1995 by Daniel Stern and Nadia Bruschweiler- Stern.

response, guided by a tentative consciousness. He or she can visually fixate a nearby "out-of-the-body" object and can track ... with steps of head and eyes and pulsing arm and finger extensions, performing fluid, rate controlled "pre-reaching"' Trevarthen (2002a: 2). The child is not really grasping an object, but the seeking behavior is there. Even if no real object can be perceived, searching actions can occur, '... generated within the time and space of a spontaneous imagination, a cerebral "motor" image for activity of the whole body' (ibid). I will return to this point when I describe the phenomenon of mirror neurons. Attempts in experimental situations proved that the baby is '... groping, seeing, listening and tasting with purposeful discrimination, showing rudiments of a conscious "subjectivity", and an ability to learn from movements that bring reward. But, of all these activities ... the most deliberate and effective are those that reflect affectionate interest from a parent seeking intimate communication. The baby exhibits "innate human intersubjectivity"' (ibid).

Bråten introduced the notion *altercentric participation* which means '... sensory-motor perception in a participatory sense, involving virtual co-enactment of the model's movements as if the infant were the co-author of the model's movements and moved with the model's movements in the same direction' (1998: 106). On the foundation of this ability researchers like Bråten (1988, 1998), Heimann (1997, 1998), Trevarthen (1998, 2002a, 2002b), Whiten and Brown (1998) and others proved that imitation occurs in neonates and in autistic and mentally handicapped people.

DEFINING INTERSUBJECTIVITY

Earlier in this paper I talked about intersubjectivity without presenting a clear description of the term. At least two pairs of intersubjective notions can be distinguished: one-way versus two-way intersubjectivity (the relational side of intersubjectivity); and emotional versus intellectual intersubjectivity (the way in which intersubjectivity is revealed).

ONE-WAY VERSUS TWO-WAY INTERSUBJECTIVITY

The meanings of intersubjectivity are most clearly explained in an article by Gómez (1998). He defined subjectivity as the way we perceive, think about, and feel about the world. Someone becomes intersubjective when their subjectivity is capable of taking the subjectivity of others as its object, that is 'when my mind thinks about the minds of other subjects, or when I feel about the minds or the feelings of others' (Gómez, 1998: 245). In this case, it is a question of one-way intersubjectivity. The above-mentioned work of Stern presented this one-way intersubjectivity. A second expression of intersubjectivity appears when two people are reciprocally aware of each other's awareness—when they are in dialogue—the so-called two-way or second-person intersubjectivity. In other words '... not all interactions between social agents necessarily entail intersubjectivity' (Meltzoff & Moore, 1998). They gave the following example: If a baby climbs on the shoulder of its mother, using her simply as a footstool, one can not speak of intersubjectivity because it is not the other's mind that has been taken into account. Much of the purposeful contact of autistic people is, in consequence, not intersubjective. As far as I know, Gómez is the first to explicitly make this distinction between one-way and two-way intersubjectivity. Properly speaking, every therapeutic relationship has to develop into two-way intersubjectivity for it to be called a full-fledged relationship.

COGNITIVE VERSUS AFFECTIVE INTERSUBJECTIVITY
Gómez went on to describe, from a developmental psychological perspective, two kinds of intersubjectivity. First, there is the *theory of mind* (TOM) notion: according to this, some authors think that any appraisal of another's subjectivity must be based on some sort of theoretical knowledge of the other person's mind—as opposed to direct perception or primary representation—whereas others share the idea that knowledge of other minds must be based on some kind of abstract representations, usually referred to as *meta-representations* (Gómez, 1998: 246–7). Both cases deal with theoretical constructs that are not directly observable. This approach of intersubjectivity focuses on the thinking side of people, as perceived by the observer. This is, at least partly, in accordance with Stern's original 1985 notion of intersubjectivity '... beginning around nine months of age with the advent of interattentionality (e.g., pointing), interintentionality (e.g., expecting motives to be read) and interaffectivity (e.g., affect attunement and social referencing)' (Stern, 1985/2000: xxii).

The second kind of intersubjectivity deals with different approaches that focus on *the perception and feeling of emotions*, rather than on the construction of theory of mind, which according to Gómez (1998) was the original notion of intersubjectivity. This second notion of intersubjectivity is especially observable in children at a very early stage:

> The subjectivity of others is *felt* by infants, who are capable of attuning themselves to it, in the same way as they display their own subjectivity by means of emotional behaviors to which adults adjust themselves. ... an emotional intersubjectivity precedes and is inseparable from the 'intellectual' intersubjectivity studied by authors working under the label of 'theory of mind'. This emotional intersubjectivity is usually displayed in dialogical situations …. (p. 247)

This overlaps with Stern's later notion of intersubjectivity which stated that new evidence on other-centered participation, as well as the new findings on mirror neurons and adaptive oscillators, convinced him '… that early forms of intersubjectivity exist from almost the beginning of life' (Stern, 1985/2000: xxii). This primary intersubjectivity as Stern, in imitation of Trevarthen, called it '… starts from the beginning, as does the sense of an emergent self, as does the sense of a core self …' (ibid).

Gómez is the first who explicitly distinguishes the emotional and intellectual intersubjectivity on the one hand, and on the other, connects them as being inseparable from each other.

For TOM theorists, the earliest manifestation of intersubjectivity 'is usually taken to occur at around 9–12 months, when infants start pointing out things to people and engaging in a number of behaviors that are identified under the label of "joint attention"' (Gómez, 1998: 248). These theorists underlined the cognitive side of intersubjectivity. Advocates of the emotional approaches of intersubjectivity (the *primary* intersubjectivity, already extant before three or four months) emphasized the expressive and affective components, that is they not only speak in terms of reaching, pointing, or looking to the face 'but also in terms of complying with instructions, accepting assistance, acquiescing, resisting, or making facial expressions' (ibid: 249). In this view, one can certainly speak of awareness of … and of symbolization, which could, of course, be preverbal.

In Gómez (1998) we saw that, based on an innate capacity, children in a very early phase of their development learn to behave intersubjectively. One of the intersubjective behaviors is the mutual imitation between mother and child (others are, for instance, the development of empathy and the working of mirror neurons). A very early expression of intersubjectivity is seen in the imitation of observed behaviors by the neonate, imitation which is at first elicited in social relationship with the mother who, in her turn, imitates behaviors of the child.

Bråten (1998) showed that even two-hour-old children consciously and unconsciously imitate movements, sounds, and behaviors of parents in a dialogical relationship, the so-called *altercentric participation*. Kugiumutzakis (1998) described experimental studies which show that imitation can be observed with neonates less than 45 minutes old. Drawing from Trevarthen (1998), the following description of early infant imitation is possible: *imitation is the innate capacity to communicate observed behavior in an increasingly purposeful way in face-to-face exchanges, by emitting effectively coordinated vocal and oral expressions and behaviors*. In the same publication Trevarthen emphasized '... the primacy of motor co-ordinations and endogenous rhythms in the epigenesis of sucking, neonatal looking, prereaching, "prespeech" and primary gestures' (ibid: 34).

According to Heimann the neurological foundation of imitation is '... a direct process at a subcortical level where visual, auditory and somatosensory information share the same neural maps or even the same multimodel neurons' (1998: 103).

A NEUROPHYSIOLOGICAL BASIS FOR INTERSUBJECTIVITY

Heimann's statement seems to fit with the discovery of *mirror neurons* by an Italian research group under the direction of Vittorio Gallese. He extended the studies carried out by Oram and Perret (1994), Perret, Harries et al (1989), and Perret, Mistlin et al (1990) on the working of motor neurons. Mirror neurons are a special kind of motor neurons. When monkey A observes monkey B executing an action—for example, picking up an object—almost immediately, the motor neurons related to that kind of action become active in monkey A. This happens only if the observed action stems from a goal-related behavior: '... these neurons do not respond to static presentations of hand or objects, but require, in order to be triggered, the observation of meaningful, goal-related hand–object interactions' (Gallese, 2000a: 2). This means it is the goal-oriented motor activity, not the visual perception of the object, which is decisive for activating these mirror neurons. In other words, if the goal-oriented motor activity is not subconsciously recognized by the observer no mirror neurons will be activated or, as Gallese stated 'When the kinematics of the agent is different from that of the observer—as in the case of the mechanical observer, or for mirror neurons, in the case of grasping achieved by using a tool—the observed action cannot be matched on the observer's motor repertoire, and therefore the intended goal cannot be detected and/or attributed to the mechanical agent' (2000a: 3). The latter is partly refuted by, among others, Gilbert. He demonstrated that the use of tools gives the same results *when the observer can perceive the goal-oriented nature of the action*. 'This is facilitated by incorporation of the tool in the body scheme. Body scheme is the way in which the neural control (the brain) configures the body' Gilbert (2004: 63). In general Gilbert gave a valuable, critical evaluation of the research on mirror neurons, especially in relation to the work of Arbib and Gallese.

The same phenomenon has been observed in human subjects. Studies executed with techniques such as transcranial magnetic stimulation (TMS), EEG, MRI and magnetoencephalogram (MEG) '... suggested that humans have a "mirror matching system" for actions similar to that originally discovered in monkeys' (Gallese, 2000a: 4). Buccino et al (2001) showed that when we observe goal-related behaviors executed with effectors as different as the mouth, the hand or the foot, different specific regions of our premotor cortex became active. Or, as Gallese (2003a) stated:

> ... the sensorimotor integration process ... instantiates an 'internal copy' of actions utilized not only to generate and control goal-related behaviors, *but also* to provide—at a prereflexive and prelinguistic level—a meaningful account of behaviors performed by other individuals. ... Especially Broca's region appears to be involved in this prereflexive and prelinguistic analysis of other's behavior. ... Although we do not overly reproduce the observed action, our motor system becomes nevertheless active *as if* we were executing that very same action that we are observing. ... This implicit, automatic, and unconscious process of embodied simulation enables the observer to use his/her own resources to penetrate the world of the other without the need of explicitly theorizing about it. (p. 174)

In summary, fundamental functional qualities of most neurons in certain areas of the brain do not discharge in direct relation to primary feelings, but rather to the observation of goal-oriented behaviors. This implicit process of pre-reflexive, simulated action is of great interest for the development of behavior from birth onwards (for instance with regard to imitation), for the recognition of behavior of one's own species (social identity) and for the development of one's own identity (I-identity),[2] in short, for the development of intersubjectivity.

This implicit process is the more important one. Gallese pointed out that research findings revealed that not only are motor neurons involved, but also that audiovisual mirror neurons act in the same way. They laid the neurobiological foundation to identify oneself with the other while maintaining one's own identity (= empathy). I can understand the other, because my neural mechanism (motoric and audiovisual) evokes an activation pattern corresponding with that of the other: '... the other is experienced as another being as oneself through an appreciation of similarity' (2003a: 176).

Gallese continued to develop his Shared Manifold Hypothesis (Gallese,

---

2. Although Gallese is not quite clear with reference to the development of I-identity I think the following is meant: as an *individual* organism we experience our I-identity which '... is articulated into three phenomenological properties: *mineness* (I consciously experience *my* body as having always phenomenally belonged to me); *selfhood* (I am directly acquainted with the contents of my self-consciousness); and *perspectivalness* (phenomenal space is organized around a centre ...)' (2000b:. 34).

As belonging to a larger community we are influenced by members of that community and in an intersubjective relation we develop our I-identity.

2001, 2003a, 2003b). In summary this means that when we enter in a mutual relationship with others, we share a multiplicity of states with them which Gallese defined as 'implicit certainties'. 'We share emotions, our body schema, our being subject to somatic sensations such as pain. ... It is just because of this shared manifold that intersubjective communication, social imitation and ascription of intentionality become possible' (Gallese, 2003a: 177).

One of the levels that the shared manifold can be operationalized on is the phenomenological or empathic level: 'Actions, emotions and sensations experienced by others become implicitly meaningful to us because we can share them with others' (ibid). He argues for an extended notion of empathy, '... conceived as an intentional form of perception by analogy' (p. 175).

Although Gilbert does not disapprove Gallese's thesis, he poses some objections regarding the extrapolation from laboratory findings to the intersubjective functionality (Gilbert, 2004: 57–66). Moreover, the transition from behavioral actions to the reciprocity of empathic understanding is not quite clear, though interesting, and seems to be a 'hypothesis by analogy'.

SOME FINAL REMARKS

The innate intentionality from birth onwards, the reciprocity in imitative behavior, and the supposed mirror-matching system, mean that children are more actively involved in relationships than has been thought until recently, and that they have manipulative power to shape relationships. Also Van IJzendoorn (2001), in his article on attachment and therapy, stated that the child develops an image of the educator as someone who is at the child's disposal and is sensitive, and that the child perceives himself or herself as a valuable individual who can explore the world at ease. However, I would like to add that the child also perceives themselves as someone who accepts that they can influence and control the world around them and that they will have to experience that this is accepted by the persons close to them. In other words, parents should give a feeling of security when the child behaves congruently in their own way, even when this behavior is not seen as pleasant or appropriate by the parents, such as crying to get something. Many adults are not inclined to give this sense of security in everyday life when they feel themselves manipulated, even though it is a basic way of dealing with others, even by infants. As I pointed out earlier (Peters, 2003), Gergely and Watson (1996) showed extensively that neonates already influence and control environmental stimuli, while Bråten (1988, 1998) referred to a dialogical relationship at that age.

Another point of interest is the way in which imitation takes place. As Vliegen and Cluckers (2001) stated, it is never a matter of strict imitation. On one hand the imitation is colored by the empathy the mother experiences in relation with her child and, on the other hand, by her congruent way of responding. When the mother imitates the behavior of the child she adds something from herself to the utterances of the child. In doing so, the child experiences that it is their mother who communicates with them. This is in line with research on mirror neurons as we saw before. For Gallese stated that because of our neural mechanism an activation pattern corresponding with that of the other is evoked: '... the other is experienced as another being as one self through an appreciation of *similarity*' (2003a: 176). This corresponds to the *as if* condition in the notion of empathy.

What this all has to do with Pre-Therapy is explained in the last section of this article.

THE INNATE CAPACITY FOR INTERSUBJECTIVE IMITATION IN RELATION TO PRE-THERAPY

INTRODUCTION TO PRE-THERAPY

For those who are not familiar with Pre-Therapy I will give a short description of the practical application of pre-therapeutic reflections (the theoretical underpinning of Pre-Therapy I have described in an earlier article, see Peters, 1999).

Pre-Therapy, as a form of client-centered/experiential psychotherapy, is applied to clients with severe innate or acquired contact disturbances, for whom the more conventional forms of therapy such as talking therapy and behavior therapy are not (yet) applicable. The almost complete absence of contact—Prouty (1994) called this *existential autism*—makes the application of these kinds of treatment impossible. So the therapist, at first, has to establish or restore the client's very basic contact functions, which I earlier described as the *primary application* of Pre-Therapy (Peters, 1999). Because some form of contact is a precondition (therefore the use of the prefix 'pre' in Pre-Therapy) for the more conventional forms of therapy, the question is how to bring this contact into being with clients who are severely disturbed, have hallucinatory psychoses, and are retarded with contact disturbances, and so on, for whom contact is the goal of the pre-therapeutic treatment. This is done by the application of pre-therapeutic reflections, the so-called *contact reflections*. From his or her own congruence, the therapist mirrors the minimal behavioral utterances of the client, expressions he or she also bodily 'radiates' but which are not bodily experienced. There are four contact reflections.

SITUATIONAL REFLECTIONS

Situational reflections serve to facilitate contact. It is the beginning of the possibly very primitive or primary interaction of the client with his or her environment. For instance, a client sits in a catatonic position, stares in a stony way in front of him or her, and hardly reacts to stimuli from his or her environment. Situational reflections are remarks made by the therapist that refer to the concrete situation:

> You are sitting on the floor.
> Noises are coming from outside.
> A dog barks.

The purpose is, by means of a situational reflection that affects the client, to give them an opportunity to express a first reaction to something that happens in the real world.

FACIAL REFLECTIONS
Facial reflections concern the reflecting of facial expressions. For instance:

> You look angry.
> You have a big smile on your face.
> Your eyes are closed.

The therapist verbalizes the feeling that is implicitly stated by the client's face. This helps the client express pre-expressive affect and helps them come into affective contact with themselves.

WORD-FOR-WORD REFLECTIONS
Word-for-word reflections involve the literal repetition of what the patient says: sounds, words, or entire sentences. This process brings the patient to communicational speech, giving them the experience that they are the one who is giving expression to communication. 'These are reflections of social words and sentences in the stream of incoherent language' (Prouty & Pietrzak, 1988, p. 427). For instance, the hallucinating client makes the following statements and the therapist gives a literal repetition of the remarks:

> C: *Careful. Pink elephant there.*
> T: *Careful. Pink elephant there.*
> C: *Look out-Hurt-gonna get.*
> T: *Look out-Hurt-gonna get.*
> C: *They are big and pink and ugly.*
> T: *They are big and pink and ugly.*
> C: *They laugh and yell and hurt you.*
> T: *They laugh and yell and hurt you.*
> (Ibid: 435)

BODY REFLECTIONS

Actions expressed bodily by the client are reproduced or reflected as accurately as possible. Also dependent on the communication level of the patient, this can be a record of the position and actions of the patient (e.g., 'You are moving back and forward. Your arms are tense.'), as well as the nonverbal imitation of these expressions (e.g., shrugging the shoulders, sitting and looking at one's feet, tapping on the floor, etc.). This process expresses a sympathetic attunement to the client, on the level of his or her identity with his or her own body.

These four techniques are generally followed by, or are coupled with, reiterative reflections: reflections used earlier, which afforded contact, are now repeated. Thus it is really not a new technique but it is the principle of repetition, which is central here.

In general, in association with the expressive possibilities of the client, the therapist tries to restore the client's contact with herself and her surrounding world. In illustration, I will describe a part of a Pre-Therapy session which I published previously (Peters, 1999). *WW* stands for word-for-word-reflections, *FR* for facial reflections, *BR* for body reflections, *SR* for situational reflections and *RR* for reiterative reflections. *L* is the client, *H* the therapist.

L: *mmmm*
H: *(WW) mmmmm Leny says*
L: *Fedat*
H: *(WW) Fedat*
H: *(FR) Leny, looks at the window Leny, looks at the window*
L: *mmm*
H: *(WW) mmm Leny says*
  (FR) Leny looks at the window; Leny looks out of the window
  (SR) Leny hears uh uh uh
  (FR) Leny looks out of the window
  (FR) Leny looks at the door
  (BR) Leny taps at the chair
  (BR) hand to the mouth
L: *mmm*
H: *(WW) mmm*
  (FR) Leny looks at me
L: *mmmm*
H: *(WW) mmmm, Leny says*
  (BR) Leny taps at her bed

>   (BR) Leny nods
>   (FR) Leny looks at the door
> L: mmmm
> H: (WW) mmmm, Leny says
>   (FR) and looks out of the window
> L: Betoe
> H: (WW) Betoe
> L: Passé ...
> H: (WW) Passé, betoe
> L: Ne we passé
> H: (WW) Ne we passé
> L: Te ba na toe and knocks at the wall
> H: (BR) [Leny knocks. Leny beats on bed. H imitates the response.]

This vignette (more extended examples can be found, among others, in Krietemeyer & Prouty, 2003; Peters, 1999, 2005; Prouty 2001, 2003; and Prouty, Van Werde & Pörtner, 2002) gives an impression of the way in which Pre-Therapy is originally applied. Many utterances of the client are not recognizable words; however, the therapist gives back the client's sounds. In association with the expressive possibilities of the client, the therapist tries to restore the client's contact with herself and her surrounding world. Reflections that are the most effective, the so-called reiterative reflections, are very often repeated.

Apart from this, there is what I have earlier named a *secondary application* of Pre-Therapy (Peters, 1999). In the primary application of Pre-Therapy, the contact reflections serve primarily to establish or to restore the very basic contact functions. When a certain level of contact is possible, especially word-for-word, the facial reflections can play an important role in the current, individual verbal therapies. This is what I call the secondary application of Pre-Therapy. Just mentioning what you see on the client's face or repeating their words, without interpretation, judgment, and so on are ways of approaching the client other than, for instance, asking why they are beating themselves, saying that they have no reason to be angry, or telling them that they do not need to be afraid because you are with them, as very often happens in daily life. The reflections give them an opportunity to elaborate their anger, panic, or whatever else is happening within the client. It is a reflection on their momentary level of functioning.

> EXAMPLE
> Some years ago I saw a video of an autistic man sitting at the table while eating some bread. Most of the day he was in contact with his

environment, although the contact was very flighty. In the video, he gave the impression of being occupied with compulsive thoughts (he was very tense, murmured some words, stared at some points on the table, and so on). Ward personnel told me that this could lead to severe tantrums. It was as if he wound himself up in stereotypic compulsive thoughts. We decided to use facial and body reflections such as 'Wim drinks', 'Wim looks at me', 'Wim takes a slice of bread', and so on. The tension slowly flowed away, there was more reciprocity in the contact, and a tantrum was prevented. Why do I mention this example? On one hand, I will show that there need not always be an enduring, massive contact disturbance to apply Pre-Therapy in a meaningful way. On the other hand, the value of Pre-Therapy in the application of stereotypic and compulsive behavior, at least with people who are mentally handicapped, is highly underestimated. Stereotypic and/or compulsive behaviors may be very understandable from the client's point of view; however, that does not mean that he is not suffering from this emitted behavior.

INTERSUBJECTIVITY, IMITATION, AND PRE-THERAPY

As we saw before, Pre-Therapy is a kind of client-centered/experiential psychotherapy aiming at restoring or bringing about primary or secondary contact in an intersubjective context. The relation between intersubjectivity and Pre-Therapy can best be understood by a quote by Prouty:

> You can say that:
> Pre-Therapy is a form of attunement,
> Pre-Therapy is intersubjective contact,
> Pre-Therapy is intersubjective relatedness,
> Pre-Therapy is a one-way intersubjectivity which is pre-mutual intersubjectivity.
> Mirror neurons are the biological basis for Pre-Therapy. (Prouty, 2006)

Pre-therapy is almost exclusively applied to people with (severe) contact disturbances—that is a nearly total lack of contact with themselves and with the surrounding world. In daily life, it is obvious that a large part of the target group consists of people with a severe mental handicap and/or people with an autistic contact disturbance. This means that the therapist often takes the initiative to have contact with the client, which is a kind of one-way intersubjectivity, hoping that this will lead to two-way intersubjectivity. With people suffering from a severe contact crisis, especially with people who are mentally handicapped, the cognitive disturbance is predominantly present. This means that the second form of intersubjectivity, which focuses on the perception and feeling of emotions, is the central topic in this kind of treatment and not the cognitive form of intersubjectivity. This second form of intersubjectivity exists already in the neonate.

We also noticed that imitation, and to a greater extent the development of intersubjectivity, belongs to the neonatal capacities of people, including those with a mental and/or an autistic handicap. This means that the therapist, in applying pre-therapeutic contact reflections, does not only join in the remaining behaviors the client still exhibits, but also appeals to innate skills people have at their disposal: imitation and intersubjectivity are archaic potentialities people have. These capacities, which develop relatively spontaneously in the neonate, differ from those of the client with severe contact disturbances in that in the latter these capacities are blocked in such a way that they have to be evoked. The imitation of the limited utterances of the neonate by the mother with the aim of coming to a mutual intersubjectivity corresponds with the application of pre-therapeutic reflections by the therapist. Mother and therapist link onto behaviors that are close to the person and from which is to be expected that they would elicit responses. This is the foundation of the success of pre-therapeutic interventions.

An obvious question is whether the pre-therapeutic reflections rest too much on a mechanical imitation of the client's behavior. One can ask the same question concerning the imitative behavior of the mother. We already saw that the imitation by the mother is not a strict imitation of the child's behavior, but her imitation is colored by her empathic feeling and by her congruent way of responding. This is identical to the application of pre-therapeutic reflections. The therapist approaches the client in an empathic and accepting way, joins to the basal rest behaviors the client exhibits; however, at the same time, the therapist approaches the client from his or her own congruence so that therapist and client do not coincide. It is what Rogers (1962) and Kohut (1977) called *mirroring*. The difference between those two authors is that Rogers explained mirroring as an empathic response from the therapist to the client, whereas Kohut, and this seems important for my thesis, in 1977 already explained mirroring from a developmental perspective as he stated that:

> The psychologically healthy adult continues to need the mirroring of the self by self-objects ..., and he continues to need targets for his idealization. No implication of immaturity or psychopathology must, therefore, be derived from the fact that another person is used as a self-object—self-object relations occur on all developmental levels and in psychological health as well as in psychological illness. (p. 188)

With reference to infants, Gergely and Watson (1996) thought that there was proof that infants are extremely sensitive to the difference between their own affective-expressive utterances and those of the parents. The child at a very early stage is able to see the responses of the mother as corresponding with his or her own feelings and behaviors, but also as differing from them. This is analogous to the application of pre-therapeutic reflections. Characteristic in applying pre-therapeutic reflections ought to be that the therapist links up with the often deformed behaviors of the client but acts so in empathic directedness to the client and from his or her own congruence. This gives the client the largest opportunity to recognize the behaviors of the therapist as part of himself or herself, which will facilitate the client to respond. On the other hand, the client has to distinguish his or her affective-emotional utterances as differing from those of the therapist. This is essential because the client has to learn that the reality contact is his or her reality within the context of his or her existence and not the therapist's.

SUMMARIZING CONCLUSIONS

My tentative conclusions are the following:

- As seen in the aforementioned work of authors such as Bråten, Trevarthen, Kugiumutzakis, Heimann, Meltzoff and Moore, and others there is sufficient proof that imitation and intersubjectivity are innate human capacities.
- These capacities are accessible from the very first hours of life.
- These basic capacities also exist in people who are autistic and mentally handicapped (the strong tendency by children with Down's syndrome to imitate is especially well known); and with these clients, as well as with the clients who are severely contact disturbed, the emotional view of intersubjectivity is far more important than the intellectual one. In other words, approaches wherein the perception and feeling of emotions are central (which is, according to Gómez [1998], the original conception of intersubjectivity) is situated on an earlier level of age in which pre-speech and proto-conversation play a relatively important role.
- The neonate has the capacity to distinguish the responses of the adult as differing from as well as corresponding with their own behaviors.
- Research has shown that imitation has to be seen as a mutual influencing and dialogical process, which connects well with the concept of Pre-Therapy, the ultimate goal of which is to bring about a contact dialogue, after which the more regular forms of psychotherapy are applicable.

- Pre-therapeutic reflections therefore are in line with the very basic imitative and intersubjective capacities which exist in human beings from birth.

- Similar to the imitation of the utterances of the child by the mother, where the imitation of the child's behaviors is not a pure mechanical repetition of these behaviors, in Pre-Therapy too the therapist reflects from an empathic stance and in their own congruent way the often-minimal behaviors of the client.

According to the above-mentioned concept, Pre-Therapy can be seen from a developmental frame of reference in which the success of the application of pre-therapeutic reflections, even with adults, proceeds because it is attuned to the basic potentialities we have since birth.

REFERENCES

Atwood, G & Stolorow, R (1984) *Structures of Subjectivity: Explorations in psychoanalytic phenomenology.* Hillsdale, NJ: The Analytic Press.

Bråten, S (1988) Dialogic mind: The infant and the adult in protoconversation. In M Carvallo (Ed) *Nature, Cognition and System. 1,* 187–205. Torino: Meynier.

Bråten, S (1998) Infant learning by altercentric participation: The reverse of egocentric observations in autism. In S Bråten (Ed) *Intersubjective Communication and Emotion in Early Ontogeny* (pp 105–27). Cambridge: Cambridge University Press.

Buccino, G, Binkofski, F, Fink, GR, Fadiga, L, Fogassi, L, Gallese, V, Seitz, RJ, Zilles, K, Rizzolatti, G & Freund, HJ (2001) Action observation activates pre-motor and parietal areas in a somatotopic manner: An fMRI study. *European Journal of Neuroscience, 13,* 400–4.

Gallese, V (2000a) Action, goals, and their role in intersubjectivity: From mirror neurons to the 'shared manifold' hypothesis. Retrieved 23 October 2004, from www.mpipf-muenchen.mpg.de/MPIPF/MECA/docs/gallese.doc

Gallese, V (2000b) The inner sense of action. Agency and motor representations. *Journal of Consciousness Studies, 7,* 23–40.

Gallese, V (2001) The 'Shared Manifold' hypothesis. From mirror neurons to empathy. *Journal of Conscious Studies, 8,* 33–50.

Gallese, V (2003a) The roots of empathy: The shared manifold hypothesis and the neural basis of intersubjectivity. *Psychopathology, 36,* 171–80.

Gallese, V (2003b) The manifold nature of interpersonal relations: The quest for a common mechanism. *Phil. Trans. R. Soc. Lond., 358,* 517–28.

Gergely, G & Watson, JS (1996) The social biofeedback theory of parental affect-mirroring. The development of self-awareness and self-control in infancy. *International Journal of Psychoanalysis, 77,* 1181–212.

Gilbert, J (2004) De cognitieve dimensie van bewustzijn en spiegelneurale effecten. Een onderzoek naar de bijdrage van spiegelneuronale werking tot de realisatie van be-weten. Unpublished Masters thesis, University of Ghent. Ghent: Belgium.

Gómez, JC (1998) Do concepts of intersubjectivity apply to non-human primates? In S. Bråten (Ed) *Intersubjective Communication and Emotion in Early Ontogeny* (pp 245–60). Cambridge: Cambridge University Press.

Heimann, M (1997) The never ending story of neonatal imitation. Poster presented at the VIIIth European Conference on Developmental Psychology, Rennes, France.

Heimann, M (1998) Imitation in neonates, in older infants and in children with autism: Feedback to theory. In S Bråten (Ed) *Intersubjective Communication and Emotion in Early Ontogeny* (pp 89–105). Cambridge: Cambridge University Press.

Kohut, H (1977) *The Restoration of the Self.* New York: International University Press.

Krietemeyer, B & Prouty, G (2003) The art of psychological contact: The psychotherapy of a mentally retarded psychotic client. *Person-Centered and Experiential Psychotherapies, 2,* 151–61.

Kugiumutzakis, G (1998) Neonatal imitation in the intersubjective companion space. In S Bråten (Ed) *Intersubjective Communication and Emotion in Early Ontogeny* (pp 63–89). Cambridge: Cambridge University Press.

Meltzoff, AN & Moore, MK (1998) Infant intersubjectivity: Broadening the dialogue to include imitation, identity and intention. In S Bråten (Ed) *Intersubjective Communication and Emotion in Early Ontogeny* (pp 47–63). Cambridge: Cambridge University Press.

Oram, MW & Perret, DI (1994) Responses of anterior superior temporal polysensory (STPa) neurons to 'biological motion' stimuli. *Journal of Cognitive Sciences, 6,* 99–116.

Perret, DI, Harries, MH, Bevan, R, Benson, PJ, Mistlin, AJ, Chitty, AJ, Hietanen, JK & Ortega, JE (1989) Framework of analysis for the neural representation of animate objects and actions. *Journal of Experimental Biology, 148,* 87–113.

Perret, DI, Mistlin, AJ, Harries, MH & Chitty, AJ (1990) Understanding the visual appearance and consequence of hand actions. In MA Goodale (Ed) *Vision and Action: The control of grasping* (pp 163–80). Norwood, NJ: Ablex.

Peters, H (1999) Pre-Therapy: A client-centered/experiential approach to mentally handicapped people. *Journal of Humanistic Psychology, 39,* 8–30.

Peters, H (2003) Enkele gedachten over vroegkinderlijk imiteren en intersubjectiviteit in relatie tot aspecten van psychotherapie. *Tijdschrift Cliëntgerichte Psychotherapie, 41,* 84–115.

Peters, H (2005) Pre-Therapy from a developmental perspective. *Journal of Humanistic Psychology, 45,* 62–82.

Prouty, G (1994) *Theoretical Evolutions in Person-Centered/Experiential Therapy. Applications to schizophrenic and retarded psychoses.* Westport, CT: Praeger.

Prouty, G (2001) The practice of Pre-Therapy. *Journal of Contemporary Psychotherapy, 31,* 31–40.

Prouty, G (2003) Pre-Therapy: A newer development in the psychotherapy of schizophrenia. *The Journal of the American Academy of Psychoanalysis and Dynamic Psychiatry, 31,* 59–73.

Prouty, G (2006) Personal communication.

Prouty, G & Pietrzak, S (1988) Pre-Therapy method applied to persons experiencing hallucinatory images. *Person Centered Review, 3,* 426–41.

Prouty, G, Van Werde, D & Pörtner, M (2002) *Pre-Therapy: Reaching contact-impaired clients.* Ross-on-Wye: PCCS Books.

Rogers, CR (1962) The interpersonal relationship: The core of guidance. *Harvard Education Review, 3,* 426–41.

Stern, DN (1985/2000) *The Interpersonal World of the Infant: A view from psychoanalysis and developmental psychology*. (Second edn, 2000, with new Introduction). New York: Basic Books.

Stolorow, RD, Brandchaft, B & Atwood, GE (1987) *Psychoanalytic Ttreatment. An intersubjective approach*. Hillsdale, NJ: The Analytic Press.

Trevarthen, C (1998) The concept of foundations of infant intersubjectivity. In S Bråten (Ed) *Intersubjective Communication and Emotion in Early Ontogeny* (pp 15–47). Cambridge: Cambridge University Press.

Trevarthen, C (2002a) Human nature before words. Unpublished Manuscript.

Trevarthen, C (2002b). Sensing self and other out of body and in the future: Exceptional explanations for everyday human experiences. Paper presented at the Conference, Fundacio Bial 'Research on brain and experience: Tools of science for understanding exceptional experience'.

Tronick, EZ (1998) Dyadically expanded states of consciousness and the process of therapeutic change. *Infant Mental Health Journal, 19*, 290–300.

Van IJzendoorn, MH (2001) Gehechtheid en therapie: Mentale representaties van gehechtheid in psychotherapie en interventies. *Tijdschrift Cliëntgerichte Psychotherapie, 39*, 182–98.

Vliegen, N & Cluckers, G (2001) Baby observatie en therapeutisch proces. Van een historisch perspectief naar een actueel verband. In N Vliegen & C Leroy (Eds) *Het Moederland? De vroegste relatie tussen moeder en kind in de psychoanalytische therapie* (pp 21–45). Leuven/Leusden: Acco.

Whiten, A & Brown, J (1998) Imitation and the reading of minds: Perspectives from the study of autism, normal children and non-human primates. In S Bråten (Ed) *Intersubjective Communication and Emotion in Early Ontogeny* (pp 15–47). Cambridge: Cambridge University Press.

CHAPTER 6

Pre-Therapy and the Pre-Expressive Self

GARRY PROUTY

INTRODUCTION

The *necessary* condition of a therapeutic relationship is that the therapist and the client be in psychological contact (Rogers, 1957). However, Rogers fails to provide a conceptual or practice definition of 'psychological contact.' Furthermore, it is a gratuitous assumption that all clients possess this attribute. Evolving from these issues, Pre-Therapy is a theory of psychological contact. It provides a practice description (contact reflection)a description of client internal function (contact functions) and a description of measurable behaviors (contact behaviors). Its primary application is to 'contact impaired,' regressed, low functioning and chronic clients, such as the developmentally disabled, schizophrenic, dissociated or Alzheimer's populations.

CONTACT REFLECTIONS

Contact reflections are extraordinary literal and concrete reflections to reach the severely withdrawn or regressed client described as contact impaired. Examples of applications with psychotic and retarded persons are to be found in Prouty (1976, 1990); Prouty and Kubiak (1988a, 1988b); Prouty and Pietrzak (1988); Prouty and Cronwall (1990); and Van Werde (1989,1990).

Situational Reflections (SR) are reflections of the client's situation, environment or milieu. They are a 'pointing toward the world.' Their theoretical function is to facilitate reality contact. An example would be 'Johnny is riding the bike' or 'Mary opened the door.'

Facial Reflections (FR) are reflections of pre-expressive feeling embodied in the face. An example is: 'You look sad' or more literally, 'You are smiling.' Their theoretical function is to facilitate affective contact.

Word-for-Word Reflections (WWR) are reflections of single words, sentence

---

Prouty, G (1998) Pre-Therapy and the pre-expressive self. *Person-Centred Practice,* 6 (2), 80–8. By kind permission of The British Association for the Person-Centred Approach.

fragments and other verbal disorganization so characteristic of brain damaged and psychotic persons. Their intent is to develop communicative contact. The client may say 'tree,' (mumble) 'horse,' (mumble) 'car,' (mumble). The therapist reflects the clear language even if meaning is not clear. Occasionally, the therapist may also reiterate sounds.

Body Reflections (BR) are reflections of pre-expressive 'bodying,' such as catatonic statuesque behavior or other bizarre body expressions. Their purpose is to integrate body expression within the sense of self. The reflections are mostly verbal, but can be done with the therapist's own body.

Reiterative Reflections (RR) embody the principle of re-contact. If any of the contact reflections are successful, then apply them again. The purpose is to expand the 'island' of meaningful experiential contact.

These reflections, when combined, provide a 'web' of psychological contact for the regressed, isolated and contact-impaired client. Contact reflections facilitate the contact functions (client process) which result in the emergence of contact behaviors (measurement).

CONTACT FUNCTIONS

The contact functions refer to the client process in psychological contact. They represent an expansion of Perls' (1969: 14) concept of 'contact as an ego function.' They are awareness functions and are described as reality, affective and communicative contact. The development or restoration of the contact functions are the *necessary* conditions of psychotherapy. Their functioning are the theoretical goals of Pre-Therapy. Reality contact (world) is the awareness of people, places, events and things. Affective contact is described as the awareness of moods, feelings and emotions. Communicative contact is defined as the symbolization of reality (world) and affect (self) to others.

VIGNETTE

Dorothy is an old woman who is one of the more regressed women on X ward. She was mumbling something (as she usually did). This time I could hear certain words in her confusion. I reflected only the words I could clearly understand. After about ten minutes, I could hear a complete sentence.

Client: *Come with me.*

Therapist: *(WWR) Come with me.*

[*The patient led me to the corner of the dayroom. We stood there silently for what seemed to be a very long time. Since I couldn't communicate with her, I watched her body movements and closely reflected these.*]

C: *[The patient put her hand on the wall.] Cold.*

T: *(WWR-BR) [I put my hand on the wall and repeated the word.] Cold.*

[She had been holding my hand all along; but when I reflected her, she would tighten her grip. Dorothy would begin to mumble word fragments. I was careful to reflect only the words I could understand. What she was saying began to make sense.]

C: *I don't know what this is anymore. [Touching the wall –* REALITY CONTACT.*] The walls and chairs don't mean anything anymore. [Existential autism]*

T: *(WWR-BR) [Touching the wall.] You don't know what this is anymore. The chairs and walls don't mean anything to you anymore.*

C: *[The patient began to cry –* AFFECTIVE CONTACT. *After a while she began to talk again. This time she spoke clearly –* COMMUNICATIVE CONTACT.*]
I don't like it here. I'm so tired ... so tired.*

T: *(WWR) [As I gently touched her arm, this time it was I who tightened my g r i p on her hand.]
You're tired, so tired.*

C: *[The patient smiled and told me to sit in a chair directly in front of her and began to braid my hair.]*

This vignette begins to express Pre-Therapy as a therapeutic theory and philosophy. It illustrates the use of contact reflections to facilitate the contact functions (reality, affect, communication).

CONTACT BEHAVIORS

Contact behaviors are the emergent behavioral changes that are the operationalized aspect of psychological contact. Reality contact (world) is operationalized as the client's verbalization of people, places, things and events. Affective contact (self) is operationalized as the bodily or facial expression of affect. Communicative contact (Other) is operationalized as the client's verbalization of social words or sentences. Exploratory studies have provided evidence for reliability (DeVre, 1992) and construct validity (Prouty, 1994). Positive effects for therapy have been measured by Hinterkopf, Prouty and Brunswick (1979) and Dinacci (1997). Full scientific and theoretical descriptions can be found in Peters (1986); Leijssen and Roelens (1988); Prouty (1976, 1990, 1994), and Prouty, Van Werde and Pörtner (1998/ 2002).

THE PRE-EXPRESSIVE SELF

The pre-expressive self is an intuitive and heuristic concept derived from the author's personal experience, as well as clinical and quantitative case studies of Pre-Therapy.

THE PRE-EXPRESSIVE SELF

As a young boy, I lived with my mother, step-father and mentally retarded/psychotic brother. I have long recognized the influence of my brother on the personal formation of Pre-Therapy. One day, when I was eleven or twelve years old, I invited a friend to visit my home. We were talking when I said 'I wonder if he [brother] understands what we are saying?' To my intense surprise, he responded, 'You know I do, Garry' and then lapsed back into a regressed and autistic state. For years the experience 'haunted' me, giving me a feeling there was 'somebody in there.' It was not until *after* the publication of my first book that the importance of that experience became clear. In the foreword of that text, Luc Roelens, a Belgian psychiatrist, arguing against the medical understanding of psychotic states, relates similar case descriptions. I read them and realized the similarity. He describes several cases of clients suddenly expressing contact. One case concerns a woman patient with a chronic and severe catatonic state. When informed that her husband had fallen from the roof and broken both legs, she immediately responded with her intention to go home and take care of everything. There was no relapse. At four- and ten-year follow-ups she displayed only mild autism. Another reported case concerned a mute male schizophrenic who had been in a dementia-like state. He was being fed by a nurse when he choked and spat all over her. He immediately responded by saying, 'Excuse me, I did not mean to do that', and then relapsed back into his previous state. My brother, and these cases express the presence of a 'pre-expressive self' that underlies the autism, regression, psychosis, brain damage, retardation, senility, etc. There is somebody 'in there'.

PRE-EXPRESSIVE SIGNS

Signs of a pre-expressive self are derived from the verbal process of psychotic expression. Using word-for-word reflections of psychotic content results in movement toward reality. For example, a young, male catatonic expresses himself by saying 'Priests are devils.' By carefully and precisely reflecting this, it eventually processes to the reality of a homosexual overture from a local priest. This highly condensed metaphor 'contained' latent reality content. The movement from a highly condensed psychotic metaphor to the manifestation of latent reality content is called 'pre-expressive process.' The psychotic metaphor is 'pre-expressive.' It contains reality in a pre-expressive form.

The semiotic structure of such initial psychotic expression can be characterized in the following way. These pre-expressive forms have *no context* to derive meaning from and they have *no referent* to complete their symbolic function. This means the expressions lack reality sense and appear to be void of a reality source. Without understanding that the latent reality is 'packaged' in a pre-expressive way, the therapeutic potential of psychotic expression is not envisioned.

Further signs of the pre-expressive self are derived from individual case histories and quantitative studies. All of these have the feature of movement from fragmented, incomplete, bizarre, incoherent expression to fuller cogency and congruence-movement from a pre-expressive to an expressive state.

The Pre-Expressive Self refers to a *potentiating*, structure of experience and expression. It is characterized primarily by is *organismic, pre-symbolic* thrust toward reality, possibly a manifestation of the self-formative tendency (Rogers, 1978). It is the polar opposite of the Freudian concept of regression. The organismic pre-symbolic thrust toward reality is distinctly opposite to the regressive concept of movement away from reality. The energy is directed forward instead of being a downward fixation as described by Freud. The concept of regression is a *developmental* concept; whereas, pre-expressive is a *therapeutic* concept. These concepts have a different functional context. They also lead to radically different understandings of psychotic process for the psychotherapist. The picture resulting from a pre-expressive understanding senses a 'buried' self, expressing meaning and reality in a *different symbolic structure* capable of being therapeutically processed by more 'primitive' reflections (Pre-Therapy).

MULTIPLE PERSONALITY

Roy (1991, 1997) describes the use of Pre-Therapy as an adjunctive method in the treatment of multiple personality disorder. Within the context of a person-centered/experiential therapy, she describes the application of contact reflections to develop and assist the integration of a dissociated self and repressed memories. According to Roy, such personality fragments often lack in an experiential felt sense and may be expressed in halting, primitive symbolizations (pre-expressive). As an example, a client would express singular words such as 'face,' 'dark,' 'window,' 'cellar,' 'door,' 'hurt,' 'bleeding,' etc., which Roy would reflect contactfully through word-for-word reflections. Roy goes on to describe an important facial reflection: 'You look angry.' According to the client, this helped make contact with important angry feelings. They were embodied pre-expressively in her face. Roy further states: 'Dissociated material, whether it is as distinctive as a separate personality, or much less so, must be experienced and *allowed to live in the world.*' She also points out that a non-directive, non-interpretive approach reduces the possibility of suggestion, one of the major problems in the treatment of repressed, dissociated memories. Coffeng (1995, 1997) describes the application of contact reflections with multiple personality clients, as well as those with severe trauma and sexual abuse.

A NON-VERBAL CLIENT

McWilliams and Prouty (1998) report the application of contact reflections with a non-verbal, profoundly retarded woman. The contact work was supplied by her stepmother. The stepmother used body reflections involving finger, head and arm movements, as well as non-verbal sounds. She would also literally reflect facial expressions such as happiness. All of these were combined with the principle of reiteration. This contact work was woven into daily living in contrast to a 'session.' Positive results for the 'client' included a sharp increase in contact with the world, self and other. Her increased contact with the world was evidenced through her attention to environmental situations, such as looking out the car window. Her contact with the other was expressed through her being less isolated, being more 'present' with her family, resulting in increased mutuality. Her improved contact with self was evidenced in a shift from a non-responsive mode of seeing herself in the mirror, to a smiling, satisfied mode of looking. The net result of the contact work was a decrease in psychological isolation and an increase in psychological presence, enhancing for 'client' and family.

HALLUCINATORY VOICES

Prouty (1977, 1983, 1986, 1991; Prouty & Pietrzak, 1988) describes the theory and practice of pre-symbolic experiencing as it applies to the integration and processing of visual hallucinations. Often, during lectures on visual hallucinations, people would ask about the application of contact reflections to audio hallucinations. Until Jill Prouty presented this case material there had been no evidence for this possibility.

VIGNETTE

C: The voices. [Client puts hands on head.]

T: (BR) Your hands are on your head.

C: [Moves hands to cover face.]

T: (FR) Your hands cover your eyes.

T: (BR) You're breathing deeply.

C: [The client removes her hands from her eyes and looks at the floor.)

T: (SR) You're looking at the floor.

T: (SR) There is a green carpet in this room.

C: [No response.]

T: (SR) We're standing here together.

T: (BR) You're breathing easier now.

C: [The client looks directly at the therapist.]

T: (SR) You looked directly at me.

C: [The client puts her hands on the side of her head and over her ears.]

I hear voices.

T: (WWR) You hear voices.

C: The voice says 'You die, you should kill yourself'

T: (WWR) The voice says 'You die, you should kill yourself'

T: (RR) You said earlier you heard voices.

[Looking directly at the therapist, the client began her story about an actual sexual abuse.]

Reality contact had been established and communicative contact about the voices had been developed. The therapist was then able to use classical psychodramatic technique, that is developing the roles for the drama and setting the scene. Sufficient psychological contact had been established to proceed with therapy. The therapist then asks:

T: Is it one voice or many?

C: One.

T: Male or female?

C: Male, my brother.

Therapist: Choose someone in the group to be your brother.

The client was able to release rage at her brother for not protecting her from sexual abuse during his presence. In addition, the client was able to process guilt and anger over this, which was the origin of the voices. The vignette illustrates the use of voices as a therapeutic process and the use of Pre-Therapy as an adjunctive method of contact to enable therapy.

SOME FURTHER THOUGHTS

LACAN

A theoretical observation can be made concerning postulation of a 'mirror stage' of 'I' development (Lacan, 1977). Lacan reports observations of human infants and how they respond to mirrored images of themselves. He starts by describing how monkeys lose interest in their own mirrored image. In contrast, human infants continue to recognize and respond to their own mirrored image. They see themselves. This differentiation, he concluded, reveals a *human* stage of development he calls 'the mirror stage.' He characterizes this as a stage of a primordial integration of the 'I' (self). Pre-Therapy also seems to lead to a primordial integration. Both seem to indicate an integration of self at primitive levels. Perhaps Pre-Therapy facilitates self-integration at a 'mirror stage' of development. Perhaps this may account for the success with non-verbal, profoundly retarded clients (see McWilliams & Prouty, 1998).

MINKOWSKI

Still another interesting observation can be made concerning the theoretical interface between Pre-Therapy and the phenomenological description of schizophrenia offered by Minkowski (1970). Minkowski describes schizophrenia as a lack of *vital contact* between the person and reality. He describes vital contact as the person's *experiential penetration* of the phenomenon. Next, he describes a *relatedness* between the phenomenon and the person as characterized by an ebb and flow, a mutual process of attending and receiving. Another quality of vital contact or the person's involvement with the phenomenon is *sympathy* (empathy). Finally, there is the characteristic of 'horizon' as *infinitely nuanced*. Our meanings are continuous. The last element of vital contact concerns *synchronicity*. Things, as well as ourselves, move forward in time, in a 'parallel' fashion. Schizophrenia, for Minkowski, is the absence of this *vital contact*.

There is a marked parallel between Minkowski's formulation concerning the lack of vital contact as central to the nature of schizophrenia and Pre-Therapy's empathic contact as central to its treatment. What this brings together is a description of treatment (Pre-Therapy) that corresponds to the problem (lack of vital contact).

SUMMARY

This paper has described techniques to develop psychological contact with regressed, isolated, 'pre-relationship' and 'pre-process' clients. The concept of the 'pre-expressive self' is introduced. The application of these techniques was originally targeted for schizophrenic and developmentally disabled clients. They have been recently expanded to Alzheimer's victims as a tool for communication, as well as to processing multiple personality clients along with those suffering from severe trauma and abuse. The hallucinatory work has been expanded from purely visual experience to include auditory experiences. Possible interfacing between Pre-Therapy and the observations of Lacan and Minkowski are described.

REFERENCES

Coffeng, T (1995) Experiential and pre-experiential therapy for multiple trauma. In U Esser, G Pabst & G Spierer (Eds) *The Power of the Person-Centered Approach* (pp 185–204). Köln, Germany: GWG Verlag.

Coffeng, T (1997) Pre-experiential contact with dissociation (Video). IVth International Conference for Client-Centered & Experiential Therapy. Lisbon, Portugal.

Dinacci, A (1997) Ricerca sperimentale sultrattamento psicologico dei pazienti schizofrenic con la Pre-Therapia. Dr. G Prouty. *Psychologia Della Persona*. 2 (4). Maggio. Bologna, Italy.

DeVre, R (1992) Prouty's Pre-Therapy. Master's thesis, Department of Psychology, University of Ghent, Belguim.

Hinterkopf, E, Prouty, G & Brunswick, L (1979) A pilot study of Pre-Therapy method applied to chronic schizophrenic patients. *Psychosocial Rehabilitation Journal*, 3, 11–19.

Lacan, J (1977) The mirror stage as formative of the function of I as revealed in psychoanalytic experience. In *Ecrits* (pp 4–7). New York: WW Norton.

Leijssen, M & Roelens, L (1988) Herstel van contactfuncties bij zwaar gestoorde patienten door middel Van Prouty's Pre-Therapie [The contact functions of Prouty's Pre-Therapy.] *Tijdschrift Klinische Psychologie*, 18 (1), 21–34.

McWilliams, K & Prouty, G (1998) Life enrichment of a profoundly retarded woman: An application of Pre-Therapy. *The Person Centered Journal*, 5 (1), 29–35.

Minkowski, E (1970) Schizophrenia. In *Lived Time* (pp 281–2). Evanston, IL: Northwestern University Press.

Perls, FS (1969) *Ego, Hunger and Aggression*. New York: Random House.

Peters, H (1986). Prouty's pre-therapie methods en de behandeling ven hallucinaties een versalg [Prouty's Pre-Therapy methods and the treatment of hallucinations]. *RUIT,* (March), 26–34.

Prouty, G (1976) Pre-Therapy, a method of treating pre-expressive psychotic and retarded patients. *Psychotherapy: Theory, Research and Practice*, 13, 290–94.

Prouty, G (1977) Protosymbolic method: A phenomenological treatment of schizophrenic hallucinations. *Journal of Mental Imagery, 1* (2), 339–42.

Prouty, G (1983). Hallucinatory contact: A phenomenological treatment of schizophrenics. *Journal of Communication Therapy, 2* (1), 99–103.

Prouty, G (1986) The pre-symbolic structure and therapeutic transformation of hallucinations. In M Wolpin, J Shorr & L Krueger (Eds) *Imagery, Vol 4* (pp 98–106). New York: Plenum Press.

Prouty, G (1990) Pre-Therapy: A theoretical evolution in the person-centered/experiential psychotherapy of schizophrenia and retardation. In G Lietaer, J Rombauts & R Van Balen (Eds) *Client-Centered and Experiential Psychotherapy in the Nineties* (pp 645–58). Leuven: Leuven University Press.

Prouty G (1991) The pre-symbolic structure and processing of schizophrenic hallucinations: The problematic of a non-process structure. In L Fusek (Ed) *New Directions in Client-Centered Therapy: Practice with difficult client populations* (pp 1–18). Chicago, IL: The Chicago Counseling Center.

Prouty, G (1994) *Theoretical Evolutions in Person-Centered/Experiential Psychotherapy: Applications to Schizophrenic and Retarded Psychoses.* Westport, CN: Praeger (Greenwood) Publications.

Prouty, G & Cronwall, M (1990) Psychotherapy with a depressed mentally retarded adult: An application of Pre-Therapy. In A Dosen & F Menolascino (Eds) *Depression in Mentally Retarded Children and Adults* (pp 281–93). Leiden: Logan Publications.

Prouty, G & Kubiak, M (1988a) The development of communicative contact with a catatonic schizophrenic. *Journal of Communication Therapy, 4* (1), 13–20.

Prouty, G & Kubiak, M (1988b) Pre-Therapy with mentally retarded/psychotic clients. *Psychiatric Aspects of Mental Retardation Reviews, 7* (10), 62–6.

Prouty G & Pietrzak, S (1988) Pre-Therapy method applied to persons experiencing hallucinatory images. *Person-Centered Review, 3* (4), 426–41.

Prouty, G, Van Werde, D & Pörtner, M (1998) *Prä-Therapie.* Stutgaart: Klett-Cotta. [English edn (2002) *Pre-Therapy: Reaching contact-impaired clients.* Ross-on-Wye: PCCS Books]

Rogers, CR (1957) The necessary and sufficient conditions of therapeutic personality change. *Journal of Consulting Psychology, 21* (2), 95–103.

Rogers, CR (1978) The formative tendency. *Journal of Humanistic Psychology, 18,* 23–6.

Roy, BC (1991) A client-centered approach to multiple personality and dissociative process. In L Fusek (Ed) *New Directions in Client-centered Therapy: Practice with difficult client populations* (pp 18–40). Chicago, IL: The Chicago Counseling Center.

Roy, BC (1997) An illustration of memory retrieval with a DID client. Paper presented at Eastern Psychological Association, Washington DC.

Van Werde, D (1989) Restauratie van het psychologisch contact bij acute psychose. *Tijdschrift voor Psychotherapie, 5,* 271–9.

Van Werde, D (1990) Psychotherapy with a retarded schizo-affective woman: An application of Prouty's Pre-Therapy. In A Dosen, A Van Gennep & G Zwanikken (Eds) *Treatment of Mental Illness and Behavioral Disorder in the Mentally Retarded: Proceedings of International Congress, May 3rd & 4th* (pp 469–77). Amsterdam: Logon Publications.

Part IV

Related Developments

Editor's Commentary on Margaret Warner and Judith Trytten

Warner (2002), following the highly concrete 'word-for-word' approach of Pre-Therapy, finds new ways of understanding schizophrenic cognitive processing and ways of understanding the particular effectiveness of Pre-Therapy. She suggests that schizophrenic 'thought disorder' is actually a hybrid of normative metaphoric processing and normative logical processing, and carries within it the potential for significant reality-oriented therapeutic outcomes.

Traditional psychiatric models have emphasized ways that schizophrenic processing is deficient because it follows faulty logics. Von Domarus (1944), Arieti (1955) and others have observed that schizophrenic people tend to follow a particular sort of irrational, 'paleologic' style of thinking that creates false syllogisms like the following:

a. My mother's hair is red
b. Your hair is red
c. You are my mother

Warner notes that—unlike syllogistic logics, which operate with clear definitions and clear relations among phenomena—metaphors, similes and the like pick up on broad similarities among complex, multifaceted phenomena. They tend to define phenomena that are 'like' each other or have an 'as if' relation to each other. For example, the faulty syllogism cited above would make sense if expressed as a likeness rather than as a clear fact:

a. My mother's hair is red
b. Your hair is red
c. You are 'like' my mother

Metaphors have a particularly powerful function in processing. Things that are not yet clear can be captured and held in attention by metaphors, allowing people to connect with their felt sense of the whole of their experience.

Warner suggests that clients experiencing thought disorder tend to form statements as if they related to clearly defined phenomena or syllogistic logics, but then, to a significant degree, continue to process them as if they were metaphors or similes.

She calls these hybrid thought forms 'metaphacts' and 'metacauses.' For example, Luke might say 'I realized today that my father is the Boston strangler on the sly.' As a literal fact this is implausible (his father isn't a serial killer), but as a metaphor it seems to be highly attuned to Luke's felt sense of his situation with his father. Certainly, if he had expressed this in a more ordinary metaphoric form Luke's statement wouldn't sound irrational at all. For example, he could quite sensibly say 'I think my father is so angry at me that (it's as if) he could strangle me.'

Warner notes that, given the close empathic following that is provided by Pre-Therapy, Luke tends to proceed by bringing to mind a variety of scenes relating to the metaphor (his father being angry enough to strangle him) and to ultimately clarify what bothers him about the situation. For example, after touching on a variety of scenes relating to his father and to his father's anger, Luke might say, 'My father wants me to stop smoking and I just don't want to. He drinks too much and I don't complain about that.'

Notably, Warner, in her close analysis of Luke's process over a number of years, is finding significant positive potentials for productive processing and for human actualization implicit in the 'thought disorder' that is characteristic of schizophrenia. Trytten (2002), in a research analysis of a single Luke session, finds an overall progression of the session that parallels that of more high-functioning clients. Warner and Trytten suggest that psychiatric models that actively discourage the non-normative 'crazy-sounding' schizophrenic process are actually cutting clients off from the possibility of clarifying their thoughts and feelings and in the process greatly intensifying their alienation from themselves and others.

REFERENCES

Arieti, S (1955) *An Interpretation of Schizophrenia.* New York: Robert Brunner.

Trytten, J (2002) Schizophrenic client process: Phase and cognition patterns in a client-centered therapy session. Unpublished clinical research project, Illinois School of Professional Psychology of Argosy University, Chicago.

Von Domarus, E (1944) The specific laws of logic in schizophrenia. In JS Kasanin (Ed) *Language and Thought in Schizophrenia* (pp 104–44). Berkeley, CA: University of California.

Warner, MS (2002) Luke's dilemmas: A client-centered/experiential model of processing with a schizophrenic thought disorder. In JC Watson, RN Goldman & MS Warner (Eds) *Client-Centered and Experiential Psychotherapy in the 21st Century: Advances in theory, research and practice* (pp 459–72). Ross-on-Wye: PCCS Books.

CHAPTER 7

Metaphact Process: A new way of understanding schizophrenic thought disorder

MARGARET WARNER AND JUDITH TRYTTEN

Clients diagnosed with schizophrenia often organize their thoughts in strikingly unusual ways, a form of thinking traditionally labeled as 'thought disorder.' 'Luke,' a client we[1] have studied intensively over a more than ten-year period, often forms his thoughts in ways that are typical of the 'thought disorders' described in the psychological literature. Luke's therapy has been client-centered, utilizing Garry Prouty's very literal contact reflections as the primary mode of empathic responding (Prouty, 1994).

In one such therapy session, Luke—who actually comes from a well-established Irish-American family—expressed the following sequence of thoughts (slightly condensed here):

The trouble with the world is that there are too many Spaniards. My father is a Spaniard. When he talks, I only understand about a third of what he says. I think that that's because he comes from another country. On the other hand, you seem to understand me perfectly well. That must be because we come from the same country.

Traditional analyses of thought disorders have focused on the ways that such thinking doesn't make normative sense. Surely, Luke's father is not really a Spaniard, and if Luke and his father have communication difficulties, these are not caused by their having differing nationalities. These sorts of flaws of reasoning have been extensively described and researched in the literature on schizophrenia. However, the research hasn't come to a definitive understanding of the cause of such thought disorders or any clearly helpful therapeutic response. Many psychotherapeutic traditions discourage responding directly to such 'thought-disordered' formulations out of the belief that such

---

1. The conceptualization of 'metaphact processing' as an alternative way of understanding thought disorders was developed by the primary author, Margaret S. Warner, PhD. Judith D. Trytten, PsyD, conducted the first numerical research on hypotheses relating to Luke. The development of the conceptual model has been greatly assisted by textual analyses of Luke's process conducted within the doctoral research projects of the following students of the Illinois School of Professional Psychology: Jim Collins, Kim Mandel, Sheila Senn, Chin Teoh, and Robin Young.

responding is likely to encourage non-reality-based ways of thinking. When therapists do connect with such psychotic material, they often see this as a way of achieving some other purpose, such as arriving at a therapeutic alliance, making relevant symbolic interpretations, or helping the person gain the existential courage to face reality (see, for example, Pao, 1979 and Bellack, Mueser, Gingerich et al, 1997). Person-centered therapists, especially those following the work of Garry Prouty (1994), are quite distinct in this regard, since they see a strong therapeutic value in very close empathic responding to psychotic material, and see such psychotic material as having positive change potential in and of itself.

In our studies of Luke's process within client-centered therapy, we have come to a way of understanding the positive change potential inherent in such schizophrenic 'thought disorders,' a mode of experiencing which we call 'metaphact processing.' We propose that 'metaphact processing' is an exceedingly difficult but productive mode of processing experience that utilizes metaphors[2] and complex wholes to clarify experience at times when the client is having difficulty using clearly defined units and unit-logics.

This understanding of metaphact processing has been developed through an intensive analysis of a single case, which may seem to offer slender grounds for the formation of such a generalized model. However, schizophrenic thought disorders take such distinctive and characteristic forms that it seems likely that they have strong biological underpinnings. Not only is Luke's way of forming his thoughts very typical of schizophrenic thought disorders described in the literature, but he is free of numerous other psychological syndromes that could complicate the picture. Given these factors, we think that the deep patterns that we find within Luke's process may well be characteristic of many other clients experiencing such 'thought disorders.'

In our pilot research, we find that this sort of 'metaphact processing' occurs through a complex interaction between typically right hemisphere and typically left hemisphere modes of thinking.[3] This is particularly notable since this kind of collaboration between typically right hemispheric and typically left hemispheric modes of thinking has been found to be associated

---

2. We are using the word 'metaphor' in its broad sense throughout this paper, including those figures of speech that indicate some broad similarity rather than a clearly defined identity. More specific figures of speech such as similes and personification will be subsumed in the terms metaphor and metaphoric distance.

3. The actual brain organization of these phenomena is complex. For simplicity's sake we will be using the terms 'left hemisphere' and 'right hemisphere' in reference to monosemantic and polysemantic cognitive functions in which the dominant (usually left brain) and non-dominant (usually right brain) typically dominate respectively.

with highly productive therapeutic processing in more normatively functioning clients (Iberg, 1990; Hendricks, 2001).

We argue that collaboration between typically right and left hemisphere processes is essential to a person's ability to form a coherent sense of his or her own emotions, intentions, and strategies, as well as those of others, phenomena that are sometimes called a 'theory of mind' (Baron-Cohen, 1997). Brune (2005) summarizes recent research which supports the proposition that, in general, schizophrenic clients have particular difficulties in forming a 'theory of mind.' This difficulty in articulating a sense of their own and others' feelings, wants, intentions and the like is thought to connect with other difficulties typically associated with schizophrenia such as extremes of social withdrawal.

The theory of metaphact processing that we are presenting has been developed through textual analysis of numerous sessions audio taped over more than ten years of Luke's psychotherapy. In this chapter we will offer an in-depth qualitative and quantitative analysis of Luke's process in one relatively typical session in the year 2000. We will use this session to explore the ways that Luke's 'thought disordered' process relates to characteristically right and left hemispheric modes processing, to his development of 'theory of mind,' and to his ability to initiate positive social relationships.

CONCEPTUALIZATIONS OF THOUGHT DISORDER

After more than a century of research, theorists remain uncertain as to whether schizophrenia is a single syndrome or, more likely, a cluster of related syndromes affecting brain and behavior. Harrow and Quinlan (1985) find that 'bizarre-idiosyncratic' thinking is commonly, though not universally, found in acutely schizophrenic patients. It tends to lessen in prevalence and severity as patients improve, but manifestations again increase in chronic phases of schizophrenia. While this 'bizarre-idiosyncratic' quality is hard to define precisely, Harrow and Quinlan (1985) find that quite ordinary people serving as coders are able to agree on its presence with high reliability. While most clearly marked in schizophrenia, varieties of bizarre-idiosyncratic thinking are also found in acute manic episodes and various states of dementia.

The term 'thought disorder' tends to be applied to a subset of 'bizarre-idiosyncratic' expressions in which clients make characteristic sorts of conceptual errors in formulating their thoughts. The exact nature of such conceptual confusion and its relation to various sorts of brain processing remains a subject of debate. Several factor analyses of schizophrenic patients isolate a 'disorganization' syndrome, with some sort of thought disorder being a major constituent of this factor (McKenna & Oh, 2005).

In some of the earliest work analyzing schizophrenic thinking, Bleuler (1911) notes that patients suffering from any of the schizophrenias tend to have associations that become 'weak and disconnected.' He suggests that, as a result, schizophrenic people are often unable to select which of many possible thoughts or word meanings would make sense in the light of the task they are pursuing. Vygotsky (1934, 1962) conducted cognitively oriented research showing that schizophrenic patients have a marked difficulty with tasks that require them to sort objects by category (such as all of the green objects), tending to see each green object as unique, or to be caught up in associations irrelevant to the definition at hand.

E. Von Domarus (1944) builds on this work, noting that schizophrenic clients very often make a very characteristic error in thinking. One of the best known classical forms of logic, the syllogism in the form of 'Barbara,' only works when one phenomenon is a clear instance of some larger class of phenomena (Bateson, 1988: 4). For example, one can sensibly say:

> Men die
> Socrates is a man
> Socrates will die

Gregory Bateson (1988: 6) notes that:

> The basic structure of this little monster—its skeleton—is built upon classification. The predicate ('will die') is attached to Socrates by identifying him as a member of a class whose members all share that predicate.
>
> The syllogisms of metaphor are quite different and go like this:
>
>> Grass dies
>> Men die
>> Men are grass

Bateson notes that:

> I understand that teachers of classical logic strongly disapprove of this way of arguing and call it 'affirming the consequent' ... Von Domarus long ago pointed out that schizophrenics commonly talk and act in terms of syllogisms [like the above] ... If I remember rightly, he does not notice that poetry, art, dream, humor and religion share with schizophrenia a preference for this [second sort of] syllogism. (Ibid)

The crucial point here is that syllogistic logics depend on clearly defined classes and qualities that are associated with those classes by definition. Metaphoric modes of thinking rely on sensing similarities that emerge when two phenomena are placed in some sort of comparative relation to each other. But, such metaphoric modes of thinking function in quite different ways from syllogistic logics, ways that can be highly effective within their own realm.

Straube and Oades (1992) note that a number of later research studies fail to confirm that schizophrenic patients have difficulty using classical syllogistic logics per se. This suggests that the basic structures that go into making logical deductions are not problematic for most schizophrenic clients. Rather, Straube and Oades note, schizophrenic people often seem to form the units that go into their logical deductions in non-normative ways. As a result, when they use syllogistic logics, they don't come to sensible conclusions. Several theorists propose that various sorts of distraction may bring schizophrenic clients to form faulty premises (Harrow & Prosen, 1978; Friths, 1970, cited in Straube & Oades, 1994).

McKenna and Oh (2005) suggest that a primary source of such faulty premises may lie in a conceptual over-inclusiveness characteristic of clients with thought disorders. Using the work of Maher (1983), they propose that 'spreading activation' brings clients to draw on too broad a net of associations when they try to use their semantic memories:

> ... in the sentence *Bees make honey*, associations to the word bee might include sting, wasp and hive, and those to honey might include sweet and comb. Were such associations routinely incorporated into speech, the sentences which resulted such as *Bees make sweet* would strike the listener as distinctively odd. (Maher, 1983, cited in McKenna & Oh, 2005)

This sort of over-inclusiveness, then, seems likely to generate the sort of 'paralogical' thinking originally cited by Von Domarus, in which there is a confusion between units that are clearly defined instances of a larger class and those that share certain similar qualities.

In our example from Luke, he doesn't seem to sense the difference between his father's *being* a Spaniard and his father's *having some qualities* that he associates with Spaniards. It is worth noting here that Luke's phrases relating to Spaniards and to people who come from foreign countries seem to do more than simply offer a metaphoric expression for Luke's overall experiences of not feeling understood. They also point to more complex aspects of his relationships with his father and with his therapist that he has not yet put into words.

BRAIN HEMISPHERE RESEARCH AND THOUGHT DISORDER

Numerous research results point to some sort of disruption in right and left hemispheric functioning in schizophrenia (Straube & Oades, 1992; Rotenberg, 1994). Such hemispheric laterality is not absolute. Rather, these tend to be functions in which the dominant (usually the right) hemisphere or non-dominant (usually the left) hemisphere is more fully represented. Rotenberg (1994) notes that a characteristically left hemisphere form of processing creates a 'monosemantic context':

> 'Left hemisphere' or formal logical thinking so organizes any sign material (whether symbolic or iconic) as to create a strictly ordered and unambiguously understood context ... Such a strategy of thinking makes it possible to build a pragmatically convenient but simplified model of reality. (p. 489)

On the other hand, a characteristically right hemisphere form of processing creates a 'polysemantic context':

> ... the function of right-hemispheric or image thinking is a simultaneous 'capture' of an infinite number of connections and the formation due to this capture of an integral but ambiguous context ... Individual facets of images interact with each other on many semantic planes simultaneously ... The advantages of this strategy of thinking manifest themselves only when the information itself is complex, internally contradictory and basically irreducible to an unambiguous context. (Ibid: 489)

Straube and Oades (1992) note the difficulties in discerning the actual source of difficulties with functions associated with right or left hemispheres, since such difficulties could result from:

> 1. Over- or underfunctioning of one hemisphere
> 2. A compensatory process in response to a contralateral dysfunction
> 3. Impaired information transfer between hemispheres (p. 610)

Rotenberg (1994) notes that functional hyperactivation of the left hemisphere has been found in many investigations of schizophrenia (Gur, Resnick, & Alavi, 1978; Liddle, Friston, Frith, Hirsh, Jones, & Frakowiack, 1992, both cited in Rotenberg, 1994). He suggests that thought disorder can be understood as resulting from right hemisphere dysfunction, in which the right hemisphere is unable to select relevant information. As a result the left hemisphere is overwhelmed with irrelevant and inappropriate information: '... positive symptoms may represent an intensive but irregular and misdirected search activity, which tries to compensate for the right hemisphere insufficiency' (p. 492).

Seidman et al (1999, cited in Cozolino, 2002: 120) note that schizophrenic patients and their close relatives tend to have reduced volume in a number of left hemisphere brain areas, including the hippocampus and the amygdala. Shenton et al (1999, cited in Colozino, 2002: 120) find a significant correlation between increases in thought disorder and decreases in left hemisphere neuronal volume. Cozolino (2002) suggests that aberrant perceptual experiences such as hearing voices talking may be seen as right hemisphere language (related to primary process thinking and/or implicit memories) breaking into left hemisphere awareness. This would suggest an underfunctioning in the left hemisphere.

Straube and Oades (1992), on the other hand, suggest that the primary difficulty may be in impaired coordination within or between the hemispheres. They note that since for the majority of schizophrenic patients, sensory input and knowledge of general rules seem to be intact,

> ... the primary failure may be in the matching process ... we propose here that the prominent clinical and experimental features are not caused by a breakdown of function at a single location but arise through impaired coordination of the frontal and temporal-limbic axes. (p. 612)

In a similar vein, Goldberg (2001) notes that studies using functional neuroimaging have found a pattern of 'hypofrontality,' lower blood flow than would be expected to the frontal lobes among schizophrenic patients. The frontal lobes have a major role in coordinating activities among brain functions and this activity is particularly pronounced in relation to novel tasks. Notably, such novel tasks tend to elicit stronger right than left hemisphere engagement. One would expect, then, that therapy situations, in which clients are trying to sort out situations that are not yet clear, would be particularly likely to elicit this sort of frontally mediated right hemisphere involvement.

METAPHACTS AND METACAUSES AS CONCEPTUAL HYBRIDS

Analysis of Luke's therapy sessions offers an opportunity to consider these issues in the light of his ongoing processing of real-life issues. We have observed that, when Luke is already clear about a subject, he often seems quite capable of using facts and metaphors in a normative way. But, when he tries to process material that is emotionally important, but not yet clear, he uses hybrids of two forms of thinking that would ordinarily be clearly separated—metaphoric ways of speaking and more clearly defined facts or causes. This would suggest that Luke's fundamental difficulty doesn't come from the lack of an ability to use logic or to use metaphors, so much as a difficulty that occurs when he tries to use these two modes—the sort of holistic thinking typical of the right hemisphere and the more linear, sequential, language-based units typical of the left hemisphere—in close collaboration with each other.

We have named these hybrid forms 'metaphacts' and 'metacauses' with the operation of the two together being termed 'metaphact processing.' When Luke is using metaphacts, he typically *sounds* as if he were speaking about clearly defined units (or facts) and clearly defined causal relations. For example, he states that his father *is* a Spaniard and that he is having trouble understanding his father *because* his father comes from another country. He seems to be trying very hard to make some kind of cause-effect sense out of the phenomena at hand.

Yet, notably, Luke's whole train of thought—that seems so unreasonable when seen as a rendition of facts and causes—would make sense if it were reformulated in terms of the kinds of broad similarities characteristic of metaphors or similes rather than more clearly defined identities. To make sense linguistically, one would have to add the cues that indicate that one is speaking of such metaphoric similarities—creating a kind of 'metaphoric distance.' Thus, a person might quite sensibly say:

> *The trouble in the world is that too many people behave* as if they were *Spaniards. I feel as if my father is like that. He* seems as if *he comes from another country. He* might as well *be speaking Spanish; I only understand about a third of what he says. Somehow, you and I seem like we come from the same country. You seem to understand me perfectly well.*

We also find that, while Luke *sounds* as if he were speaking in a logical, cause-effect way, the actual progression of his thoughts follows the broad metaphoric similarities involved in the phenomena he is talking about more than the exact facts and causes. He doesn't consider factual possibilities that might go with his father being a Spaniard—such as thinking about more exact qualities of Spanish culture or considering whether communication would be improved if Luke were to learn Spanish.

Rather, he follows up on his *broad sense* of speaking or not speaking the same language and calls to mind other experiences that do or do not share that same broad sense. In this segment, he moves from sensing into the way that it seems as if he and his father don't speak the same language to sensing the way that interactions within his therapy sessions feel different from those with his father. We suggest that it is exactly this potential for metaphoric processing—for bringing up material that has broadly similar qualities or feeling tone—that gives 'metaphacts' and 'metacauses' such importance.

The same sort of conflation of factual and metaphoric functions applies to Luke's other 'positive' schizophrenic symptoms, such as hearing voices and seeing hallucinations. When expressed as literal facts, they don't seem realistically sensible. For, example, Luke once noted that a dinner guest had devils on his shoulders, which seems unlikely as a realistic description of the situation. Yet these hallucinatory images seem to capture Luke's overall sense of this dinner guest in a metaphoric way. This person seemed to Luke as if he were under the influence of some devils. After hearing Luke's description of this person, I (Warner) felt that I might well have felt the same way about him if I were in Luke's situation.

Often metaphacts seem to come freshly, as in the example given at the beginning of this chapter. Luke had never seemed to think of his father as a 'Spaniard' before, and he didn't hold onto that image for more than a few weeks. Nevertheless the image was remarkably rich in its ability to capture the broad view that Luke seemed to have of his father at that time, as a dominant, haughty, somewhat autocratic personality who was hard to understand, much like a stereotypical Spanish conquistador. Using that image as a 'handle' for his sense of his father then allowed him to operate with it in various ways.

At other times, Luke develops stable metaphacts that capture his broad feel for issues with images that remain relevant to him over a number of years. Often, some concrete detail of a crucial life situation comes to serve as an image for the whole of that situation and of similar situations that come up later.[4] For example, during the actual psychotic break, paramedics twisted Luke's knee while trying to get him into the ambulance. Luke very commonly uses the term 'knee-twister' to refer to a whole broad cluster of situations in which people are ill or not right with themselves.

---

4. Jim Collins (2003) refers to Luke's use of situational details to create metaphact images of larger wholes as 'metasynechdoche.'

METAPHACT PROCESSING AND GENDLIN'S PHILOSOPHY OF THE IMPLICIT

The role of metaphor in this sort of metaphact processing can be understood more clearly when considered in the light of more ordinary psychological processing. Gendlin (1964, 1968) emphasizes that making sense is a whole-body process.

When clients feel safe they are very likely to spontaneously attend to aspects of their experience that are immediately felt, but unclear,[5] Gendlin (1964, 1968) notes that the sorts of words and images that come to clients in response to this sort of vague sensing are often very vivid and idiosyncratic. Scenes, images, metaphors, idiosyncratic words and the like provide a 'handle' that allows the person to hold onto those immediately felt experiences long enough to let more come—more feelings, images, memories, thoughts and the like. These handle words or images are particularly likely to come in a metaphoric form.

For example, a woman client might say:

> *My new job is everything I've always wanted. Still, something doesn't feel right, somehow. I can feel a tightness in my stomach as I say that ... (pause). I have the image of sinking into quicksand, as if I will get swallowed up and disappear from sight. Like maybe I will get so involved in this that I won't have any room at all for my friends, for my family ...*

Gendlin (1964, 1968, 1995) is very clear that metaphors like 'sinking into quicksand' in the above example don't operate by an exact matching. The whole organism responds when a word or image 'works' as a handle for a particular experience. And, the body holds a richness of implicit meaning that might be 'carried forward' in more than one way.

A number of studies have found that the sort of processing that Gendlin describes—in which clients attend to a 'felt sense' of the whole of their immediate experience—is associated with various measures of overall productivity in therapy (Hendricks, 2001).[6] In these sorts of moments of active and productive processing, clients seem to engage in a complex collaboration between the two quite different modes—feeling into a sense of the whole, (which would be typical of the right hemisphere and would often be experienced metaphorically), and finding an articulated voice that

---

5. Practitioners of focusing-oriented psychotherapy may also take more active steps to encourage or foster such attention to immediately felt experience, as described in Gendlin (1996).
6. This is not, of course, to say that this form of processing is the *only* way that therapy can be productive.

carries forward the felt sense of the whole (that would be typical of the left hemisphere and would tend to be formed in more clearly defined units and causal logics).

Yet, ordinarily clients *know* when they are speaking metaphorically. For example, if the woman described above feels *as if* she is sinking into quicksand, she has the metaphoric distance that lets her know that she is not *really* sinking into quicksand. On the other hand, when material is articulated in a way that has clear units and clear relations (as when she says she is afraid that she will get so caught up in the new job that she won't have time for friends or family), she *knows* that she is *not* speaking metaphorically.

We would suggest that some form of processing that incorporates typically right and left brain modes of thinking is needed to form a 'theory of mind'— a sense of one's own and of others' feelings, intentions, beliefs, plans and the like. It is not as if these phenomena already exist someplace in a person's body and simply need to be labeled. Rather, the body contains the totality of the person's lived experience in an implicit form. But, this vast complexity only comes into a full and personally integrated voice through a complex and ongoing collaboration between dominant and non-dominant modes of cognitive process.

We hypothesize, then, that Luke is trying to process in much the way that more high-functioning clients might. But, at certain moments of active processing, which require a collaboration of right and left hemisphere modes, the two modes collapse into the single hybrid mode that we call metaphact processing.

EXPLORATORY DATA ANALYSIS FOCUSING ON A SINGLE LUKE SESSION

OVERVIEW OF LUKE'S THERAPEUTIC HISTORY

Luke is a Caucasian man in his mid forties, who grew up in a prosperous Midwestern, Irish-American family. He suffered a psychotic break in his third year of attending a competitive California university. After a period of intensive therapy and family support, he attempted a return to the university. However, he suffered another psychotic break almost immediately. Luke then lived in a series of supported residential settings and hospitals for the next 15 years. In the early 1990s, his medication was changed to Clozaril® and he came to the Midwest to live in a supported residential setting closer to his home, which enabled him to live closer to his father.

At the time that I (Warner) began seeing Luke, he was cooperative and able to come to therapy on his own. He appeared quite schizophrenic in his mode of dress and reported relatively frequent incidents of feeling overwhelmed and frightened by psychotic symptoms (for example, on his way to therapy, he would see the bus engulfed in flames and need to get off and wait for another bus) and by negative reactions from others in public. In the early years, therapy sessions tended to focus almost completely on reactive issues, such as Luke's responses to others' expectations of him, rather than more proactive issues relating to how Luke himself would like his life to be. Luke's communication has always seemed prototypic of schizophrenic 'thought disorder' particularly when he is processing material that is emotionally significant but not yet clear to him. He hears voices and has both longstanding and more ephemeral hallucinations. He has never shown signs of systematic or longstanding paranoid delusions, mood disorders, substance abuse, or more severe 'borderline' sorts of emotional dysregulation.

Over the years, Luke has stopped dressing in ways that seem odd. He now typically wears a conservative suit and tie. The voices and hallucinations which he experiences can be moderately disturbing to him, but they have stopped being overwhelming or alarming. Now, they tend to be experienced as useful or comforting, as when he hears the voices of family members who are deceased. While he sees himself as having had a difficult life, he now fundamentally views himself as a happy and contented person, and often puzzles over the persistent unhappiness of other people that he knows. His round of activities is very limited in comparison to that of most higher-functioning people, but he takes great pleasure in the activities of his week. He seems to have worked through the trauma of the original psychotic breaks and has an ongoing sense of confidence that such things are unlikely to happen to him again. In the last six years, Luke has become strikingly more pro-social, spending increasing amounts of therapy time in thinking about which sorts of personal contacts, social activities and trips he would like for himself.

SELECTION OF A LUKE SESSION FOR EXPLORATORY ANALYSIS

We have chosen a fairly average Luke session, a session from the spring of 2000 for exploratory qualitative and quantitative analysis. We chose this particular session since it shows metaphact processing as Luke uses it to process more ordinary, day-to-day confusions and frustrations (rather than choosing a session involving a more dramatic life crisis). This Luke session is compared to a session with a more normatively functioning client previously analyzed by Jim Iberg (1990).

In Luke's session, he talks about having gone to the airport to take a trip to the East coast to see relatives, but the flight was cancelled due to severe rain. Luke waited the whole day as successive postings put the time of the flight back further and further until, ultimately, the flight was cancelled altogether. Luke's brother suggested that he could reschedule the flight, but by this time Luke had had enough and declined the offer. Luke behaved in perfectly normative ways throughout this mini-ordeal, but afterwards he begins to wonder if he has somehow done something wrong.

The session being analyzed here comes about midway in the therapy process described in the previous section. At the time of this session, Luke still feels quite overwhelmed by his fears of having another psychotic break, but he is just beginning to claim his own positive desires for social outlets and to take personal initiatives to get these to happen.

CODING OF THE CLIENT SESSION

For the quantitative part of this analysis, Judith Trytten (2002) divides Luke's session into 52 client/therapist 'utterances' which she codes using measures of the client's relation to an immediate felt sense, a coding system developed by Jim Iberg (1990). Iberg's coding system is deeply grounded in Gendlin's (1964, 1968) theories of experiencing.

The first of Iberg's (1990) coding categories is 'pregnancy' or storytelling processing. This refers to segments in which the client, while perhaps personally engaged, speaks in a relatively matter-of-fact way. Iberg notes that, while clients often describe their experiences in ways that seem thematic and clearly defined, their stories are likely to be 'pregnant' with issues that are not yet clear to the client. The second, 'parturiency' is coded when the client seems to be attending directly to immediate, bodily felt experiencing often with higher levels of struggle as to what exact words or images fit. Iberg is using the image of childbirth here. When clients attend to aspects of their experience that are troubling or not yet clear they often pause more and seem to struggle to find words or images that fit with their immediately felt sense of the situation. The third code, 'nascency' applies to segments in which the client has reached some closure, often conveying a sense of relief or insight. When new meanings have been 'born' that are congruent with the client's whole-body sense of their lived experience, they are able to operate with these meanings more easily, often using them for problem-solving or relating them to other meanings in their lives. Trytten (2002) uses a coding system that allows ten coders to rate each segment on more than one of these categories, so that each utterance is rated as having higher or lower levels of each of these three experiencing qualities.

Trytten (2002) also uses two cognitive measures developed by Iberg, which examine the use of typically right hemisphere and left hemisphere functions during processing. Noting suggestive patterns in the cognitive variables from Iberg's (1990) research, Trytten (2002) also developed a measure that we are calling 'right-left pairing.'[7] This is a measure in ratio form of the difference between the two variables measuring characteristically right hemisphere and left hemisphere styles of cognition. When this ratio is close to 1.0, dominant and non-dominant modes of cognition are being used relatively equally; when the ratio is close to 0.10, one mode of cognition is being used almost exclusively.

Margaret Warner developed a code for metaphact language in the summer of 2006 so that Trytten's (2002) measures could be related more clearly to Luke's metaphact processing. Since this is a new coding system and she is the only rater to date, findings using these codes are offered with some tentativeness. To code for metaphact language, Warner counts instances of three sorts of metaphact usage and creates a combined total for each utterance. (If the same usage is repeated more than once in the utterance, she only counts it once.) She counts instances in which Luke uses non-normative[8] words or phrases when he is clearly trying to describe or analyze his personal experience as 'metaphacts' (i.e. these are not simply word plays or strings of associations). When Luke describes his experience using non-normative language that he has used in stable ways over numerous sessions, she codes these as 'stable metaphacts.' When Luke makes causal attributions that would not be seen as reasonable by normative standards as he describes or analyzes his experience, she counts these as 'metacauses.'

SINGLE-SESSION COMPARISONS OF LUKE AND A MORE NORMATIVE CLIENT

Trytten (2002) completed an analysis comparing the selected Luke session with a session with a more normatively functioning client. This analysis shows broad similarities between the two clients in the ways that characteristically dominant (left hemisphere) and non-dominant (right hemisphere) cognitions function within the flow of the particular therapy sessions analyzed. Trytten (2002) and Iberg (1990) each divide the client sessions being analyzed into relatively equal segments, choosing the exact dividing lines of the segments by looking at a graph of the three phase variables and maximizing the meaningfulness of the segments relative to the three processing phase variables. This results in four segments in Luke's session, and three in the Iberg session, which was a shorter session. Both Luke's session and the Iberg session show increases in right-left pairing through the first session segments, followed by a decrease during the last segment of the session. (See Figure 1.)

---

7. In Trytten's (2002) research she called this measure 'crowding.' We call it 'right-left pairing' here to emphasize the crucial, though delicate collaboration that seems to occur between these two quite different modes of mental process when they work together within a single therapy utterance.

8. Our use of 'non-normative' here is equivalent to the category of 'bizarre or idiosyncratic usage' as described by Harrow and Quinlan (1985).

Figure 1: Graph of mean of right-left pairing in Luke session (Trytten) and Iberg session for each session segment

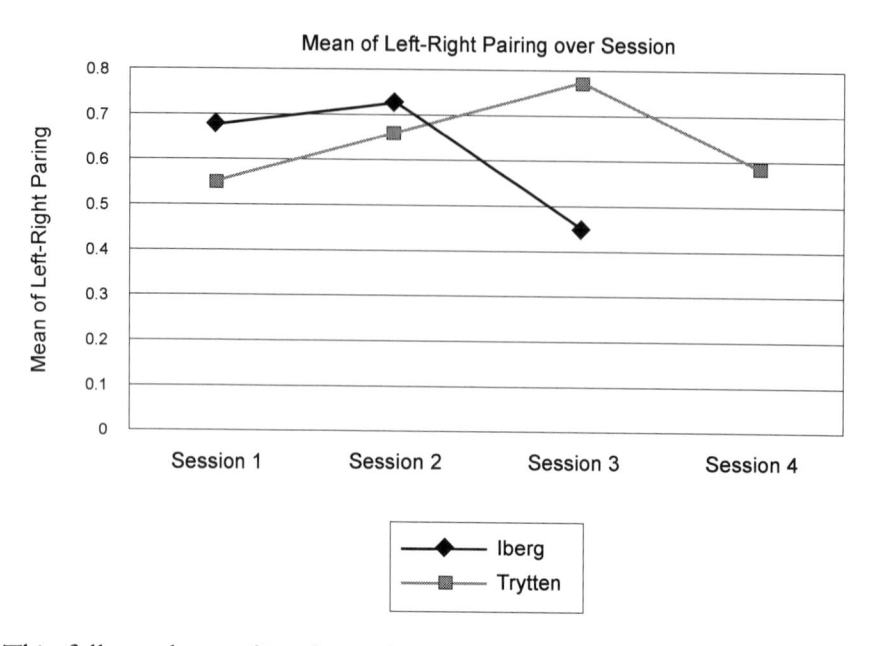

```
                    Mean of Left-Right Pairing over Session
```

This follows the predicted trend, suggesting that these clients are both exploring issues that are not yet clear to them with increasing close use of left-right pairing until they reach a level of clarity. Once this level of clarity is reached, both clients move, in their last session segment, toward using a lower level of left-right pairing. In addition, in this last therapy segment, both clients show an alternation from primarily non-dominant (right hemisphere) to primarily dominant (left hemisphere) cognition that seems, along with the decrease in pairing, to be suggestive of a turn-taking by utterance of the two kinds of cognition replacing the high level of pairing in the section before.

Notably, in Luke's session the increase in right-left pairing is statistically significant in the third section, the section in which the highest levels of 'parturience' (or searching for words with some felt immediacy) are measured. In addition, in the immediately following or last section the highest levels of nascency (or closure on issues) are found by the raters. Both clients show a strong positive correlation between pregnancy (i.e. a matter-of-fact, or storytelling style of process) and dominant, left hemisphere cognition, as well as a correlation between parturience (processing which involves immediate bodily sensing and searching for words) and non-dominant, right hemisphere cognition. A further similarity is that both clients show peaks of parturience at times during their sessions which seem to signal significant shifts in the overall patterns of processing within the sessions. Unlike the Iberg client, Luke shows an even stronger positive correlation between parturiency and dominant cognition than between parturiency and non-dominant cognition. Trytten (2002) notes that this finding fits with Rotenberg's (1994) suggestion that when schizophrenic clients are having difficulty processing, they may attempt to compensate by over-using left hemisphere modes of processing.

These findings suggest that Luke is processing in a way that is strikingly similar to that of a more normative client, but that he does this in a somewhat slower or more complicated way than does the more normative client that Iberg studied. To understand these complications better we will first look at the results of the metaphact analysis.

METAPHACT ANALYSIS

In our preliminary analysis using the new metaphact rating system, which codes levels of schizophrenic language in each utterance, we find a highly significant correlation of .43 between metaphacts and dominant thought (Pearson Correlation p test < .001). In addition, we find a significant correlation of .37 between metaphacts and parturiency (Pearson Correlation p test < .01). These correlations offer support to the hypothesis that Luke's use of metaphacts increases as his level of parturiency increases, i.e. as he searches for words that connect to his immediate felt sense of his situation. At the same time the correlations support the hypothesis that Luke tends to try to use the sorts of clear units and cause-effect logics that would be typical of the dominant (typically left) hemisphere when he is trying to put words to his experience in these moments.

The relationship between metaphact processing and right-left pairing is more complex. When whole segments of the therapy session are considered, the mean for metaphacts exactly follows the pattern of the mean for right-left pairing, with the lowest mean in section one, a higher mean in section two, the highest mean in section three, and a somewhat lower mean in the fourth section. Yet, right-left pairing does not show a correlation with metaphacts utterance by utterance. Rather, the levels of right-left pairing are quite varied in these high metaphact utterances. Sometimes, Luke seems to use metacauses in an attempt to create a clear cause-effect rationale for what is happening (albeit with flawed ideas about plausible sorts of causation). In these utterances a dominant or left brain style of processing predominates. Sometimes Luke seems to use metaphacts in a more descriptive way, putting words to his sense of the situation being considered (albeit with a confusion of metaphors and facts). In these utterances a non-dominant, right hemisphere style of processing predominates. And, sometimes, he does both at once, with high levels of right-left pairing being coded in those utterances.

Overall, high levels of right-left pairing seem to occur immediately before and after Luke's highest metaphact utterances. Descriptively, relatively equal levels of dominant and non-dominant thought occur as Luke begins to describe situations that are bothering him. His use of schizophrenic language is low to moderate at this point. Yet, as he gets to the core of issues that he can't make sense of in the situation at hand, he uses much higher levels of schizophrenic language, with very varied levels of right-left pairing as noted above. This seems to bring to his mind a range of scenes that are thematically related to the issues that are of concern to him, which help him differentiate his sense of the issues. These 'differentiating scenes' are high in right-left pairing and lower in metaphact language. At certain points, Luke pulls together a sense of the crux of the issues that he has been considering. These 'crux statements' tend to be high on right-left pairing and low in metaphact language. To understand these patterns better, let us look more closely at the session itself.

ANALYSIS OF THE TEXT OF LUKE'S SESSION

THE FORMATION OF THE PROBLEM

In the beginning of the session, Luke describes the circumstances leading up to the flight cancellation in completely normative language (Utterances 1–3). Luke seems engaged, but matter of fact and not particularly vulnerable. These utterances are low in metaphact language, in parturience, and all have non-dominant thought as the primary rated thought. In Utterance 3, Luke comments on the results of the long day's waiting in uncertainty about when the flight was going to happen.

C1: *Uh huh. I would have liked to have gone doctor ... you know*

T1: *Mm hmm ...*

C2: *... I would have thought I was ... kept thinking in my mind's eye that in this day and age they can get us out to Logan. They have a big tower there ... all the planes land. They have all of them in the winter and then this rainstorm.*

T2: *Mm hmm ...*

C3: *But they said no, no we just can't do it.*

T3: *Yeah.*

C4: *... and then we all got our luggage out ...*

T4: *Mm hmm ...*

C5: *... out in the foyer there with the luggage that they had collected ...*

T5: *Sure ...*

C6: *... and then sent everyone home.*

T6: Yeah. You would have thought in this day and age with Logan Airport and everything that in your mind's eye you would have thought they could do it.

C7: Yeah.

T7: They were pretty firm about it.

C8: Yeah.

T8: They couldn't do it.

But, at this point, Luke touches on concerns about why all of this occurred and he moves quite strongly into metaphact language by Utterance 4. He is using 'metacauses' here, trying hard to logically analyze the situation without having sensible units of analysis. The segment is high both in metaphact language score and on the right-left pairing score, while it is medium in its rating of parturience. ('The judge' is a voice that Luke commonly hears.)

C1: Mmmm. It's one of those things I guess. Uh ... Course in some ways it was a discounted fare.

T1: Mm hmm.

C2: ... and God may have gotten in the way of all of it too. The Judge seemed to be saying well there're reasons why you're not going that you don't understand kind of ...

Still, this metacause language quickly leads Luke to the crux of his concern—that this trip's having gone awry will somehow mean that he won't be able to take trips in the future (Utterances 5–6). He states this in clear, quite normative language, showing moderately high levels of experiential immediacy and vulnerability (parturience) without metaphact language.

C1: Yeah. Course ... I'm pretty much keyed in on the June 16th trip to ... uh ... the Abbey with Edward that Friday ...

T1: Mm hmm ...

C2: Ummm

T2: So that's coming up pretty soon, isn't it?

C1: Yeah ... and ... uh ... Hopefully Maria won't take the canceled trip to mean that I'm never going on vacation again ...

T1: Yeah, we wouldn't want that would we?

C2: It bothered me a little bit in the subconscious today about that.

Luke tries again to reassure himself that he did OK at the airport (Utterance 7). His assessment of the situation seems completely sensible and rational, but this does not seem to reassure him. He is confused as to why the flight had to be cancelled.

BROAD FEARS ABOUT MENTAL STABILITY

Once Luke has touched on this confusion about why the flight was cancelled, he moves quickly into fears that the airport incident might be the beginning of some much broader breakdown of his life's stability. These fears are expressed with very high levels of metaphact language (Utterances 8–9), with particularly strong use of 'stable metaphacts,' and with very high parturience. Utterance 8 gives a good sense of this process, so we will analyze it in some detail:

> C1: *Right. But ... uh ... this thing about the knee twister and that uh ... the knee not exactly turned or whatever you know ...*
>
> T1: *Mm hmm ...*
>
> C2: *... is getting a little out of hand.*
>
> T2: *Yes.*
>
> C3: *I have kind of a map you know of the world in the living room there where I live and come into the living room, look at the map a little bit and then it just seems as though the whole idea of running away from home has really kind of caught on ...*
>
> T3: *Mmmm ...*
>
> C4: *... around the world almost in some ways. The whole map kind of coming out at me if you will.*

The 'knee-twister' is a stable metaphact that Luke uses to refer to his experience of being taken away in an ambulance at the time of his first psychotic break, as well as broader experiences of emotional disturbance. 'Running away from home' is a stable metaphact that refers to any abandonment of the conservative moral and religious values of his family, values that he feels help protect from chaotic life experiences. The map on the wall coming out at Luke seems to be a metaphact that refers to Luke's fears that the overall sort of breakdown represented by the 'knee-twister' and 'running away from home' may be spreading to the world at large. Utterances that reflect this sort of very broad fear of breakdown, expressed with very high levels of metaphact language, recur throughout the middle half of the session (Utterances 15, 17 and 19, 20, 25 , 26, 37, and 39). The language of stable metaphacts seems to allow Luke to revisit the trauma of his original psychotic breaks in California and to name his fear that anytime something goes wrong in his current life, it may be the beginning of the same thing happening again.

These segments are particularly interesting in the light of Trytten's (2002) finding that Luke shows even stronger correlation between dominant cognition and parturiency than with non-dominant cognition. Even though Luke seems to be feeling extreme vulnerability and he is describing some of his deepest fears in these segments, he still tries to categorize the experiences in terms of unit logics. Yet, 'the stable metaphacts' that he uses as 'units' to make sense of the experiences are images and phrases that seem to have emerged originally as metaphoric 'handles' for particular scenes. As he uses these same metaphacts to apply to a range of scenes over time, they come to function as idiosyncratic, conceptual categories with considerable depth and richness of meaning.

CLUSTERS OF DIFFERENTIATING SCENES

Luke's expression of broad fears about his own mental stability and that of the world seems to stimulate his consideration of how these fears do or do not apply to a number of more current life concerns. His broad question seems to be this: Given that he was very attracted to the excitement and pleasure of California and has trouble understanding how his life at that time led to a psychotic breakdown, what sorts of life pleasures are OK now, and what kinds of activities are likely to lead to trouble? The first such cluster relates to a visit that Joni Mitchell, a folk singer who Luke associates with the California scene at the time of his break, was making to Chicago. While he likes her music, he's not sure whether the fact that it comes from California means that it might not be safe.

> *C1: You know she's in town at the Rosemont Horizon coming up to ...*
>
> *T1: Oh ...*
>
> *C2: ... I'm not sure I think it's coming up a little bit later I'm not sure ...*
>
> *T2: Mm hmm ...*
>
> *C3: ... to have a concert and uh ... It's this whole idea of the white cobra that she brings in ... [Utterance 12]*

The 'white cobra' is a stable metaphact/hallucination that Luke experiences as relating to attractive, but dangerous California temptations, which returns him to broad mental health fears. In Utterance 15 Luke notes that

> *C1: Yeah. Umm. But ... uh ... this white cobra thing involves the running away from home I'm pretty sure something like that.*
>
> *T1: Mm hmm ...*
>
> *C2: You get that in the ambulance whatever ...*
>
> *T2: Mm hmm ...*
>
> *C3: ... and then it's ... in some ways ... uh ... hard if not impossible to shake off.*
>
> *T3: Mm hmm ...*
>
> *C4: But ...*

T4: Yeah, so you do get at that sense pretty strongly that the white cobra thing has to do with running away from home.

C5: Yeah.

T5: That you get it in the ambulance and that's pretty hard to shake off.

C6: Yeah.

T6: Mm hmm ...

Here, Luke seems to be pondering what a slippery slope California-type temptations can turn out to be, leading you to abandon your core values and perhaps even ending up having psychotic breaks. Again, he makes strong use of stable metaphacts in describing such core fears, and this segment is very high on metaphact language and parturience, with non-dominant thought being the primary cognition. Still, in Utterance 29 Luke ends up deciding that some music is very helpful to his overall sense of well-being.

C1: Yeah. [Silence ...] But I've been listening to a Vietnamese tape ... you know ... the Miss Saigon tape quite a bit.

T1: Mm hmm ...

C2: It seems to help with the legs a little bit ...

T2: Does it? Mm hmm ...

C3: Getting back inside of oneself and the ...

T3: Mm hmm ...

The second cluster of scenes relates to the question of whether it is reasonable to trust in situations in which people seem friendly. This concern seems to have been precipitated by the fact that a very attractive girl had smiled at him on the train that week. In Utterance 27 he notes that he had often been fooled by such interactions when he was in college.

C1: But ... um [Silence ...] But in some ways out in Palo Alto there you can be fooled a little bit about ... by the fellow students like you'll think some girl's giving you the come on and then she'll ... it's just the opposite or

T1: Mm hmm ...

C2: ... it's easy to get tripped with uh ...

T2: Mm hmm ...

C3: ... the sense of the radicalism out there I guess. But uh ...

And, in Utterance 28, he remembers his interaction with the police officer who ended up hospitalizing him during his psychotic break,

C1: Yeah. We talked a lot about that officer, first a smile and then ...

T1: Mm hmm ...

C2: ... just the opposite uh ... But ... uh ...

T2: Yeah.

C3: Hard to know ...

T3: Talked about him somewhat that at first it was a smile and then turned out to be so much the opposite ...

What is striking here is the fact that Luke's pondering his fears of total breakdown in highly idiosyncratic schizophrenic language seems to stimulate a positive processing step. Each of the two series of scenes, by bringing up related situations in which he has had somewhat the same feelings, allows him to differentiate his wishes and fears relating to these more concrete current-life situations.

And, it is notable that after this intensive pondering of a variety of wishes and fears, Luke comes up with a remarkably clear statement in Utterance 30 about his exact feelings and desires in response to the original airport situation:

C1: But this idea of paranoia, it's more like a claustrophobia ... sometimes comes up like ... explaining to Thomas that I wasn't going on the American Airline flight the next day and ...

T1: Mm hmm ...

C2: ... and feeling kind of trapped ... not ...

T2: Mmmm ...

C3: ... a hundred percent but ...

T3: Mm hmm ...

C4: ... uh ... as you know I haven't had much of a vacation in a while ...

T4: Yeah.

C5: But um ...

T5: Yeah, so there was some ...

C6: course ...

T6: ... trapped feeling there.

C7: Yeah.

T7: In talking to Thomas about the American flight and stuff like that ...

C8: Yeah.

T8: But you really haven't been on a vacation for a while.

C9: No. Pretty much where I am in the scheme of things.

Luke moves from here to another long cluster of scenes relating to the question of whether he might be in trouble at his residence for canceling his trip, and whether things are emotionally safe there overall. In Utterance 40 he notes that he is not always sure why people get thrown out.

> C1: No. [Silence ...] But they claim all the people who leave Harper Place are going on to something else but I think in some ways on the sly that they kind of being given the boot out the door there ...
>
> T1: Mmm ...
>
> C2: Some of them ...
>
> T2: Mmmm ...
>
> C3: But ... uh ...
>
> T3: So that they claim that people who leave are going on to something else?
>
> C4: Yeah.
>
> T4: But then you think well maybe on the sly that they're giving you the boot out the door ...

And, in Utterance 45 he notes that one other resident planned a trip and had it cancelled for reasons that are unclear to Luke:

> C1: But see Ruth was supposed to go spend the night with her boyfriend in a hotel or something ...
>
> T1: Mm hmmm ...
>
> C2: ... and she made all the plans ...
>
> T2: Mm hmm ...
>
> C3: ... and then at the end of it somehow or other it got cancelled ...

Again, it is notable that the series of scenes that come to Luke's mind all relate to ways that he has had bad or mistrustful feelings at his residence in ways that might bring him to think that he could get in trouble for not rescheduling the current trip. He doesn't seem to come to these scenes by any usual process of abstraction. Rather, they come to his mind spontaneously in response to scenes in which his more drastic fears have been framed in stable metaphact language.

After pondering the situation at his residence at some length (Utterances 38–43) Luke then comes up with a modest proactive plan to deal with his concerns. He decides to ask his cousin to call the residence to be sure that their upcoming trip doesn't get cancelled. (He seems to take for granted that the staff will listen to his cousin when they would not listen to him.) He worries briefly that he might be like his aunt who spent most of her life in hospitals. But in the end he decides that everything is probably OK.

C1: *Yeah. That's pretty much seems to be the latest from Midway. The voice there on that ... uh ... But ... uh ... yeah I'm ... I'm, as Dad pointed out ... uh ... points out I'm just trying to be myself kind of thing and then ...*

T1: *Mm hmm ...*

C2: *... hopefully everything will go well.*

T2: *Mm hmm ...*

C3: *I don't know ... how to explain it exactly ...*

T3: *Yeah. As your dad put it you really are just trying to be yourself ... [Utterance 48]*

It is particularly interesting here that Luke seems to have resolved his original dread arising from the cancelled flight. He seems to have done this by developing a conceptualization of his worst general fears using stable metaphacts, and by pondering several series of thematically related scenes associated with ways that those wishes and fears play out in his current and past life. Yet, he never did figure out in a more rational-analytic way why the flight might have been cancelled. And his resolution of the sense of dread doesn't seem to involve becoming any clearer in his understanding of those sorts of factual-analytical issues. It is notable that this is the utterance which was rated as showing the most nascency (the coding category that suggests closure, relief) in the session by the raters.

Luke then moves to an extended description of his attempts to set up dinner dates now that he is home for the week. In spite of his disappointment about the cancelled trip he has responded by making a series of very positive, pro-life pleasure and pro-social initiatives (Utterances 44–52).

T1: *Mm hmm ...*

C2: *I was calling all my friends over the weekend cause I wanted to go out for dinner ...*

T2: *Mm hmm ...*

C3: *... and none were available kind of thing.*

T3: *Ohhh ...*

C4: *I even called Heather Shoreland ... um ... Mary's sister ...*

T4: *Mm hmm ...*

C5: *... related to the Mill's not actually through blood but ...*

T5: *Mm hmm ...*

C6: *... she's a sister of Mary Shoreland who's going to marry Pat Mill. But ... um ...*

T6: *Mm hmm ...*

C7: *... she said she had a roommate with her, a girl roommate from college and so she ...*

T7: Mmmm ...

C8: ... couldn't come around ...

T8: Mmmm ...

C9: ... and then I tried to buckle down Edward and then he was going over to the Chicago Yacht Club ...

T9: Uh huh ...

C10: ... and then there's maybe this disease kind of out there. It's not really within me that's saying like ... uh ... well we can't ... we're going to do something else other than seeing Luke ...

T10: Mmmm ...

C11: ... and it will all be OK ... it'll all work out and ... [Utterance 50]

In this sequence, Luke is very clear about what he wants and assertive about reaching out for it in normative, pro-social ways. He can't seem to get anything arranged at the last minute. He dips into a bit of metaphact language in expressing his disappointment (there's maybe this disease out there ... we're going to do something other than seeing Luke ...), but he seems relatively philosophical about things not working out. This sequence is particularly notable when it is compared to Luke's early years in therapy in which he virtually never made social initiatives on his own.

Despite the newness of this material, Luke doesn't seem to have given the kinds of verbal cues that would lead the raters to code highly through the section for 'nascency' (i.e. sense of closure, relief, new insight), even thought nascency is significantly higher overall in the section than it was during the rest of the session. Perhaps this is because he doesn't frame the shift in a cognitive, analytic way. Still, this last, sustained cluster of utterances (49–52) shows the pattern of right-left cognition that Iberg found in periods of nascency with his more normative client. Luke has shifted to utterances that are more clearly dominated by either right brain or left brain modes of cognition and alternate frequently from one mode to the other, which suggests an easy turn-taking as opposed to the more intense pairing in the same utterance that occurred in sections two and three. In addition, as at the beginning of the session, more utterances are primarily non-dominant, as contrasted to the third section in particular in which more utterances are primarily dominant. This suggests that Luke no longer feels so pressed to sort out an issue, but rather feels fairly content with what he has figured out here. It should also be noted that in this section the metaphact processing is greatly decreased in comparison to the second and third sections, in which he was processing more intensely.

LUKE'S METAPHACT PROCESSING AS IT RELATES TO THEORY OF MIND AND PRO-SOCIAL BEHAVIOR

It is notable that steps relating to 'theory of mind' and 'pro-social behavior' emerge out of metaphact processing rather than seeming to be impeded by it. Stable metaphacts seem particularly powerful in allowing Luke to get a sense of what his deepest fears are and to develop a personally meaningful account of what sorts of things he should be concerned about in his current life. Series of related scenes seem to allow Luke to develop a more refined version of what exactly these wishes and fears are. These seem deeply personal and congruent, despite the fact that he continues to have limitations in his ability to make sense of the facts of the situation. It is also striking that when Luke comes to understandings of the crux of his feelings about these situations, his understandings tend to be expressed in very normative and sensible language. The fact that Luke spontaneously moves to taking social initiatives, once he has processed his deepest fears and become clear about what he would like, is also particularly striking in this session and in Luke's therapy process as a whole.

LUKE'S METAPHACT PROCESSING AND PROUTY'S THEORY OF PSYCHOLOGICAL CONTACT

Building on Rogers' first 'necessary and sufficient condition for psychotherapy,' Garry Prouty (1994) observes that clients cannot participate in therapy effectively if they are out of psychological contact with 'self, world or other.' We suggest that Luke's style of processing, (and perhaps thought disorder in general), can be thought of as manifesting a very particular kind of difficulty with psychological contact which is amenable to a particular application of Pre-Therapy. Luke is very clearly oriented in relation to the basic facts of his life. He knows who he is and where he is. He comes to therapy independently and values the process. Given all of this, many more basic 'contact reflections'—such as facial, bodily, environmental or reiterative reflections—would seem superfluous. Yet, in a way that is typical of schizophrenic thought disorders, many of Luke's exact words are very unusual and don't make normative sense. He is 'out of contact' in the very particular sense that he does not fully distinguish facts and metaphors when actively processing.

In therapy sessions, I (Warner) found that I began staying very closely with Luke's exact words from the pragmatic sense that Luke found even mild paraphrasing of his words confusing. If, for example he said that he was 'mad' and I said he was 'angry,' he was likely to say something like 'I don't know Doctor. You know more about these things than I do.' I find that responses that are very close to Luke's own words don't seem odd to him. In fact, such very close reflecting seems crucial in allowing both of us to stay connected to the complexities of what Luke is saying. In Luke's case, I have the sense that this sort of Pre-Therapy 'word-for-word' responding lets him hold his words in attention in a way that lets them process further. In recent years, as he has become more confident of his own viewpoint and more willing to correct me if my empathic response is not exactly what he meant, I have felt freer after responding with his exact words, to also paraphrase the point of what he is saying or to ask questions about his process. (For example, I asked him if he actually sees the snakes that he talks about, and he seemed pleased to give me detailed explanations of what they look like and what meaning they carry for him.)

It is worth noting that, while Luke benefits greatly from contact reflections, in other ways he uses therapy much the way any normatively functioning client might. He comes to sessions, surveys issues that are on his mind in any given week, explores them with increasing emotional depth, and considers alternate solutions to problems. In this sense Luke's sessions don't seem to be a 'pre' therapy. Rather he might be considered to be a client who has severe contact difficulties relating to metaphact processing whose participation in 'real' psychotherapy is greatly enhanced by contact reflections.

REFERENCES

Baron-Cohen, S (1997) *Mindblindness: An essay on autism and theory of mind.* Cambridge, MA: MIT Press.

Bateson, G (1988) *Mind and Nature.* New York: Bantam Books (cited online at www.oikos.org/angelsmental.htm).

Bellack, AS, Mueser, KT, Gingerich, S & Agresta J (1997) *Social Skills Training for Schizophrenia: A step-by-step guide.* New York: Guilford Press.

Bleuler, E (1911) *Dementia Praecox or the Group of Schizophrenias.* (Translated into English in 1950 by Joseph Zinken, MD). New York: International Universities Press.

Brune, M (2005) 'Theory of mind' in schizophrenia: A review of the literature. *Schizophrenia Bulletin, 31* (1), 21–42.

Collins, J (2003) Narrative Theory and Schizophrenia: The construction of self via non-normative processing. Unpublished Clinical Research Project. Illinois School of Professional Psychology of Argosy University/Chicago.

Cozolino, L (2002) *The Neuroscience of Psychotherapy.* New York: WW Norton & Co.

Gendlin, ET (1964) A theory of personality change. In P Worchel & D Byrne (Eds) *Personality Change* (pp 100–48). New York: John Wiley.

Gendlin, ET (1968) The experiential response. In E Hammer (Ed) *The Use of Interpretation in Treatment* (pp 208–27). New York: Grune & Stratton.

Gendlin, ET (1995) Crossing and dipping: Some terms for approaching the interface between natural understanding and logical formulation. *Minds and Machines,* 5 (4), 547–60.

Gendlin, ET (1996) *Focusing-Oriented Psychotherapy.* New York: Guilford Press.

Goldberg, E (2001) *The Executive Brain.* Oxford: Oxford University Press.

Harrow, M & Prosen, M (1978) Intermingling and disordered logic as influences on schizophrenic 'thought disorders.' *Arch Gen Psychiatry, 35,* 1213–18.

Harrow, M & Quinlan, D (1985) *Disordered Thinking and Schizophrenic Psychopathology.* New York: Gardner Press.

Hendricks, MN (2001) Focusing-oriented/experiential psychotherapy. In DJ Cain & J Seeman (Eds) *Humanistic Psychotherapies: Handbook of research and practice* (pp 221–51). Washington, DC: American Psychological Association.

Iberg, J (1990) Ms. C's focusing and cognitive functions. In G Lietaer, J Rombauts & R Van Balen (Eds) *Client-Centered and Experiential Therapy in the Nineties* (pp. 173–204). Leuven: Leuven University Press.

Maher, BA (1983) A tentative theory of schizophrenic utterance. In B Maher & W Maher (Eds) *Progress in Experimental Personality Research Vol XI* (pp 1–52). San Diego, CA: Academic Press.

McKenna, P & Oh, T (2005) *Schizophrenic Speech: Making sense of bathroots and ponds that fall in doorways.* Cambridge: Cambridge University Press.

Pao, P-N (1979) *Schizophrenic Disorders: Theory and treatment from a psychodynamic point of view.* New York: International Universities Press.

Prouty, G (1994) *Theoretical Evolutions in Person-Centered/Experiential Psychotherapy: Applications to schizophrenic and retarded psychoses.* Westport, CT: Praeger.

Rotenberg, V (1994) An integrative psychophysiological approach to brain hemisphere functions in schizophrenia. *Neuroscience and Biobehavioral Review, 18* (4), 487–95.

Straube, E & Oades, R (1992) *Schizophrenia: Empirical research and findings.* San Diego, CA: Academic Press.

Trytten, J (2002) Schizophrenic client process: Phase and cognition patterns in a client-centered therapy session. Unpublished clinical research project, Illinois School of Professional Psychology of Argosy University, Chicago.

Von Domarus, E (1944) The specific laws of logic in schizophrenia. In JS Kasanin (Ed) *Language and Thought in Schizophrenia* (pp 104–44). Berkeley, CA: University of California.

Vygotsky, LS (1934) Thought in schizophrenia. *Arch Neurol & Psychiat, 31,* 1036.

Vygotsky, LS (1962) *Thought and Language.* Cambridge, MA: MIT Press. (Original work published 1934)

Warner, MS (1997) Does empathy cure? A theoretical consideration of empathy, processing and personal narrative.' In AC Bohart & LS Greenberg (Eds) *Empathy Reconsidered* (pp 125–40). Washington, DC: American Psychological Association.

Warner, MS (2006) Toward an integrated person-centered theory of wellness and psychopathology. *Person-Centered and Experiential Psychotherapies 5* (1), 4–20.

Editor's Commentary on Ton Coffeng

Morton Prince (1906), the American psychiatrist who pioneered the clinical concept of dissociation, observed similarities between psychosis and dissociation. Ton Coffeng describes similarities between the treatment of psychosis (Pre-Therapy pre-symbolic processing) and the therapy of dissociation.

Coffeng has successfully expanded the whole concept and application of Pre-Therapy to dissociation. First, as in the treatment of psychosis, he applies Pre-Therapy as a first stage in treatment. Two reasons for this are that dissociated clients often do not have access to their experiencing, and secondly, they often cannot articulate their experience and are pre-expressive. Coffeng explains that both access to experiencing and articulation of experience are goals of Pre-Therapy. Then he applies pre-symbolic processing, which was originally used for hallucinatory images, to flashback imagery. Coffeng also demonstrates the pre-experiential property of the contact reflections as they precede experiential focusing (Gendlin, 1996). Coffeng has successfully expanded the clinical range of Pre-Therapy/pre-symbolic methods as first steps in the treatment of dissociation, to be followed by more traditional experiential/client-centered work.

REFERENCES

Gendlin, E (1996) *Focusing-Oriented Psychotherapy: A manual of the experiential method.* New York: Guilford Press.

Prince, M (1906) *The Dissociation of a Personality.* New York: Longmans, Green & Co.

CHAPTER 8

The Therapy of Dissociation: Its phases and problems

TON COFFENG

Therapists working with dissociated and traumatized clients commit themselves to a long project. The therapy of these clients is long and intensive. Its beginning is difficult, when clients, being used to isolation, have to share their inner life. Therapists understand the client's problem with talking and are happy with what can be said. They accept crises, extra sessions or phone calls, since their clients have no other ways of coping. When trust and attachment develop, clients begin to communicate more, and the exchange becomes easier. On this basis, the trauma can be addressed properly. After some time clients begin to integrate their trauma, and dissociative symptoms and flashbacks decrease.

In this latter stage, however, incidents may occur that disturb the ongoing process. Clients function as they did in a previous stage. They dissociate again, having been integrated already. They don't express themselves as they did, or become mute. Some clients become demanding or reluctant to proceed. The therapy is stranded. Therapists are surprised, as they didn't expect problems at this stage. They are confused also, not being able to talk with the client as before. They try interventions from an earlier stage, but discover that these do not work. They become discouraged, seeing their client deteriorating. These incidents need a more directive approach, so that their background can be explored. When this problem is solved, the therapy can resume its course. The incidents have to be placed in a context, as part of the extended therapy of dissociation. Therefore we start with a description of the therapy. In this case, it is a client-centered/experiential therapy, with two experientially different phases. However, the sequence of the article is not intended to suggest that the late incidents are specific to the therapy model presented here. They seem to occur to other therapists also, independent of their approach or style.

Previously published as Coffeng, T (2005) The therapy of dissociaton: Its phases and problems. *Person-Centered and Experiential Psychotherapies* 4 (2), 90–105. By kind permission of The World Association for Person-Centered and Experiential Psychotherapy and Counseling.

THE PHASIC CHARACTER OF THERAPY

According to the official 'state of the art,' the therapy of dissociation has three phases: (1) stabilization and symptom reduction; (2) treatment of traumatic memories; and (3) reintegration and rehabilitation (van der Hart, van der Kolk & Boon, 1998). These phases are planned and have a protocol of what a therapist does in each phase. Roy (1991) introduced a different and client-centered approach, in which the client's process was followed rather than directed. Inspired by her, I developed a therapy that included various elements (Coffeng, 1996). These elements appeared to have their own time in the therapy. Watching the processes of clients during the course of therapy, I could distinguish two experientially different phases, each having its own pace and language (Coffeng, 2002a, 2002b).

FIRST PHASE

In the beginning of therapy, clients have frequent dissociative switches, which interrupt their memory and consciousness. They lose track of the day. Some clients have a Dissociative Identity Disorder (DID), a severe form of dissociation (Ross, 1997). They have different identities, alter-personalities or 'alters' inside, with different names, ages, characters, each carrying a part of the trauma memory. The multiplicity leads to internal discussion, conflict, chaos and the hearing of voices. Alters take their turn to control the clients' behavior; clients have only partial control over this.

In addition, clients have traumatic flashbacks, which disturb their consciousness as well. During a flashback victims re-experience their trauma as if it is happening again, being unaware of the present. At those moments, clients cannot talk about it (van der Kolk, 1996). Moreover, as their traumatic memory is affected by dissociation, victims have fragmented flashbacks, which they don't recognize as parts of their trauma (Braun, 1986).

The functioning of dissociative clients at this stage reminded me of Prouty's psychotic clients (Prouty, 1994). He found them *pre-experiential*: they don't have access to feelings yet. Their process is basic, slow, and repetitive, being a stage before the experiencing of neurotic clients. They are also *pre-expressive*: they cannot express their experience yet. Prouty attributed these difficulties to a lack of *psychological contact*. Psychological contact is the ability to have contact with reality, with one's feelings, and to communicate with others. Prouty developed a method to restore contact, called *Pre-Therapy*. It consists of specific *contact reflections*, of which there are five types. (Situational reflections describe the environment and support contact with reality; body reflections describe the body posture of the client and assist contact with one's body, oneself and with reality; facial reflections describe what can be seen on the client's face and support contact with feelings; word-for-word reflections duplicate exactly what the clients say, and support their communicative contact; and reiterative reflections repeat reflections which had an effect before, and reinforce the process.) These reflections are simple, slow and repetitive, and they fit with the slow and repetitive process of psychotic clients. They are based on Rogers' conditions, but adapted to their language. Reflections need time and have to be repeated, before any effect can be seen. Results were reported in pilot studies, clinical vignettes and videos (a complete list of references can be obtained from the author). Most clients improved in contact. Some could have psychotherapy afterwards; others could discuss their psychotic experience. Pre-Therapy has been implemented in several clinical settings (Prouty, Van Werde & Pörtner, 2002).

I noticed similarities with dissociative clients. Their initial process is also pre-experiential. It is slow and repetitive, although it seems hectic sometimes from the outside. When re-experiencing their trauma during a flashback, clients cannot discuss or process it: they are pre-expressive. Dissociative switches and flashbacks disturb their psychological contact. Therefore, I characterized the first phase of therapy as *pre-experiential*. I followed clients with slow, repetitive and literal reflections, calling these the therapeutic language of the first phase. Contact reflections belong to this phase also. They support the clients' impaired contact during switches and flashbacks, giving them a foundation. I assumed that clients wouldn't need to dissociate so much when this foundation was stronger. It should enable them afterwards to address their trauma.

Prouty's phenomenological approach to hallucinations is also important. He observed that these had a process, which he called *pre-symbolic*. His therapy, *pre-symbolic processing*, has four stages with stage-specific reflections. Initially, the shape of hallucinatory images changed, when they were reflected literally. In the second stage, clients perceived affect in their hallucinatory image, and both affect and images were reflected. In the third stage, clients noticed affect in themselves instead of outside, which was reflected also. Another shift followed, when the hallucinatory image changed into a flashback of a past (traumatic) event. Clients were shocked when they realized they had had that experience themselves. They needed to integrate it, which occurred afterwards in a typical experiential therapy, that being the fourth and final stage. This procedure has been illustrated with clinical vignettes (Prouty, 1994, 2004).

A similar process can be observed in dissociated clients, when their traumatic flashbacks are reflected literally, without going into their content. It is trusted that the traumatic story will explain itself in due time, like the hallucinations of Prouty's clients did. Gradually, memory fragments come together and they become a complete memory of the trauma, which corresponds to the third stage of the pre-symbolic process. Slow reflections help to pace the emotional turmoil when this complete flashback occurs.

The clients' distinct dissociative states are reflected literally as well, and not explored. More precisely, they are reflected phenomenologically. It is expected that these personalities will explain themselves afterwards. Therefore, the first phase of therapy is characterized as *pre-symbolic*. *Pre-symbolic processing* fits into this stage, being its corresponding therapeutic language.

Summarizing, the process of the first phase is pre-experiential and pre-symbolic. The therapeutic language consists of contact reflections (Pre-Therapy) and pre-symbolic processing. Contact reflections support the process in general, while pre-symbolic processing is attuned specifically to the content of the process.

CRITICAL EPISODE

At the end of the first phase, clients improve in various aspects. Owing to contact reflections, they have more contact with reality, with others and with themselves. There is trust in the therapist, who has passed tests of reliability. The relationship is stronger. Having more contact, clients don't need to dissociate so much. Dissociative barriers between alter-personalities become permeable, and these alters can't ignore each other any longer. With the decreasing dissociation comes an improvement of memory. Flashbacks, being parts of their traumatic memory, come together. When their memory of the trauma becomes complete, it is still a frightening flashback. Clients are shocked to realize that they experienced that trauma themselves. They cannot escape or dissociate as they did before, and have to face it. But they cannot cope with the intense emotions of it either. They begin to notice feelings, but don't know yet how to deal with them. They are unfamiliar with feeling experientially. They are not used to expressing feelings in symbolic language. In short, they are in no-man's land. This episode corresponds with the third stage of Prouty's pre-symbolic process. I called it 'critical', as it requires the strong presence of the therapist. This necessity is not recognized often, as therapists assume that their client won't need help at this stage. They may go on holiday without arranging for a back-up or replacement. In this stage of therapy, it is particularly important that therapists are available or that they arrange a solid replacement. Support, extra sessions or phone calls are needed, sometimes even a short admission. Clients should be informed about the critical episode and possible facilities. *Clearing a space* (CAS), the first step of focusing (Gendlin, 1996), is a valuable supportive technique at this moment. An emotional distance is created between the client and the traumatic experience. McGuire (1984) added imagery to CAS for distressed clients. She asked if they ever had a positive experience, and encouraged them to imagine as if they were at that place. The positive image helps them to feel space and to recover, while the traumatic experience is placed at the edge of the positive image. CAS has the effect of pacing, so that the working on the trauma can be postponed.

Usually, the shift from the first to the second phase is rapid, making the critical episode short. Sometimes, the change is gradual, leading to a distinct intermediate phase, resembling 'the grey zone' of Van Werde (2002). In that case, it has features of both first and second phases, and so reflections of the first phase have to be alternated with those of the second.

SECOND PHASE

In the second phase of therapy, the process shifts from pre-experiential to experiential. Clients get contact with feelings and are more curious than afraid of them. They want to learn focusing (Gendlin, 1996). The need to dissociate decreases. In fact, clients find switching more disturbing than helpful: they begin to integrate. Having more contact with reality, they are less afraid of flashbacks, realizing that these come from the past. As their amnesia decreases, they remember more and want to remember more. The memory of the traumatic event becomes complete, being still a flashback. Clients face their trauma, and have to integrate it. Instead of being in the trauma, they learn to look at it, knowing it is in the past. The traumatic memory has to become a narrative memory. The shift, from re-experiencing the trauma to feeling it experientially, is accompanied by strong emotions. Clients fear they will explode or lose their boundaries, if they feel what really happened to them. For such critical moments, Pesso (1988) offers a psychomotor technique of 'holding and containment.' Group members, acting as supporting figures, hold the client, saying that they will protect her from exploding and that they are assisting her to endure strong feelings. They protect the ego-skin of the client, forming an 'ego-wrapping.' When supported in this way, clients are able to contact their feelings, without the fear of getting lost.

These supportive figures however, are absent in individual therapy. Instead, their help can be asked for in the form of an image, but this is often not sufficient. Verbal support or the contact reflections of the therapist also fail. The client needs physical support. So the therapist takes the role of a supportive figure. Physical contact by therapists, however, is controversial, especially in circles of traditional therapy. But body techniques can be offered safely and professionally as long as preconditions are observed (Bohun, Ahern & Kiely, 1990; Durana, 1998; Hunter & Struwe, 1998; Stenzel & Rupert, 2004). The body support and the stronger therapeutic relationship provide a context in which the working through of the trauma can take place (Coffeng, 2002b). This process resembles the process of grief.

Three emotional themes are apparent in the second phase. At first clients experience anxiety, being shocked about what happened; in a later stage, they feel pain, realizing how it has hurt them emotionally and physically; and finally they feel sadness, when they see what they have lost.

Focusing is relieving. When clients are assisted in staying with an anxiety-provoking problem *and* in attending to their felt sense of it, they feel a relief. There is also a change: the problem feels different afterwards (Gendlin, 1996). The trauma can be digested with small, experiential change steps (Gendlin, 1990). Clients focus on the vague felt sense, which contains all aspects of their traumatic experience. It is felt that it happened. Clients are reassured when they learn that the flashback was a remnant of a past event, and not a sign of madness. Their body knew it. When clients have contact with their body, they have access to the body's healing capacity. Their felt sense can be consulted to repair or reconstruct the traumatic experience. Their body has a 'blueprint' (Gendlin, 1993), or an inner knowing about what should have happened, and what should not have happened. It knows that children should not be raped, and that lies should not be believed. The body is the center of truth (Pesso, 1990). Because of brainwashing, the mind of victims is mixed up with false moral rules (Spiegel, 1986). The therapist assists in restoring their blueprint by mentioning proper rules. Clients check with their felt sense whether these rules fit.

The process has changed also from pre-symbolic into symbolic. Clients use symbolic language to express feelings and so the therapeutic language becomes symbolic. Images are helpful to express feelings. These contain more aspects of the felt sense than words (Gendlin, 1996). Words, having limited meanings, may also evoke self-criticism, especially with victims. Images give more emotional space, which appeared helpful for grieving clients (Coffeng, 1992). Trauma clients can use imagery when they ask their blueprint: 'What should have happened?' They can imagine ideal caregivers. Therapists assist with their imagination. A court can be imagined, where justice is done. Trauma clients like imagery; they have symbolic energy, bringing drawings, paintings, etc. that have a symbolic meaning.

INCIDENTS IN THE SECOND PHASE

Since the language of the second phase has become experiential and symbolic, the interaction with the therapist becomes quick and flexible. There are fewer misunderstandings. The work on the trauma is intensive, but it gives a change and relief. The relationship being steady, therapists relax and enjoy the improvement. They look forward to seeing the end of therapy, having had a long journey with the client. In any case, they don't expect problems. They are surprised when incidents happen that contradict what they supposed. Some clients slip back into pre-experiential functioning and start to dissociate again. I was confused when this happened to me: the same client, who was integrated before, now seemed far away and did not respond to symbolic language. My second reaction was doubt: had I been too optimistic? Had we not reached the second phase? I tried to be patient again and returned to the slow speed and to the contact reflections of the first phase. This appeared to be unproductive. Clients continued to dissociate. Their alters complained and had many wishes to be fulfilled, as if time was endless. My third reaction was despair. It was as if nothing had been done. The end of therapy seemed far away. My fourth reaction was anger. I confronted the clients with their complaints, the limits of my age, and the waste of time. I became impatient and practical. To my surprise, it worked. Clients appeared able to work hard, to grieve and even to discuss the end of therapy. Sessions could be hectic, but clients could understand and integrate what happened. I shall describe the different backgrounds with vignettes. There are exceptions, where more patience and empathy are needed. Examples of these are given as well.

HIDDEN ALTER

A client had already had nine years of therapy when I replaced her therapist, who had become ill and could no longer continue with her. The client had a Dissociative Identity Disorder from early traumas, and she also had a physical handicap. She arrived with the smile of a happy patient. As the weeks passed, the smile changed into a depressed and annoyed look. She would sink into her chair with a deep sigh, complaining about her physical disease. She visited academic hospitals to get a second opinion and to hear about new medical developments. She also consulted experts on heredity and fertility. Each time she told how disappointing these visits were. Hearing this week after week, I became exhausted. I asked how long she was going to continue this medical journey before we could start therapy. I said that I feared I would be retired before that moment. I also said that I had difficulty with her annoyed look, which suggested she did not expect help from me either. It discouraged my optimism. The client seemed embarrassed, but she admitted I was right. She had stuck to her patient role, believing it was the only way to get attention from her family and from me. She feared I wouldn't like her when she showed her real self. Our contact improved, but she remained depressed and skeptical about therapy. I was not convinced that the air was clear. Remembering Kluft (1986), I inquired if there was another dissociated part of her who I didn't know, and who was responsible for this mood. She was irritated, as if this question was not allowed, but then the unknown alter appeared. He did not trust people, and expected I would fail like other people and send them away. He was waiting until I was finished; then, he would carry out his plan to commit suicide. He was depressed, and I asked the reasons for his depression. He explained it was because he carried the blame of past events. I could understand him and he felt himself being taken seriously. I asked if he could let me know when his death wish was strong, before he killed himself and the other alters. He did not expect I would be available at such moments. I told him my possibilities and limits, and we made a deal for emergency calls. However, I confronted this alter with another problem: we could not proceed with therapy if he would not give us a chance. He gave me the benefit of the doubt. After that, the therapy went well. More incidents followed, but the personal confrontation and direct response cleared the air. The client dared even to announce the end of therapy by herself. We ended nicely after half a year.

Kluft (1986) discovered 'new' alter-personalities when he confronted dissociative clients with their unproductive behavior during the last part of therapy. These alters had been hidden and frustrated change. Kluft negotiated with these alters until they agreed to cooperate. From that moment, therapy went well. Kluft's discovery is helpful when the therapy becomes chronic. It is also important to know the hidden alter, as this personality may have crucial information: a missing part of the traumatic memory, or the knowledge about dynamics between alters.

LAYERING OF MEMORIES

The appearance of new traumatic memories can be shocking for therapists who supposed they knew the entire story. These new memories usually come after an incident. I was confronted by this years ago. A client underwent a traumatic narco-analysis when an adolescent. She remembered the psychiatrist carrying a tape recorder while he brought her to the basement of the hospital. When she awakened again, she was afraid that she might have disclosed things she hadn't wanted to disclose. The doctor gave her electro-shocks afterwards, supposedly 'to forget the incest story.' She disliked this authoritarian doctor, as he had made erotic insinuations to her. Years later, another memory emerged. My co-therapist saw the client during my absence. At that time, the client accompanied somebody to hospital: the same hospital where she had had the narco-analysis. While her relative was examined, she went downstairs to find the narco-analysis room. There, the flashback of the original story returned. By carrying a tape recorder, the psychiatrist had *pretended* narco-analysis, but in the room he had forced sex on her. When she resisted, he had injected drugs, had fastened her on a stretcher and had raped her. Afterwards, he had told her that nobody would ever believe her. Shocked and confused, she had run away. She was fetched by nurses and punished by the doctor. He gave her electro shocks so she would forget *this* event! The client was shocked when she realized what had happened. She also felt reassured that the original memory had come back, and that my co-therapist believed her. She blamed me for having believed the first story of the 'narco-analysis'. The original memory had not come to the surface earlier, as she had expected that I would not believe her, as the abusive doctor had predicted.

The layering of traumatic memories has been observed in victims of the holocaust (van Ravesteijn, 1978), and in those of sexual abuse (Brown & Fromm, 1986; Terr, 1994). The memory of the original trauma is concealed under cover or screen memories. The cover memory is supposed to be a defense against the fear of being not believed, or against feelings of shame about the trauma. Another cause of the layering of memories is the connection of repeated traumatic experience with the emotional development of children (Coffeng, 1992). It becomes linked with it while it interferes with it as well. Attachment is affected also (Schore, 2003; Sinason, 2002). Because of these mechanisms, trauma memories don't come back as a story, but in the shape of problematic interaction or transference (Brown, 1997). This phenomenon resembles the reappearance of the trauma story in the re-enactment of children: 'behavioral memory' (Terr, 1994). The trauma is visible in their play, while the children are amnesic about the story and unable to tell it.

Dissociation contributes to the layering of traumatic memory, as trauma experience goes together with 'peritraumatic dissociation' (Marmar, Weiss & Metzler, 1998). It causes a split between the 'Emotional Person', who carries the traumatic memory, and the 'Apparently Normal Person', who is amnesic about the trauma (Nijenhuis, van der Hart & Steele, 2001). These mechanisms account for the various expressions of traumatic memory. Some victims have alternating flashbacks and amnesia, while others recover their memory after a long amnesic period (Harvey and Herman, 1996). Clients with a Dissociative Identity Disorder have alters who carry a trauma fragment, separated by dissociative barriers from other alters who don't know. The split between alters can be on different levels of experience, knowledge and sensation: some alters know the content of the story, while others carry feelings of the trauma, or images (Braun, 1986). When therapists attend to incidents, these alters may appear with their part of the story.

Due to the layering of memory, the original story appears late in therapy. Therapists don't expect to hear a new version of the traumatic story. Having been amnesic about this part of the memory, clients are shocked as well. The example given shows that one should not assume that one knows the whole story from the first telling. The client's behavior, the interaction, or countertransference feelings can give a cue of traumatic memories not yet revealed.

'THE UNSPEAKABLE'—THE EFFECT OF TRAUMA ON LANGUAGE

The term 'pre-expressive' has been used for the language of psychotic patients (Prouty, 1998). Their words are concrete and hard to understand. Later in therapy, when more words are added, the earlier words make sense. They appear to have announced a crucial message and to have implied experience. Dissociative clients are pre-expressive in the same sense. Having flashbacks and switches, they use telegram words. Unable to feel the whole complexity of their trauma, they cannot describe it in semantic language. Clients become expressive in the second phase. They use experiential language. Previous and pre-expressive words come back, but now together with their explanation. Their words cover different aspects of experience and no longer just concrete things.

There are exceptions. A client grew up with a chronic psychotic father, who depended on her and who abused her sexually. Her mother denied the problems; she would run away when the father's psychosis was critical, leaving the client alone with him. The client dissociated, behaving as if she could manage and ignoring her own anxiety. She was confronted with confusing ideas and double binds (Spiegel, 1986). Her father told her he would come back after his death to collect her, so the client anticipated his return when he finally committed suicide. Having been blamed by her mother for having made her father psychotic, the client believed she could make other people ill, and she closed her eyes whenever people passed.

When she came to therapy, she hardly spoke. She had frequent dissociative switches which prevented her from continuing a sentence or answering a question. It was as if she had to cross a busy highway before she could speak again. Her language was poor: she spoke in few words which could mean many things.

When we reached the second phase of therapy, her speech remained simple. I needed to teach her to use more words. When her language became richer finally, there was another surprise. She became mute again. After an incident, she explained the silence. It had to do with what had happened seven years before, when her brother had killed himself. I had supported her at that time and assisted her with grieving; but I had not realized the impact of the loss. It had been like a bomb, and had destroyed her language. It had triggered memories of the previous suicide of her father. The loss was also catastrophic, because her brother was the only witness of her traumatic childhood. She was left as the only one who knew the story. Losing him, she lost the hope of telling it to other people, fearing they would not believe her. Hence, she lost the perspective to escape from her dissociative isolation. She was without words again. I had to stay with 'the unspeakable,' her existential inability to speak.

The unspeakable is an important aspect of traumatic experience. It is related to *alexithymia*, a term introduced for psychosomatic patients. It is the inability to have contact with feelings and to express them. Alexithymia has been used also for trauma victims (Hyer, Woods & Boudewyns, 1991). The crash of the trauma makes it impossible for victims to address their feelings and to share them: it is too much. There are no words to describe the intensity and complexity of the trauma, in which fantasy and reality have been mixed up (Laub & Auerhahn, 1993). Victims of concentration camps used psychological defenses to survive in the middle of repeated trauma and danger (Bluhm, 1999). These mechanisms are difficult to change afterwards. It is hard to contact their feelings and to integrate the trauma. La Mothe (2001) described 'Freud's Unfortunates': clients who are well adapted and who remember all details of the holocaust. When they talk about it, it is in a detached way. On the other hand, they have traumatic nightmares and flashbacks that do not change and that they cannot discuss. The catastrophic knowledge of the trauma is unexperienced experience that paradoxically stands for an indescribable core of an event that undermines the self in relation and the concomitant capacities for language, narrative and knowledge. Laub and Auerhahn (1993) connect language—the capacity to symbolize—with the presence of an internalized, empathic other person. The more the victim is in the middle of horror, the more the empathic other person is felt to be absent, and the more language becomes impossible. The victim is kept in traumatic images and nightmares, unable to put these experiences into words. There is a gradation in the severity of traumatization and loss of language. The more a person has a distance from the trauma, the more language and fantasy are preserved. Children of holocaust survivors are more remote from the trauma than their parents, but still too near to be able to talk about it. At the end of the spectrum are people who were not involved. Their language and fantasy are intact. They have access to their feelings: they can imagine the trauma and empathize with the victim. The empathy involved in the therapy situation, however, makes these listeners (therapists) vulnerable at the same time (Wilson & Lindy, 1994).

Another cause of the unspeakable is the strange experience of victims returning from the traumatic environment to the safe world (Cyrulnik, 2002). It is as though they come from another planet. They cannot feel 'normal' again in the normal world. There is still the other reality of the traumatic experience. If they had a safe childhood, it is difficult to reconnect with that time. There is a gap. Arriving in a safe world, they remember the unsafe world. When they try to make language about it, this language seems not applicable to the safe world and may not be understood there either.

The unspeakable can happen during the second phase of therapy. Thus, clients who make progress on all aspects of therapy may remain without words at crucial moments. The human presence of the therapist is essential then. One tries to stay with what cannot be told.

PSYCHOSIS?

A client was integrating from a Dissociative Identity Disorder, and she reached the end of a long therapy. Suddenly, she asked me to send her to hospital. I was surprised, because she seemed to be doing well. I hesitated also because she had had a bad hospital experience previously. But she insisted, fearing a violent alter-personality would take over. Moreover, she was afraid of becoming psychotic; she had had a psychosis ten years ago. I offered extra sessions and phone calls, ready to arrange admission any moment. Before I could see her again, however, she had already been admitted. She was said to be psychotic with hallucinations and delusions. I couldn't believe it. She recovered quickly and we resumed therapy. But her fears of becoming psychotic remained. I challenged her to address 'the psychosis' and to find out what it was about. She would choose an image that symbolized it and focus on that image. She had a drawing of her first psychosis that she had made previously. She imagined the drawing in front of her and focused on it. After a silence, she burst into laughter, exclaiming: 'That I have been always afraid of that!' She had believed she had a psychotic core, because her father had told her so. By telling her she was crazy, he had tried to justify his sexual abuse. Now, she could see through his false accusation and she was relieved to be rid of that burden. Afterwards, the reasons for her two 'psychotic attacks' also became clear. After this clarification, she relaxed completely and she could end her therapy without fears.

I had assumed that dissociative clients could not become psychotic, having been told that dissociation would exclude a psychosis, dissociation being a coping strategy to prevent it. However, dissociative psychoses do exist (van der Hart, Witzum & Friedman, 1993). The border between dissociation and psychosis doesn't seem sharp. Another example came recently from Prouty (2004), who reviewed a therapy together with the client. At that time, she had hallucinated a python. Looking back however, she realized she had had more hallucinations than that of the python alone. Somebody made a picture of all the hallucinations. The picture resembled the constellation of alters of a DID client!

DISCUSSION

It is hard to find reports of incidents late in therapy with dissociative clients. Sakheim, Hess and Chivas (1988), who mentioned crisis episodes in the course of therapy, did not foresee problems in the last part of therapy. Chu (1988, 1994) discussed various difficulties, which do not seem to be related to the end phase either. The question could arise of whether the late problems are a consequence of my therapy model. This is unlikely as I heard of similar problems from therapists who use other approaches. It is also unlikely since these incidents have different causes and do not occur with every dissociative client.

The examples given are typical for clients who experience trauma and dissociation. They differ from problems late in any therapy. Regression is a common phenomenon, when clients fall back into a rigid functioning. It is due to their stress of integrating new experiences and changing old concepts. Fearing that they may lose control, they try to control their process. They lose contact with their bodily experience and become 'structure-bound' (Coffeng, 1991). With an adequate therapist response, however, clients regain their flexibility quickly.

Negative therapeutic reaction, a standstill near the end of therapy, is another problem (Hahn, 2004). Clients expect to be devalued by the therapist if they become really known. They re-experience the shame which they felt during the early affective misattunement from their former caregivers. The shame prevents them from showing their autonomy and from moving forward. Trauma victims have also feelings of shame that may prevent change (van Ravensteijn, 1978). It is a different shame, however, coming from their humiliation during the trauma.

Since the late incidents may contain different and crucial information, it is important to address them. Therapists must notice them, confront their client with them, and explore the background together with the client. This requires alertness, energetic action and curiosity. Some therapists are too tired at the end of a long therapy, and not ready for new problems. They miss incidents or become bored. This can be a reason to consider a replacement therapist, a colleague who can deal with the incident with fresh energy. The new therapist can move freely, not being fixed in the patterns of the previous relationship. He or she can afford to confront and to be ignorant of existing patterns of interaction.

I have felt the freedom when I have replaced colleagues, as shown in the first vignette. I had a similar experience when I assisted a colleague. She was tired from a long therapy that did not seem to be moving. I joined her in the sessions, focused on other things than the ones they were using, and suggested new options. The colleague regained her energy, and the therapy started moving again. I felt the difference also of being the first therapist. Exasperated after a long therapy, I announced the end of it. To my surprise, my flexibility returned. It felt as if I had stepped out of our old relationship. Interventions became easier, and we could end therapy. Another surprise was that I became open again to the comments of colleagues. I had not heard them before, being locked up in the old relationship.

There is another reason to consider replacement. Many therapists stop working with trauma clients after some time (Sussman, 1995). They are disillusioned, or burn out. Vicarious traumatization is one cause (Wilson & Lindy, 1994). Another might be that they were stuck in an interaction pattern with the client. It is difficult to escape from this pattern, despite supervision. Thus, the rule that the same therapist should do such a long and intensive therapy alone needs to be questioned. When replacement is possible, therapists can stop in time, instead of being 'condemned' to the same client. They can preserve their energy and optimism.

It is hard to find therapists for dissociative clients, or to find a replacement therapist, especially when the first had problems. This difficulty adds to the isolation of trauma therapists. It is better to organize replacement in a network. This is a supervision group in which participants are co-therapists for one another and they know one another's clients. Co-therapists replace the therapist during holidays or illness, and they can assist in sessions. Co-therapists should be ready also to replace a therapist completely. When they offer to take over, the first therapists feel really supported and they 'get some air'. When recovered, they are ready also to replace a colleague. It is a mutual commitment. This spirit reminded me of some of my previous supervisors. They came to meet with me in person during night duties, instead of advising by telephone only.

Dealing with late incidents is a difficult enterprise, but it is also interesting. The difficulty lies in the combination of being energetic and sensitive at the same time. Expressions of the client should not be taken for granted but need to be questioned again and again. It is not a matter of believing but of exploring, as previous expressions of the client may have a new meaning. A balance has to be found between patience and curiosity. This balance resembles what McCann and Coletti (1994) called 'the dance of empathy.' In their wish to understand, they circle around a client with questions. Responses of the client help them to learn more and to empathize. From there they ask the client new questions, in order to understand better. It begins with a circular dance with the client, but over time it becomes a spiral movement as the therapist comes nearer to the client. The combination of curiosity and checking—recommended by the authors as a way to prevent empathic strain—is also an excellent way to deal with the late incidents.

The concept of two phases can help therapists to find the language that corresponds to their client's process. This concept should not be used as a rigid model, but as a rough one with space for exceptions. This implies curiosity and flexibility during the whole course of therapy. Alertness is required, especially at the end. Sometimes therapists need assistance, or replacement, to maintain their curiosity. Without help, their therapy becomes a burden. With proper arrangements, it can remain a challenge.

REFERENCES

Bluhm, HO (1999) How did they survive? *American Journal of Psychotherapy, 53* (1), 96–122.

Bohun, E, Ahern, R & Kiely, L (1990) The use of therapeutic touch. Paper presented at the 7th Annual Conference on Dissociation and Multiple Personality Disorder, Chicago.

Braun, B (1986) Issues in the psychotherapy of multiple personality disorder. In B Braun (Ed) *Treatment of Multiple Personality Disorder* (pp 1–28). Washington, DC: American Psychiatric Press.

Brown, D (1997) Relationships and recollections. PAOG-AMC Workshop, Amsterdam.

Brown, D & Fromm, E (1986) *Hypnotherapy and Hypnoanalysis*. Hillsdale, NJ: Erlbaum.

Chu, J (1988) Ten traps for therapists in the treatment of trauma survivors. *Dissociation, 1* (4), 24–32.

Chu, J (1994) The rational treatment of multiple personality disorder. *Psychotherapy, 31* (1), 94–100.

Coffeng, T (1991) The phasing and timing of focusing in therapy. *The Focusing Folio, 10* (3), 40–50.

Coffeng, T (1992) Re-contacting the child. *The Focusing Folio, 11*, 11–21; *Personzentriert, 1*, 95–115; *T. Psychotherapie, 21*, 268–89.

Coffeng, T (1996) Experiential and pre-experiential therapy for multiple trauma. In U Esser, H Pabst & W Speierer (Eds) *The Power of the Person-Centered Approach* (pp 185–203). Köln: GwG.

Coffeng, T (2002a) Two phases of dissociation, two languages. In JC Watson, RN Goldman, & MS Warner (Eds) *Client-Centered and Experiential Psychotherapy in the 21st Century: Advances in theory, research and practice* (pp 325–38). Ross-on-Wye: PCCS Books.

Coffeng, T (2002b) Contact in the therapy of trauma and dissociation. In G Wyatt & P Sanders (Eds) *Rogers' Therapeutic Conditions: Evolution, theory and practice, Vol 4: Contact and Perception* (pp 153–67). Ross-on-Wye: PCCS Books.

Cyrulnik, B (2002) *Les Vilains Petits Canards*. Paris: Éditions Odile Jacob. [Dutch edn, *Veerkracht*. Amsterdam: Ambo]

Durana, C (1998) The use of touch in psychotherapy: Ethical and clinical guidelines. *Psychotherapy, 35* (2), 269–80.

Gendlin, ET (1990) The small steps of the therapy process. In G Lietaer, J Rombauts & R Van Balen (Eds) *Client-Centered and Experiential Psychotherapy in the Nineties* (pp 205–24). Leuven: Leuven University Press.

Gendlin, ET (1993) *Focusing ist eine kleine Tür.* Würzburg: DAF.
Gendlin, ET (1996) *Focusing-Oriented Psychotherapy: A manual of the experiential method.* New York: Guilford Press.
Hahn, W (2004) The role of shame in negative therapeutic reactions. *Psychotherapy, 41* (1), 3–12.
Harvey, M & Herman, J (1996) Amnesia, partial amnesia, and delayed recall among adult survivors of childhood trauma. In K Pezdek & W Banks (Eds) *The Recovered Memory/False Memory Debate* (pp 29–40). New York: Academic Press.
Hunter, M & Struwe, J (1998) *The Ethical Use of Touch in Psychotherapy.* London: Sage.
Hyer, L, Woods, G & Boudewyns, P (1991) PTSD and alexithymia: Importance of emotional clarification in treatment. *Psychotherapy, 28,* 129–38.
Kluft, R (1986) Personality unification in MPD: A follow-up study. In B Braun (Ed) *Treatment of Multiple Personality Disorder* (pp 31–60). Washington, DC: American Psychiatric Press.
La Mothe, R (2001) Freud's unfortunates. *American Journal of Psychotherapy, 55* (4), 534–63.
Laub, D & Auerhahn, N (1993) Knowing and not knowing. *International Journal of Psycho-Analysis, 74,* 287–302.
Marmar, C, Weiss, D & Metzler, T (1998) Peritraumatic dissociation and post-traumatic stress disorder. In J Bremner & C Marmar (Eds) *Trauma, Memory and Dissociation* (pp 229–52). Washington, DC: American Psychiatric Press.
McCann, L & Coletti, I (1994) The dance of empathy. In J Wilson & J Lindy (Eds) *Countertransference in the Treatment of PTSD* (pp 87–121). New York: Guilford Press.
McGuire, M (1984) Experiential focusing with severely depressed suicidal clients. *The Focusing Folio, 3,* 47–59 and 104–9.
Nijenhuis, E, van der Hart, O & Steele, K (2001) Structural dissociation of the personality. In A Hofmann, L Reddeman & U Gast (Eds) *Behandlung dissoziativer Störungen.* Stuttgart: Thieme.
Pesso, A (1988) Sexual abuse, the integrity of the body. *Bewegen en Hulpverlening, 5,* 270–81.
Pesso, A (1990) Center of truth, true scene and pilot. *Bulletin Netherlands Association Pessotherapy, 6* (2), 13–21.
Prouty, G (1994) *Theoretical Evolutions in Person-Centered /Experiential Psychotherapy: Applications to schizophrenic and retarded psychoses.* Westport, CT: Praeger.
Prouty, G (1998) Pre-therapy and the pre-expressive self. *Person-Centred Practice, 6* (2), 80–8.
Prouty, G (2004) De hallucinatie als het onbewuste zelf. *Tijdschrift Cliëntgerichte Psychotherapie, 42* (2), 85–98.
Prouty, G, Van Werde, D & Pörtner, M (2002) *Pre-Therapy: Reaching contact-impaired clients.* Ross-on Wye: PCCS Books.
Ross, CA (1997) *Dissociative Identity Disorder.* New York: Wiley.
Roy, B (1991) A client-centered approach to multiple personality and dissociative process. In L Fusek (Ed) *New Directions in Client-centered Therapy: Practice with difficult client populations* (pp. 18–40). Chicago, IL: Chicago Counseling Center.
Sakheim, D, Hess, E & Chivas, A (1988) General principles for short term inpatient work with multiple personality-disorder patients. *Psychotherapy, 25* (1), 117–24.

Schore, A (2003) *Affect Regulation and Repair of the Self.* New York: Norton.
Sinason, V (Ed) (2002) *Attachment, Trauma and Multiplicity.* Hove: Brunner-Routledge.
Spiegel, D (1986) Dissociation, double binds, and posttraumatic stress in multiple personality disorder. In B Braun (Ed) *Treatment of Multiple Personality Disorder* (pp 61–77). Washington, DC: American Psychiatric Press.
Stenzel, CL & Rupert, PA (2004) Psychologists' use of touch in individual psychotherapy. *Psychotherapy, 41* (3), 332–45.
Sussman, M (Ed) (1995) *A Perilous Calling.* New York: Wiley.
Terr, L (1994) *Unchained Memories.* New York: Basic Books.
Van der Hart, O, van der Kolk, B & Boon, S (1998) Treatment of dissociative disorders. In J Bremner & C Marmar (Eds) *Trauma, Memory and Dissociation* (pp 253–83). Washington, DC: American Psychiatric Press.
Van der Hart, O, Witzum, E & Friedman, B (1993) From hysterical psychosis to reactive dissociative psychosis. *Journal of Traumatic Stress, 6,* 43–63.
Van der Kolk, B (1996) The complexity of adaptation to trauma. In B van der Kolk, A McFarlane & L Weisaeth (Eds) *Traumatic Stress* (pp 182–213). New York: Guilford Press.
Van Ravesteijn, L (1978) De gelaagdheid van emoties. *T. v. Psychotherapie, 4* (4), 175–85.
Van Werde, D (2002) Pre-Therapy applied on a psychiatric ward. In G Prouty, D Van Werde & M Pörtner *Pre-Therapy: Reaching contact-impaired clients* (pp 61–120). Ross-on-Wye: PCCS Books.
Wilson, J & Lindy, J (Eds) (1994) *Countertransference and the Treatment of PTSD.* New York: Guilford Press.

CHAPTER 9

The Hallucination as the Unconscious Self

GARRY PROUTY

In the early 1900s, phenomenology was introduced into the field of psychiatry by the philosopher/psychiatrist Karl Jaspers (1963). This approach continued in Europe through such psychiatric writers as Binswanger (1963), Boss (1994), and Minkowski (1970). Major entry into the American psychotherapy literature was through the writings of Rollo May (1958). A brief historical review of existential-phenomenological psychiatry and psychotherapy is available in the literature (Halling & Dearborn, 1995).

Part of the phenomenological approach has been directed toward the schizophrenic hallucination (Boss, 1963; Laing, 1969; Strauss, 1966; Vandenberg, 1982). Carrying on with this tradition are the phenomenological articles of Prouty (1977, 1983, 1986, 1991), as well as Prouty and Pietrzak (1988). Those articles described methods of treatment as well as the lived experience of the hallucination. This paper attempts to describe an empathic,[1] experiential and process-oriented approach to the unconscious through the phenomenological medium of hallucinations.

The first clues as to the possibility of this emerged in actual hallucinatory work with psychotic clients (Prouty, 1994). One retarded/schizophrenic young man expressed his sense of the 'not yet conscious' in the following way:

---

1. Gallese's (2003) suggested non-reductionist model for empathy correlates the neural and phenomenological bases of intersubjectivity. He presents considerable empirical evidence for monkeys and humans that supports the concept of neural mechanisms that provide 'an implicit, automatic and unconscious' (p. 174) process of embodied simulation.

His hypothesis is that emotional sensitivity follows this same pattern of 'mirror neurons.' Phenomenologically he draws on the philosopher Husserl who postulates the body as the basis of conscious intersubjectivity. Continuing into the area of psychopathology, Gallese draws on phenomenological psychiatrists (Minkowski, Blankenberg and Paras) to formulate the view that schizophrenia is an empathic disorder, a failure in resonance with the world and with others.

Prouty, G (2004) The hallucination as the unconscious self. *The Journal of the American Academy of Psychoanalysis and Dynamic Psychiatry, 32* (4), 597–612. By kind permission of the editors. Reprinted in R Worsley & S Joseph (Eds) (2007) *Person-Centred Practice: Case studies in positive psychology* (pp 169–83). Ross-on-Wye: PCCS Books.

The evil thing is a picture. It's a purple picture that hangs there. It just hangs there and I can see it—the picture, you know. It's purple, it's very dark. So I can see it and I don't like it. I don't like it at all. It is very dark ... I don't like it at all. It's not good, this thing, whatever it is. *It's in the past* and it's very strong—the past—and it's over with and it's not coming back anymore. The *past* don't come back and this is like now. It ain't the *past*, you know. It's over with and I don't want to be tempted by it anymore. This thing, you know—has a very lot of strength to it. It's evil. You know. The thing has a very lot of strength to it. It's evil. It's no good and that's why it's no good at all. It's very evil, you know. I don't like it. It's very evil, this thing [pained laughter]. It's over with. It's *the past*, and it's not coming back anymore. (Prouty, 1994: 73–4. Emphasis added)

The client's emphasis on the past coming back is reported as a potentially imminent 'yet to be' experience. Perhaps something from the unconscious is beginning to emerge into consciousness?

THE PRE-SYMBOLIC THEORY OF HALLUCINATORY EXPERIENCE

THE PROBLEMATIC

Every conception has a starting point—a problematic (Peters, 1992; Prouty, Van Werde & Pörtner, 2001/2002). In the case of hallucinations, the problematic is posed by Gendlin (1964), who described the hallucination as 'structure-bound.' This concept has several levels of meaning. First, hallucinations are perceived, literally, 'as such' and 'not his.' Next, the experiencing is considered isolated, meaning that the experiencing is not included in the felt functioning of the organism. Finally, this implicitly felt functioning is rigid—not in experiential process. Thus, Gendlin's concept of the hallucination can be described as a *non-process structure*. The problematic is how to turn this non-process structure into a process structure—from an hallucinatory image that does not process to an hallucinatory image that *does* process, according to experiential principles.

THE PHILOSOPHICAL PRIMACY OF THE SYMBOL

The philosophical primacy of the symbol refers to an epistemological shift from *experiencing* to the *symbolizing of experience*. This philosophical primacy of the symbol is asserted by Cassirer (1955), who described the human as 'animal symbolicum.' This philosophical impulse is further expanded by Susan

Langer (1961), who described the human brain as a 'transformer.' The brain transforms 'the current of experience into symbols'. This philosophical focus allows us to think of humankind as 'motivated' to symbolize experience. This philosophical emphasis on symbolization is perhaps best represented in psychoanalysis by Kubie (1953) and Searles (1965), who both saw this capacity as the unique hallmark of humans.

THE SEMIOTICS OF ABSTRACTNESS–CONCRETENESS

These insights, however, do not produce semiotic conceptualizations about different levels of symbolization. Reichenbach (cited in Szasz, 1961) conceived such a semiotic conceptualization as levels of abstraction and concreteness. The most abstract form of symbolizing experience is the *meta-symbol*. It does not directly refer to an experience, but to a set of processes beyond direct experience. An example of a *meta-symbol* is $E = mc^2$. This process cannot be directly experienced. The next level of symbolizing experience is called *object language*. This refers to everyday ordinary cultural speech, such as book, chair and so forth. Continuing to a more concrete level, Reichenbach describes the *indexical sign*. This symbolization is a concrete experience that refers to a concrete experience; for example, cloud can refer to rain, or snow can refer to cold. Next in the continuum of concreteness is the *iconical sign*. This is a literal duplicate of the referent; a photograph or TV image, for example. An even more primitive form of concreteness is called the *pre-symbol* (Prouty, 1986). Drawing conceptualizations from Jaspers, the pre-symbol can be described in the following way: 'It cannot be clarified by someone else' and 'it is inseparable from what it symbolizes' (Jaspers, 1971: 124).

INTRODUCING THE PRE-SYMBOL

The term *pre-symbol* refers to the structure of the hallucinatory image as distinct from its processing. Psychotherapy with hallucinatory images reveals that the images contain two properties—one phenomenological and the other symbolic. This creates a definitional polarity.

1. Sartre (1956) defines the phenomenon as an experience that is 'absolutely self-indicative.' This means an experience indicates itself, refers to itself, or means itself.

2. Whitehead (1927) describes symbol as 'an experience that indicates another experience' (p. 8). Symbols are experiences that mean or refer to other experiences.

Expressed in another way, the phenomenon is 'about itself,' and the symbol is 'about something else.' These two polarities require a synthesis to describe fully the structure of the hallucination. This necessitates conceptualizing the pre-symbol.

STRUCTURAL PROPERTIES OF THE PRE-SYMBOL
EXPRESSIVE
As an expressive structure, the hallucination is described as 'self-intentional.' As already mentioned, Langer (1961) viewed the human brain as something that transforms the current of experience into symbols. This metaphor allows us to think of the hallucination as an expressive transformation of real-life experience into image form. One patient described this self-intentionality by saying, 'These images are my unconscious trying to express itself.' Another patient described it as, 'the past trying to come back.' Still another conveyed the volitional quality by saying, 'The images start in my unconscious and move towards my consciousness to be real.'

PHENOMENOLOGICAL
As an experiential structure, the hallucinatory image is described as 'self-indicating.' It is experienced as real, and as such it implies itself. Experience A implies Experience A. The hallucination means *itself as itself*. Exemplifying this, one schizophrenic patient said, 'it's real, it is … it's very real … I see it … over there … It makes sounds too.'

SYMBOLIC
As a symbolic structure, the hallucination is described as 'self-referential.' It is an experience that implies another experience. Experience A implies Experience B. The hallucinatory image (Experience A) contains its referent (Experience B) within itself. The hallucinatory image means *itself within itself*. A case example is that an hallucinatory python (Experience A) experientially processes into a real homicidal mother (Experience B). The python functions as a symbol of the mother.

HALLUCINATORY PROCESS
The following vignette (Prouty, 1991) shows how pre-symbolic experiencing is deeply rooted in the phenomenological approach and illustrates the self-intentional, self-indicating and self-referential properties of the hallucinations.

> *The patient, a male aged nineteen, was diagnosed as moderately retarded (Stanford Binet IQ of 65). He was from upper lower class origin of Polish ethnicity. There was no mental illness in the family, and the client had not been diagnosed or treated for mental illness: that is, he was not receiving any medications for psychosis. He was a day-client in a vocational rehabilitation workshop for the mentally retarded. He was referred to me for therapy because of his severe withdrawal and non-communication. The patient also behaved as though he was very frightened. He was shaking and trembling at his*

workstation and during his bus ride to the facility. At home, he rarely talked with his parents and he never socialized with neighborhood peers.

During the early phases of therapy, the patient expressed almost nothing and made very little contact with me. He was very frightened during the sessions and could barely tolerate being in the room with me. Gradually, with the aid of contact reflections, the client accepted a minimal relationship and expressed himself in a minimal way. Eventually, it became clear, the patient was terrorized by hallucinations that were constantly present to him.

The following description provides an account of pre-symbolic experiencing. It provides an outline of hallucinatory movement and its subsequent resolution about its origin.

Phase I: 'The purple demon'

Client: It's very evil, this thing. What it wants to do is to rip me apart, you know. It's very evil ... and it's very evil, this thing. That's why I don't want anything to do with it. I'm tempted by it, you know. It's so small but it has so much strength and it wants to rip me apart, you know. It wants to drive me into the past. It wants ... it wants to make the past come back and I don't want the past to come back like it did a long time ago. It's over with, you know. It's not coming back anymore. The past doesn't come back. It's over with already.

Therapist: It's evil and strong. It wants the past to come back.

C: The evil thing is a picture. It's a purple picture that hangs there. It just hangs and I can see it. I can see it ... the picture, you know. It's purple, it's very dark. It's very dark. So I can see it and I don't like it at all. It's very dark.

T: It's a dark purple picture and you don't like it.

C: And it's very tempted and I don't want to be tempted by it. It's very small. It's very evil, you know ... that's all ... It just hangs there. It don't do nothing. It's very evil, you know. It's just like a picture. A purple picture. It just stays there. It just stays there, you know ... the picture. It don't do nothing. It's evil, you know. I don't like it at all. It's not good and this thing, whatever it is. It's in the past and it's very strong, the past. ... And it's over with and I don't want to be tempted by it any more. Yeh, yeh, it's very evil, very evil and very strong and has a lot of strength to it.

T: It's evil and it's in the past. It's strong and it hangs there. You don't want to be tempted by it.

C: This thing, you know ... this thing has a lot of strength to it. It's evil, you know ... This thing has a lot of strength to it. It's evil. It's not good and that's why it's very evil, this thing.

[Pained laughter]

It's over with. It's in the past, and it's not coming back anymore. It's over with a long time ago, you know. It's not going to come back anymore. I used to talk about the trees and the flowers, grass, and its all over with. It's not coming back anymore. It's something else, the picture. The purple picture just hangs there. It's evil. No?

T: *The purple picture just hangs there. It's evil and you don't like it.*

C: *The past, it came from the past and the past is over with. It's not coming back any more, you know.*

T: *It comes from the past.*

C: *It's a picture. It's just a picture. A big, purple picture. It just hangs there. I don't think it will rip me apart. I think it's very strong, but it ain't going to rip me apart. I don't think it will rip me apart at all, no.*

T: *It's a big, purple picture. It won't rip you apart.*

C: *The thing is getting big and large. It's very big and large. It wants to get me. I won't let it. It's evil. It's like a demon, a bad demon. It wants to chop me all up. I won't let it chop me all up because it's bad. Very bad.*

[Loud sobs]

Just a temptation, like any other temptation. A temptation is a temptation. You shouldn't be tempted by it and you know I want to pull away from it. I don't want to go by it.

T: *It's big and large and evil. It wants to chop you. It's very tempting.*

C: *It's very bad and it's very destructive. It ain't good at all by it. It's like a bad demon, like a ... like a demon or evil or something. Like a demon devil and I don't care for it too much. You know, at all. I ... I don't like it too much, no. I don't like it at all, this thing. It's very bad and very evil, you know. It ain't no good. It's very bad. It's with the past and it's not going to come back any more. It's over with, you know, and talking about the trees and flowers and grass, and that's over. I mean it's not coming back, but this is right now, I mean.*

T: *It's bad and destructive, like an evil demon. It's evil and in the past.*

C: *It's not coming back, but this is right here now. I can feel it, you know. It's like air. It's up above me. It's very close up above and I can feel ... almost touch it, you know. It's so close, very close. It's like a demon, you know, demon devil or something. 'Ho, ho, hoing' and all like that, you know ... very bad, very bad. It forces me, pressing, very pressing on me ... it's very pressing, it forces, a lot of force to it and it wants to grab me, you know. It wants to grab me. The feeling wants to grab me. The feeling wants to grab me.*

T: *It's very close and it wants to grab you.*

C: *The feeling ... the feeling ... ah, it's in the picture. The feeling is in the picture. Yes, it's there and I can see it. I don't like it. It's over with, you know. It's like the past and it's not coming back any more. It's over. It's just the trees and the flowers and grass and that's over and it's not coming back.*

Phase 1 describes a purple demonic image that just 'hangs there.' The patient experiences it as evil and powerful. The image is considered destructive and wants to rip the patient apart. This phase contains the property of being self-intentional. The patient expresses: 'It wants to drive me into the past. It wants to make the past come back and I don't want the past to come back the way it did a long time ago … It's over with, you know … it's not coming back anymore … already … It's in the past and it's very strong, the past, and its over with and it's not coming back any more.' As illustrated by this example, self-intentional means the expressive transformation of real-life experiences into images.

Phase II: 'Orange square hate'
C: It's orange, the color's in a square. It's an orange color that's square. It's an orange color that's square and it hates me. And it don't even like me. It hates me.

T: It's orange and it's square and it hates you.

C: It hates me a lot, you know, and it scares me. I get scared because of that. I get scared because it hates me.

T: It's orange and it's square and you get scared a lot.

C: And because it's orange that scares me and I get scared of the bad hating.

T: The orange and bad hating scare you a lot. That hate scares you.

C: I get scared because of that. I get scared a lot. I get scared of the orange thing. It's orange.

T: You get scared of the orange thing.

C: Big orange, square thing. It's square and it's orange and I hate it. It don't like me because it hates me. It hates me and I get scared and I get excited over it too. I get very excited.

T: You get very excited.

C: It's exciting; I get excited over it too. I do. I do. I get excited over it a lot. What? I get scared a lot about it. It makes noises. It makes noises.

T: It's orange and it makes noises.

C: It makes noises … It hates me. It also gets very excited. It gets very excited. It does, it gets me very excited a lot. I get, I get, I get very excited over it. I do. I do. I do. There's so much hate and it scares me and it makes me uncomfortable. It does. And it's real … It's real, it is.

T: *It's real.*

C: *It is, it's very real.*

T: *It's very real ... You point to it. It's over on your side. You see it.*

C: *I see it. Over there. Over there.*

T: *It's over there.*

C: *It makes sounds too.*

Phase II has an image that is orange, square and has hate in it. The patient is very frightened of it. Phase II contains self-indicating properties because it is experienced as real, as a phenomenon. It implies itself. The patient's process is as follows: 'and it's real, it is ... It is, it's very real ... I see it ... Over there. Over there ... It makes a sound, too.'

Phase III: 'Mean lady'

C: *Yeah, well. Yeah, I would. I would. She's ... I don't know. There we go. What? What?*

[Auditory hallucination]

T: *OK. Let's talk about what you see.*

C: *Well, it ain't real, you know, and she ain't real, you know. What?*

[Auditory hallucination]

Ha, ha, ha.

[Sobs]

She has orange hair and yellow eyes.

T: *She has orange hair and yellow eyes.*

C: *She's very pretty. She's very pretty. She loves getting mean when I am bad. She could get ... she's mean, you know.*

T: *She's pretty and mean.*

C: *She is. She is. No, really she is. Really she is, with yellow eyes and orange hair. Boy! That scares me. That scares me a lot. That scares me a lot ... Yeah, both the meanness and the ... What?*

[Auditory hallucination]

Yeah. Aah. I can see it and I don't even want to see it. It's over with and it's not coming back any more. And I can see it.

T: *You can see it.*

C: *Yeah, that scares me. Yeah, it does. I think about it. It scares me.*

T: *When you think about it, that scares you.*

C: *I get scared. I don't want to think about it. I got it. I got it.*

T: *You don't want to think about it but you got it.*

C: *I got it. It's orange, you know. That's helping. She's helping.*

T: *She's helping.*

C: *She scares me, though, she scares me. But as long as I'm good, as long as I'm good, I am … she's a friend.*

T: *As long as you're good, she's a friend.*

C: *But she's scary.*

T: *She's scary.*

C: *Scary. Yellow eyes, orange hair she has, she does. Reminds me of a dragon, you know. Her eyes are like that.*

T: *Her eyes are like a dragon.*

C: *Almost, you know, like a dragon … Her eyes are like a dragon … She's strong … She's strong, I'm weak. And I'm good, but she's also mean. She can be mean too, see? And I'm good if I'm good and I am, I really am, but she's all … she's very mean. She can be mean … and it scares me.*

T: *She's mean and that scares you.*

C: *She looks over me. She watches over me, but she has eyes like a dragon … Right. That's like a dragon and then she scares me and I get scared.*

At this point, the patient appeared upset and wanted the tape recorder turned off. Over the next two sessions, the image processed into a nun who had beaten the retarded client because he did not understand his school lessons.

Phase III contains an image of a woman that the patient describes as pretty, mean and scary. She has orange hair and yellow eyes. This deeply frightens the patient. The significant theoretical observation of this phase is its processing to its experience of origin. The patient recaptures a real memory of being beaten by a nun who punished him for not completing his school lessons. This phase illustrates the self-referential property of hallucinations; that is, it symbolizes an experience within itself. It refers to an 'originating' event (the nun).

THE NEWER THEORETICAL FINDINGS

The following observations can be made concerning the particular case: (1) the hallucinatory structure can be processed through to an unconscious level; (2) the meaning of the hallucination can be integrated; and (3) hallucinatory processing leads to a realistic and traumatic etiology. Numerous other case histories detail the pre-symbolic processing of hallucinatory images (Boss, 1963; Prouty, 1977, 1983, 1986, 1991; Prouty & Pietrzak, 1988); these reveal insights concerning such issues as the structure of primary process and the structure of the schizophrenic self. Romme and Escher (1993) describe therapy for hallucinatory voices utilizing support groups.

PRIMARY PROCESS

Freud included both the dream and the hallucination in his concept of primary process. Assigning such limited value to consciousness, Freud paid little or no attention to the phenomenology of consciousness being developed by the philosopher Husserl. This is interesting because both were students of the philosopher Brentano. If one compares the phenomenology of dreams with the phenomenology of hallucinations, it is easy to see 'the dream is my dream' and 'I had it last night.' It is something experienced, which plays itself out within the boundaries of self, and is a memory. The hallucination is disconnected: it becomes experienced as not belonging to the self, but rather as an external reality that is immediate. Therefore, in contrast to a dream, which Freud labeled a 'projection' (within the self boundary—mine, internal etc.), I describe the hallucination as an 'extrojection' (outside of the self boundary—not mine, external etc.). On the basis of this phenomenological distinction, the dream is labeled 'projection', whereas the hallucination can be termed 'extrojection.'

A DIVIDED SELF

Polster and Polster (1974), from the perspective of gestalt psychotherapy, describe the dream as a fragment of the self. It is simple to extrapolate this perspective to understanding the hallucination. The hallucination is a self fragment split off from the self-structure—a severe rupture in the fabric of self. This presents a picture close to RD Laing's (1969) description of the 'Divided Self'—to borrow his famed title. Schizophrenia, thus, can be partially described as a severe split in the self-structure. The psychotherapy of hallucinations therefore leads to re-integration of self in schizophrenia. Many years ago, I used to see state hospital schizophrenics wandering the wards speaking and gesticulating towards 'empty' space. I now see these patients as relating to fragments of the self that contain the potentiality for re-integration. Perhaps Laing's (1969: 71) concept of the 'unembodied self' captures this picture.

THE UNCONSCIOUS

Freud described the dream as the 'Royal Road to the Unconscious'; the hallucination is also a 'Royal Road to the Unconscious.' There is an important distinction, however. Freud's data from his original inference of the unconscious were dreams, hypnosis and slips of the tongue (Boss, 1994), whereas the original datum for the description of the unconscious is the client's hallucinatory experience. This emphasis on direct experience must be considered in contrast with the psychoanalytic view of Nunberg (1955) who states *'we possess no direct evidence of the existence of the unconscious. We deduce it from indirect evidence'* (p. 6, emphasis added).

The use of an experiential hallucinatory method to approach the unconscious is predicated on several grounds. The first is accessibility. The hallucination can present itself as an immediacy to consciousness (now), whereas the dream is a past memory (last night). Closely linked to accessibility is the issue of experiential presence. Hallucinations can be well-lighted, multicolored and available for years (Havens, 1962). Their next experiential value is their capacity to be processed to their realistic origins. Finally, the hallucinatory image itself can be thought of as an experiential fragment of the unconscious, thereby providing a direct approach.

A SPATIAL PHENOMENOLOGY OF THE UNCONSCIOUS

McCall (1983), quoting the views of Heidegger, described phenomenological hermeneutics in the following manner: 'Hermeneutics is a method of *uncovering* (*unverborgen*), of remaining with the experience until it reveals its hidden truth' (p. 113). The following psychiatric description fulfills, I hope, this definition.

Medard Boss (1963) entitled a chapter of his book 'A patient who taught the author to think differently.' It is in this spirit that the evidence of a three-dimensional phenomenology of the unconscious is presented. Ellenberger (1958) outlined the various theoretical contributions to the phenomenology of spatiality. However, none of these is concerned with the hallucination per se.

The patient was a woman in her forties who was schizophrenic, homicidal/suicidal, as well as abusive of alcohol. The total length of treatment was nine years. Ten years later, the client and I spent a long time tape recording and preparing manuscripts about the therapeutic process (Prouty, 2000). In the course of the therapy, the patient had an intense hallucination of a python experientially processed to a homicidal mother (Prouty, 1994). Also, a number of smaller and less intense hallucinations were processed. In the original treatment, these hallucinations had been presented sequentially by the patient. The interesting new observation was that the therapist never realized these hallucinations were present in three-dimensional space, commingled with the patient's reality perception: they were all present at the same time. They were experienced as a unified spatial gestalt. Perhaps analogously, they could be seen as parallel to having several dreams at the same time in a single reality space.

The patient experienced eight hallucinations at the same continuing time, within real space. A realistic description is as follows: first there was a python curled in front of the table between the patient's and the therapist's chairs. This, resolved with treatment (Prouty, 1983), represented her mother's homicidal 'agent.' Concurrently, between the python and the table-lamp, appeared Sonja in an ephemeral form. The patient described her as a siren, seducing the client towards suicidal death, repeating, 'Peace, Peace.' Sonja was a tactile hallucination, and the client integrated her meaning through inserting her arm into her ephemeral body and experiencing warm 'intestine-like' sensations. The patient experienced this as disgusting, repulsive and nauseating. Sonja was also a murderous 'agent' (patient's language) for the patient's homicidal mother.

Also concurrently, another negative figure, a dwarf, was named 'The Judge.' He rendered death sentences for very minor infractions; for example, losing a rubber band. The patient described him as a 'hanging judge' who would declare her worthless, deserving to die, and so forth. He would yell 'off with her head' and 'she is guilty ... guilty ... guilty.' Again he was an 'agent' of the homicidal mother. Finally, and simultaneously, the Tasmanian Devil was a tornado-like, swirling dervish with sharp teeth. In therapy, the patient described it as her mother's chaotic anger.

At the same time, slightly behind the patient's chair and left shoulder, appeared Marie, the abused child. She was imprisoned and isolated behind bars. The child was the same age as the patient's murdered friend. Also at this age, the patient was locked in the refrigerator by the patient's homicidal mother. Further, the hallucinated child was the same age as the patient when she was sent to the darkened basement, by her homicidal mother, while a real murderer was in the neighborhood. Marie was 'healed' by the appearance of a kitten who became her best 'friend.' To this day, the client has close relationships with pet cats. In fact, she has one deceased cat preserved by a taxidermist.

There were also several 'positive' figures. Behind the therapist's chair appeared a more positive apparition called Gus. Gus was a quietly spoken, Thoreau-like fisherman, who was a gentle, down-to-earth, wise, intelligent and helpful figure. One is reminded of Jung's 'wise old man' archetype. Two young boys, like (Huck Finn and Tom Sawyer) finished the roster of the patient's spatial hallucinations. She reported that the boys felt like 'innocence.'

After the intensive experiential treatment of the python was finished (Prouty, 1983), a new, ninth image appeared. The image was of the patient's mother with the python crawling back into her breasts. Instantly, with clarity, the patient realized her mother's homicidal intent. The gestalt unity of hallucinations immediately lost its emotional intensity and passed away, presenting a normal spatiality for the office.

DISCUSSION

It is important to understand that this was a three-dimensional network of images that contained positive and negative unconscious content. Three of the pathogenic images (Python, Sonja and Judge) were co-functioning as agents of the homicidal mother. This was an organized gestalt through which therapeutic processing of hallucinations enabled direct experiential access to unconscious material (the homicidal mother). The next very important observation is that the content of the unconscious, thus far, has appeared as realistic trauma, as well as other experiential potentials of the personality, both positive and negative (Mahrer, 1996). When the hallucinatory content was integrated or became conscious, the hallucinatory self-fragment contained the unconscious. Thus, we may speak of the hallucination as a fragment of the unconscious.

CONCLUSION

This chapter has explored the psychotic hallucination from a symbolic and experiential perspective. Starting from Gendlin's (1964) conception of the hallucination as 'structure-bound' experiencing, the problem is formulated as how to develop the hallucination into process experiencing. The first step is a philosophical shift from a purely phenomenological assumption (the human is experiential) to a symbolic assumption (the human symbolizes experience). The symbolizing of experience is presented on a continuum of abstractness/concreteness ending with the pre-symbol, 'which cannot be clarified by something else' and 'is inseparable from what it symbolizes.' In phenomenological terms the pre-symbol is described as 'self-indicative' and in symbolical terms as 'self-referential,' while the motivation to symbolize experience is described as 'self-intentional.' In addition to concrete illustrations, the case material demonstrates these concepts in the therapeutic-experiential process of hallucinations.

Two aspects of schizophrenia were explored: (a) primary process and (b) the divided self. Freud described dreams and hallucinations as one concept—primary process. Failing to use phenomenology, Freud did not identify significant differences between them. The dream is something experienced within the boundary of the self; the hallucination is experienced as not within the boundary of the self. This phenomenological distinction suggests a different language of description. The dream is a 'projection' within the experiential boundaries of the self, and the hallucination is an 'extrojection' outside the experiential boundaries of the self.

Laing's famed book title *The Divided Self* (1969) finds clinical affirmation in that the hallucinatory self-fragment is severely dissociated or split off from the core self. The result, a partial understanding of schizophrenia as a profound rending of the self-structure, casts psychotherapy in the role of integrating the self-fragment into the core self.

One fundamental issue explored concerns the conceptualization of the unconscious. As described by Freud, the unconscious is an 'inference' from experience: for example, dreams, slips of the tongue and hypnosis. The unconscious as described in this paper is not an inference; it is a direct manifestation derived from the hallucinatory experiencing and processing. Perhaps it is best expressed as the 'not-conscious.'

The same case study of the clinical processing of hallucinations with a chronic schizophrenic woman revealed a spatial phenomenology that included multiple hallucinations, perhaps like several dreams within the same reality space at the same time. Her hallucinations proved capable of experiential processing to unconscious content. Because the hallucinations were fragments of the self that contained unconscious experience, it is consistent to describe hallucinations as the unconscious self. The spatial gestalt of the several hallucinations thus provides us with a spatial phenomenology for the client's unconscious.

REFERENCES

Binswanger, L (1963) Introduction to schizophrenia. In *Being-in-the-World: Selected papers* (pp 241–63). New York: Basic Books.

Boss, M (1963) A patient who taught the author to see and think differently. In *Psychoanalysis and Daseinanalysis* (pp 5–27). New York: Basic Books.

Boss, M (1994) *Existential Foundations of Medicine and Psychology*. London: Jason Aronson.

Cassirer, F. (1955) Man—An animal symbolicum. In D Dunes (Ed) *Treasury of Philosophy* (pp 227–9). New York: Philosophical Library.

Ellenberger, E (1958) Psychiatric phenomenology and existential analysis. In R May (Ed) *Existence: A new dimension in psychiatry and psychology* (pp 108–14). New York: Basic Books.

Gallese, V (2003) The roots of empathy: The shared manifold and the neural basis of inter-subjectivity. *Psychopathology, 36,* 171–80.

Gendlin, ET (1964) A theory of personality change. In P Worschel & D Byrne (Eds) *Personality Change* (pp 102–48). New York: John Wiley.

Halling, S & Dearborn, J (1995) A brief history of existential phenomenological psychiatry and psychotherapy. *Journal of Phenomenological Psychology, 26,* 1–45.
Havens, L (1962) The placement and movement of hallucinations in space: Phenomenology and theory. *International Journal of Psychoanalysis, 43,* 426–35.
Jaspers, K (1963) The subjective phenomenon of morbid psychic life. In *General Psychopathology* (p 55). Chicago, IL: University of Chicago Press.
Jaspers, K (1971) *Philosophy, Vol 3.* Chicago, IL: University of Chicago Press.
Kubie, L (1953) The distortion of the symbolic process in neurosis and psychosis. *Journal of the American Psychoanalytical Association, 1,* 57–83.
Laing, RD (1969) *The Divided Self.* New York: Pantheon Books.
Langer, S (1961) *Philosophy in a New Key.* New York: Mentor Books.
Mahrer, A (1996) *The Complete Guide to Experiential Psychotherapy.* New York: John Wiley.
May, R (1958) *Existence: A new dimension in psychology and psychiatry.* New York: Basic Books.
McCall, RJ (1983) *Phenomenological Psychology.* Madison, WI: University of Wisconsin Press.
Minkowski, E (1970) Schizophrenia. In *Lived Time: Phenomenological and psychopathological studies* (pp 272–89). Evanston, IL: Northwestern Universities Press.
Nunberg, H (1955) *Principles of Psychoanalysis: Their application to the neuroses.* New York: International Universities Press.
Peters, H (1992) *Psychotherapie bij geestelijk gehandicapten.* Amsterdam: Swets and Zeitlinger.
Polster, E & Polster, M (1974) *Gestalt Therapy Integrated.* New York: Vintage Books.
Prouty, G (1977) Protosymbolic method: A phenomenological treatment of schizophrenics. *International Journal of Mental Imagery, 1,* 339–42.
Prouty, G (1983) Hallucinatory contact: A phenomenological treatment of schizophrenics. *Journal of Communication Therapy, 2,* 99–103.
Prouty, G (1986) The pre-symbolic structure and therapeutic transformation of hallucinations. In M Wolpin, J Schorr & L Krueger (Eds) *Imagery, Vol 4* (pp 99–106). New York: Plenum Press.
Prouty, G (1991) The pre-symbolic structure and processing of schizophrenic hallucinations. In L Fusek (Ed) *New Directions in Client-Centered Therapy: Practice with difficult practice populations* (pp 1–18). Chicago, IL: Chicago Counseling, Psychotherapy and Research Center.
Prouty, G (1994) *Theoretical Evolutions in Person-Centered/Experiential Therapy: Applications to schizophrenic and retarded psychoses.* Westport, CT: Praeger.
Prouty, G (2000) Courage and self-actualization. Unpublished manuscript.
Prouty, G & Pietrzak, S (1988) Pre-Therapy method applied to persons experiencing hallucinatory images. *Person-Centered Review, 3,* 426–41.
Prouty, G, Van Werde, D & Pörtner, M (2001) *Pre-therapie.* Maarssen, The Netherlands: Elsiever. [English edn, see below]
Prouty, G, Van Werde, D & Pörtner, M (2002) *Pre-Therapy.* Ross-on-Wye: PCCS Books.
Romme, M & Escher, S (1993) *Accepting Voices.* London: Mind Publications.
Sartre, J-P (1956) *Being and Nothingness.* New York: Washington Square Press.
Searles, H (1965) The differentiation between concrete and metaphorical thinking in

the recovering schizophrenic. *Collected Papers on Schizophrenia and Related Subjects* (pp 560–1). London: Hogarth Press.

Strauss, E (1966) Phenomenology and hallucinations. In *Phenomenological Psychology: Selected papers* (pp 277–87). New York: Basic Books.

Szasz, T (1961) *The Myth of Mental Illness*. New York: Hoeber-Harper.

Vandenberg, J (1982) On hallucinating: Critical-historical overview and guidelines for further study. In J De Koning & F Jenner (Eds) *Phenomenological Psychiatry* (pp 97–110). New York: Academic Press, Grune and Stratton.

Whitehead, AN (1927) *Symbolism*. New York: Capricorn Books.

Index

A

Abraham, R 50, 70
abstractness–concreteness 166
abuse, sexual 154, 156
Adaptive Behaviour Inventory 75
affect 6, 18, 74, 107
affective
    attunement 88
    contact 17
agnosia 69
Ahern, R 151, 161
alcohol 174
alexithymia 157
Allan, K 52, 53, 72
altercentric participation 89, 91
alter-personalities 148, 150, 153, 154
Alzheimer's sufferers 105, 113 (see also dementia)
Anderson, G 64, 72
Aquilina, C 49, 70
Argyle, M 75, 81
Arieti, S 15, 20, 116, 117
Atwood, G 87, 102
Auerhahn, N 157, 162
autism, existential 18, 95, 107
Aveyard, B 50, 71

B

Baker, R 50, 71
Baron-Cohen, S 120, 144
Bateson, G 121, 144
Bayles, KA 51, 71
Bellack, AS 119, 144
Bender, M 50, 53, 71
Benner, P 60, 71
Berg, A 65, 71
Binswanger, L 164, 177
biographical approach 50
Bleuler, E 121, 144
Bluhm, HO 157, 161
body reflections (see reflections, body)
Bohun, E 151, 161

Bond, J 58, 71
Boon 148, 163
Boss, M 16, 20, 164, 173, 174, 177
Boston Change Process Study Group 88
Botorff, J 64, 72
Brain Hemisphere Research 123–4
Brandchaft, B 87, 104
Bråten, S 88, 89, 91, 94, 102
Braun, B 155, 161
Brown, D 155, 161
Brown, J 89, 104
Brown, L 75, 81,
Brown, S 50, 71
Brune, M 120, 144
Brunswick, L 6, 11, 19, 21
Bryant, B 75, 81
Buber, M i, 15, 20
Buccino, G 92, 102
burn out 160

C

care, everyday 25, 31–5
carers 31, 33, 34
Cassirer, E 165, 177
Chang, A 50, 73
Cheston, R 50, 53, 71
Chu, J 159, 161
client chart, the 80, 82
Cluckers, G 88, 94, 104
Coffeng, T 7, 8, 11, 110, 113, 146, 148, 151, 152, 155, 159, 161
Coherence Index, the 74, 78
Coletti, I 160, 162
Collins, J 126, 144
communication 6, 27, 48, 64, 74, 76, 89, 96, 97, 107, 129
    congruent 15
    difficulties 118
    distorted 69
    intersubjective 88, 94
    non-vebal 26, 29, 52, 69
    patterns 48, 61, 63

communicative
  measure 74 (see also ECPI)
  sign 74, 76, 80, 149
concreteness 69, 70
contact 8, 33
  affective 17, 18, 96, 105, 106, 107
  behaviors 15, 18, 105, 106, 107
  communicative 17, 18, 19, 20, 106, 107
  ego 17
  functions 9, 15, 17, 18, 28, 32, 33, 38, 39, 54, 58, 63, 105, 106
    level 28
    in therapy 18
  paradigm as point of reference 32–3
  psychological 6, 9, 15, 17, 18, 19
  reality 17, 18, 26
  reflections i, 9, 15–17, 18, 24, 26, 28, 33, 39, 53, 54, 55, 60, 61, 63, 65, 76, 95, 105, 110, 144, 148, 149
  sudden emotional 64–5
  work 38, 38, 52, 63, 65, 68, 110
Corner, L 58, 71
Cozolino, L 124, 144
Cronwall, M 6, 105, 114
Cyrulnik, B 157, 161

D

De Jong, A 75, 81
de Konig 60, 73
Dearborn, J 164, 178
Dekeyser, M 20, 58, 73
Deleu, C 19, 41, 46
delusions 25, 28, 158
dementia i, 48, 49, 50, 53, 58, 64, 68
  care 49, 50, 51, 52, 54
    and contact reflections 55–8
    and Pre-Therapy 68–9
    staff 58–68
dementing process 58
Department of Health 58, 71
Devil, the 40
DeVre, R 20, 107, 113
Dickson, R 60, 73
Dierick, P 51
dignity 67
Dinacci, A 8, 11, 20, 58, 71, 73, 74, 75, 81, 107, 113
Disability Assessment Schedule 75
dissociation i, 110, 146–9, 154, 155–9
Dissociative Identity Disorder (DID) 148, 153, 155, 158
divided self, the 173, 176, 177
Dodds, P 55, 60, 71
Doherty, D 50, 71
Donchin, A 66, 71
Durana, C 151, 161
dysphasia 69

E

echolalia 16
Eckman, P 75, 81
Ekman, SL 50, 71, 75
Ellenberger, E 174, 177
Elliott, R 20
embarrassment 66
empathic
  attunement 63, 88
  contact 15
  disorder 164
  response 16, 100, 118, 119
empathy 86, 87, 88, 91, 93, 94, 153, 157, 160, 164
Escher, S 173, 178
Evaluation Criteria for the Pre-Therapy Interview (ECPI) 74, 76
  calculation sheet 84
  score sheet 83
  standard score sheet 85
  technique 76
existential
  autism 18, 95, 107
  -phenomenological psychiatry 164
experiencing, structure-bound 159, 165, 176
experiential 164
  process 8, 41, 165, 167, 174
  world of dementia 52, 53, 70
Expressive Modality Index, the 74, 78

F

facial reflections (see reflections, facial)
Feil, N 50, 53, 54, 71
felt sense 63, 109, 116, 127, 130, 152
flashbacks 147, 148, 149, 150, 151, 152, 155, 156, 157
focusing 127, 150, 152
Fonagy, P 57, 73
Freud, S 109, 137, 173, 174, 176, 177
Friedman, B 158, 163
Friedman, G 15, 20
Fromm, E 155, 161

G

Gaedt, Ch 26, 36
Gallese, V 86, 92, 93, 94, 102, 164, 177
Gendlin, ET 5, 6, 25, 127, 144, 145, 146, 150, 151, 152, 161, 162, 165, 176, 177
General Interview Index 74, 80
Gergely, G 88, 94, 101, 102
gestalt
    unity of hallucinations 176
    unified spatial 175
Giel, R 75, 81
Gilbert, J 92, 94, 102
Gingerich, S 119, 143
God 39, 40, 43, 135
Goldberg, E 124, 145
Goldsmith, M 52, 71
Goldstein, K 16, 21
Gómez, JC 89, 90, 91, 101, 103
Götell, E 50, 71
Graham, J 50, 71
Graneheim, UH 65, 71
Grech, E 61, 71
grey zone 151
    functioning 28, 34
Gurwitsch, A 16, 21

H

Hahn, W 159, 162
Hallberg, IR 65, 71
Halling, S 164, 178
hallucinations 149, 158, 164–7, 174–7
    phenomenology of 173
    psychotherapy of 173
    self-referential property of 172
    somatic 39
    tactile 175
    visual 110
hallucinatory
    images 166, 167, 173
    process 167, 173
    structure 173
handle 126, 127, 137
Hansebo, G 65, 71
Harre, R 49, 73
Harries, MH 92, 103
Harrow, M 120, 122, 131, 145
Harvey, M 155, 162
Havens, L 174, 178

Heimann, M 89, 92, 103
Hendricks, MN 120, 127, 145
Herman, J 155, 162
hesitancy 63, 64
Hess, E 159, 162
hijacking 61
Hinterkopf, E 6, 11, 19, 21, 107, 113
Holloway, J 50, 71
holocaust 157
    survivors 157
        children of 157
Holtkamp, C 50, 71
Huberman, AM 60, 72
Hughes, JC 49, 70, 71
Hunter, M 151, 162
Husserl, E 7, 164, 173
Hyer, L 157, 162
hypofrontality 124

I

Iberg, J 120, 129, 130, 131, 145
iconical sign 166
I-identity 93
imitation 92, 94, 95, 99, 102
    infant 91
    intersubjective 95
implicit
    certainties 94
    philosophy of the 127–8
incest 154
indexical sign 166
Innes, A 65, 72
intersubjective
    attunement, two-way 62, 63, 65, 90
    immitation 95–101
    psychoanalysis 86
    relatedness 88
intersubjectivity 62, 63, 86, 87, 89, 91, 99, 164
    and child research 91
    cognitive versus affective 90–1
    concept of 87–95
    innate human 89
    neurophysiological basis for 92–5
    one-way 63, 89
Irblich, D 27, 36

J

Jablensky, A 75, 81
Jaspers, K 164, 166, 178
Jones, C 50, 73

K

Kendrick, KD 65, 72
Kief, M 30
Kihlgren, M 65, 71
Killick, J 52, 53, 54, 72
Kitwood, T 49, 50, 53, 54, 70, 72
Kluft, R 153, 154, 162
Knocker, S 52, 72
Koch, U 26, 27, 36
Kohut, H 100, 103
Kontos, PC 49, 72
Krietemeyer, B 17, 27, 28, 36, 98, 103
Kubiak, M 6, 16, 21, 105, 114
Kubie, L 166, 178
Kugiumutzakis, G 91, 103

L

La Mothe, R 157, 162
Lacan, J 112, 113
Laing, RD 164, 173, 178
Langer, S 166, 167, 178
Laub, D 157, 162
Lauritzen, S 50, 72
Leigh, JE 75, 81
Leijssen, M 107, 113
Leijssen, S 51
Levine, PA 30, 36
Lindy, J 157, 160, 163
linguistic disabilities, progressive 69
logic 121, 152
Lotz, W 26, 27, 36
Louw, SJ 49, 71
Lucieer, W 7

M

MacDonald, C 66, 72
MacPherson, S 66, 72
Maher, BA 122, 145
Mahrer, A 176, 178
Marmar, C 155, 162
May, R 164, 178
Mazumdar, D 16, 21
Mazumdar, T 16, 21
McCabe, L 66, 72
McCall, RJ 174, 178
McCann, L 160, 162
McCormack, B 49, 72
McGuire, M 150, 162
McKenna, P 120, 122, 145

McNiff, J 60, 72
McWilliams, K 110, 112, 113
Meltzoff, AN 90, 103
mental stability 136–7
metacauses 117, 124–6, 131, 133
metaphact/s 117, 119, 124–6, 138
    analysis 133–4
    language 131, 134, 135, 136
    processing 118, 119, 125, 127–8, 133, 143
metaphor/ic 116, 119, 121, 127, 133
    functions 126
    processing 116, 122, 126
meta-symbol 166
Metzler, T 155, 162
Miles, MB 60, 72
mind, theory of (TOM) 90, 91, 120, 128, 143
Minkowski, E 112, 113, 164, 178
mirror neurons 86, 91, 92, 95, 99
mirroring 52, 53, 54, 63, 88, 100
Mistlin, AJ 92, 103
Moore, MK 90, 103
Morse, JM 64, 72
Morton, IR 49, 51, 55, 71, 72, 73
movement 50, 53, 54
Mueller-Hergl C 67, 72
Mueser, KT 119, 144
music 50, 54
    therapy 51

N

neologisms 16
neurological change 49
NICE-SCIE 50, 72
Nijenhuis, E 155, 162
non-process structure 165
Norberg, A 65, 71
Nunberg, H 174, 178
nursing 59, 60, 64, 66
Nystrom, K 50, 72

O

Oades, R 122, 123, 124, 145
object language 166
Oh, T 120, 122, 145
Oram, MW 92, 103
Oster, H 75, 81

P

Pao, P-N 119, 145
paralogical thinking 122
Perls, FS 5, 11, 21, 76, 81, 106, 113
Perret, DI 92, 103
personality, multiple 109–10, 113
person-centered
    approach 25, 27, 31, 35, 48, 49, 50
        in dementia 53, 70
    psychotherapy 51
Pesso, A 151, 152, 162
Peters, H 7, 9, 12, 62, 63, 72, 86, 88, 94, 95, 97, 98, 103, 107, 113, 165, 178
phenomenological
    approach 164, 167
    attitude 41
    description of schizophrenia 112
    hermeneutics 174
    properties 93, 166, 167
phenomenology 7, 164, 173, 174, 177
    of hallucinations 149, 168, 173
    spacial 177
    of the unconscious 174–6
physical
    contact 68, 79, 80, 150
    coordination 77
    Expressiveness Index, the 74, 79
    safety 42
Pietrzak, S 6, 96, 103, 105, 110, 114, 164, 173, 178
Polster, E 173, 178
Polster, M 173, 178
Pool, J 50, 72
Pörtner, M i, 5, 9, 12, 15, 21, 26, 27, 28, 29, 36, 38, 39, 41, 46, 51, 59, 60, 66, 72, 98, 103, 107, 114, 149, 165, 178
Positive Person Work 50, 53, 54
pre-experiential 148, 149, 150
    contact 8
pre-expressive 148, 149, 156
    concept of 27
    functioning 42, 44, 68
    level 28, 29
    self 105, 108–9
    signs 108–9
    states 69
pre-symbol 166, 176
    properties of the 167

pre-symbolic
    experiencing 10, 110, 167, 168
    processing 149, 150, 173
    theory 165–72
    thrust 109
Pre-Therapy Interview, Evaluation Criterion for the (ECPI) 20, 74, 75
Pre-Therapy Network, the 51
primary process 173, 176
Prince, M 146
process
    -oriented approach 164
    structure 165
Prosen, M 122, 145
Prouty, G i, 5, 9, 12, 15, 18, 19, 20, 21, 25, 27, 28, 30, 36, 39, 41, 46, 53, 54, 55, 58, 59, 71, 75, 76, 81, 95, 98, 99, 103, 105, 107, 110, 112, 113, 114, 118, 119, 143, 145, 148, 149, 156, 158, 162, 164, 165, 166, 167, 173, 174, 175, 178
Prouty, Jill 7, 8, 110
psychoanalysis 87, 88, 166
psychological contact 15, 143, 148, 149 (see also contact, psychological)
Psychological Impairment Rating Schedule 75
psychosis 41, 58, 68, 146, 156, 158
psychotherapy 26–31, 32, 59, 87
    focusing-oriented 127, 146, 150
    gestalt 173
    of hallucinations 166, 173
    person-centred 48, 51, 95, 99, 106
psychotic 38, 108, 164
    break 126, 128, 129
    expression 108, 109
    hallucination 176
    material 119
    patients/clients 28, 29, 148, 149, 156, 158

Q

Quinlan, D 120, 131, 145

R

Reaction Index 74, 77
reality 74
    contact 16, 17, 18, 26, 34, 101, 105, 106, 107
Rebok, GW 50, 73

reflections, 42, 44
  body 16, 30, 33, 34, 44, 97–9, 148
  contact 15–17, 26, 30, 32, 33–5, 39, 48, 57, 67, 68, 69, 95, 105–6, 118, 148, 150
    with dementia 55–9, 60, 63, 65
  facial 16, 34, 42, 69, 96, 97, 98, 105, 110
  reiterative 16, 44, 97, 98, 106, 149
  situational 16, 31, 34, 39, 42, 56, 69, 95, 105, 148
  word-for-word 16, 34, 39, 42, 67, 68, 96, 105, 108, 116, 144, 149
regression i, 15, 108, 109, 159
reiterative reflections (see reflections, reiterative)
relational autonomy 66, 67
reminiscence 50
research 6, 9, 11, 55, 57, 60
  action 60
  Brain Hemisphere 123–4
  intersubjectivity 87–9
    and child 91
  issues 57–8
  motor neuron 92
  project 60, 68
  schizophrenia 118, 120, 121, 122
  studies 19
residential psychiatric setting 39, 66
Robinson, S 65, 72
Roelens, L 107, 108, 113
Rogers, CR 5, 6, 7, 12, 15, 21, 48, 100, 103, 105, 105, 114
Romme, M 173, 178
Ross, CA 148, 162
Rotenberg, V 123, 133, 145
Roth, A 57, 73
Roy, BC 109, 114, 148, 162
Rupert, PA 151, 163

S

Sabat, SR 49, 71, 73
Saczynski, JS 50, 73
Sakheim, D 159, 162
Sanders, P i, 10, 12, 15, 21, 39, 46
Santen, B 7
Sartre, J-P 166, 178
Scheerer, M 16, 21
schizophrenia 16, 19, 112, 118, 164, 173, 176
schizophrenic 105, 120, 122, 133, 167, 173
  cognitive processing 116

hallucination 164
symptoms, 'positive' 126
thought disorder 116, 118, 119
Schore, A 155, 163
Schwarz, R 75, 81
Searles, H 166, 178
self
  boundary of the 176
  core 91, 177
  divided, the 173, 176, 177
  -indicat/ing/ive 166, 167, 171, 176
  -intentional 167, 170, 176
  pre-expressive 105, 108–9
  -referential 167, 172, 176
  sense of 48, 49, 106
  -structure 173, 177
  unconscious 164
  unembodied 173
Senckel, B 26, 27, 36
Shakespeare, P 51, 73
Shared Manifold Hypothesis 86, 93
Sherratt, K 50, 73
Sherwin, S 66, 73
Silver, A-L 10
Sinason, V 155, 163
situational reflections (see reflections, situational)
Smith, P 64, 73
social
  constructionist perspective 49
  identity 93
Sommerbeck, L 10, 12
special needs 25
Spector, A 50, 73
speech 51, 96
Spiegel, D 152, 156, 163
Stahl, B 27, 36
Stanford-Binet IQ 19, 167
Stenzel, CL 151, 163
Stern, DN 63, 73, 88, 91, 104
stimulus-reaction 77
Stolorow, RD 87, 102, 104
Stoof, C 75, 81
Straube, E 122, 123, 124, 145
Strauss, E 164, 179
Struwe, J 151, 162
suicide 154, 156
Sung, H 50, 73
Sussman, M 160, 163
Sykes, M 50, 71

INDEX

symbol, primacy of the 165–6
symbolization 91, 166
    of experience 165, 166, 176
    of reality 17, 106
Szasz, T 166, 179

T

tension, reducing 34–5
Terr, L 155, 163
Tillen, D 60, 73
timalation 54
Tomov, J 75, 81
touch 50, 54, 74, 76
transitional objects 50
trauma 110, 147, 148, 149, 153, 154, 155, 157, 176
    language and 156–8
traumatic memories 150, 151, 154, 155
traumatization, vicarious 160
Trevarthen, C 88, 89, 91, 104
Tronick, EZ 88, 104
Trower, P 75, 81
Trytten, J 117, 130, 131, 132, 133, 145

U

unconscious 164, 167, 173, 174, 176, 177
    self 164

V

Validation Therapy 50, 53, 54, 68
Van der Hart, O 155, 158, 162, 163
van der Kolk, B 148, 163
Van IJzendoorn, MH 94, 104
Van Ravesteijn, L 155, 159, 163
Van Werde, D 1, 5, 9, 11, 15, 19, 21, 27, 28, 29, 32, 38, 39, 41, 45, 46, 49, 51, 59, 73, 98, 103, 105, 107, 114, 151, 162, 163, 165, 178
Vandenberg, J 164, 179
Vass, AA 58, 73
ventriloquism 61
verbal
    expressiveness coordination 77, 78
        Index, the 74, 78
    reflection 16, 26, 69
Verity, J 55, 73
Vliegen, N 88, 94, 104
voices, hallucinatory 110, 124, 126, 148, 173
Von Domarus, E 116, 117, 121, 122, 145
Vygotsky, LS 121, 145

W

Warner, MS 116, 117, 145
Waterman, H 60, 73
Watson, JS 88, 94, 101, 102
Weiss, D 155, 162
White, C 7, 12
Whitehead, AN 166, 179
Whitehead, J 60, 72
Whiten, A 89, 104
Wilkinson, H 58, 73
Wilson, J 157, 160, 163
Witzum, E 158, 163
Woods, B 50, 73
Woods, G 157, 162
word-salads 16
World Health Organisation (WHO) 75, 81

Z

Zarit, SH 50, 73

The Contact Work Primer
Pete Sanders (Ed) with contributions from Catherine Clarke, Penny Dodds, Marlis Pörtner, Lisbeth Sommerbeck and Dion Van Werde
2007 ISBN 978-1-898059-84-4

'Much more than a primer ... this is a superb practical introduction to Pre-Therapy and contact work that will be of value to all mental health professionals working with contact-impaired individuals.'
  Mick Cooper, Professor of Counselling, University of Strathclyde

Pre-Therapy: Reaching contact-impaired clients
Garry Prouty, Dion Van Werde and Marlis Pörtner
2002 ISBN 978-1-898059-34-9

'Pre-Therapy offers me a way of supporting someone at the edge of therapeutic viability and of bringing them back into therapeutic contact, in a way that is fully consistent with person-centred therapy. It is deeply respectful of the client and an effective way of making therapy available to those who might otherwise be excluded.'
  Margaret Brown, Counselling Manager,
  Suffolk MIND, *HCPJ*, April, 2003

Rogers' Therapeutic Conditions: Evolution, theory and practice
Volume 4: Contact and Perception
Gill Wyatt and Pete Sanders (Eds)
2002 ISBN 978-1-898059-32-5

For the first time, writers from three continents put psychological contact and the client's perception of the therapist at the very centre of the theoretical map.
  This collection of papers outlines genuine new theory and practice.
  Volume 4 in the best-selling series edited by Gill Wyatt (other volumes in the series: *Empathy*, *Congruence* and *Unconditional Positive Regard*).

www.pccs-books.co.uk